ECONOMIC INTELLIGENCE
& NATIONAL SECURITY

ECONOMIC
INTELLIGENCE
&
NATIONAL
SECURITY

Edited by Evan H. Potter

CARLETON UNIVERSITY PRESS
&
THE CENTRE FOR TRADE POLICY AND LAW

Printed and bound in Canada

Canadian Cataloguing in Publication Data

Main entry under title:

   Economic intelligence and national security

Includes bibliographical references.
ISBN 0-88629-335-9

   1. National security—Economic aspects—Canada.
2. Business intelligence. 3. Intelligence service—Canada.
4. Canada—Economic policy—1991-. I. Potter, Evan H.
(Evan Harold), date- II. Centre for Trade Policy and
Law.

HD38.7.E36 1997   327.1271   C97-900934-0

Cover Design: Coach House Printing
Typeset: Mayhew & Associates Graphic Communications, Richmond, Ont., in
association with MFL Graphic Productions

Carleton University Press gratefully acknowledges the support extended to its
publishing program by the Canada Council and the financial assistance of the
Ontario Arts Council. The Press would also like to thank the Department of
Canadian Heritage, Government of Canada, and the Government of Ontario
through the Ministry of Culture, Tourism and Recreation, for their assistance.

CONTENTS

FIGURES

TABLES

GLOSSARY

ECONOMIC ESPIONAGE: Clandestine or illicit attempts by foreign interests to assist their economic interests by acquiring economic intelligence that could be used to sabotage or otherwise interfere with the economic security of another country.

ECONOMIC INTELLIGENCE: Policy or commercially-relevant economic information, including technological data, financial, commercial, and government information, the acquisition of which by foreign interests could, either directly or indirectly, assist the relative productivity or competitive position of the economy of the collecting organization's country. The acquisition of economic intelligence becomes a security concern when the acquisition of this information by foreign interests could economically disadvantage the country concerned by jeopardizing jobs, research and development, investments, relative productivity, competitiveness, or economic growth.

ECONOMIC INTELLIGENCE COMMUNITY: This refers to all the institutions of the state that produce and/or consume commercial and economic intelligence. This community includes the intelligence services (see below).

ECONOMIC SECURITY: The maintenance of those conditions necessary to encourage sustained long-term relative improvements in labour and capital productivity and thus a high and rising standard of living for a nation's citizens, including the maintenance of a fair and dynamic business environment conducive to innovation, domestic and foreign investment, and sustainable economic growth.

ENABLING TECHNOLOGIES: This refers to the high-technology, high-skill, and high-capital-intensive sectors such as microelectronics, telecommunications, computers, biotechnology, aerospace, nuclear, chemical, and pharmaceuticals. These sectors are also referred to as strategic or key industries, because they "enable" countries to become more competitive in the world economy.

INDUSTRIAL ESPIONAGE: The use of, or facilitation of, illegal clandestine, coercive, or deceptive means by a private sector entity or its surrogates to acquire economic intelligence.

INTELLIGENCE SERVICE: This refers to only those departments and agencies of central governments that engage in clandestine activity.

SHARP PRACTICES: The use of illegal, clandestine, coercive, or deceptive means by a foreign government or entity intended to benefit the economic or commercial interests of the perpetrator. This broad category includes not only economic espionage, but other questionable practices, such as bribery and sabotage.

PREFACE

In the study of economic security, scholars of international relations, public policy, law, security intelligence, and economics rarely have the opportunity—save at the occasional interdisciplinary conference—to trade ideas in a public forum. It is rarer still to find a forum where scholars in different disciplines are brought together with practitioners to discuss the structure of national economic intelligence-gathering systems and their impact on the future economic security of nation-states.

The origins of this book can be traced to a working group on economic security that was convened in February 1995 by the Centre for Trade Policy and Law (CTPL), a think-tank that is jointly administered by The Norman Paterson School of International Affairs at Carleton University and the Faculty of Law at the University of Ottawa. The working group reviewed and commented on four research reports that make up the individual chapters in this volume. Participating in this working group were officials from the Canadian Security Intelligence Service (CSIS), the Department of Industry, the Solicitor General's Office, the Department of Justice, and the Department of Foreign Affairs and International Trade (DFAIT). We thank CSIS, Industry, the Solicitor General's Office, and DFAIT for their financial support to make this book possible.

This study is part of CTPL's on-going efforts to explore new dimensions of Canada's economic security. In this context, *Economic Intelligence and National Security* plays a particularly useful role, in that it connects domestic concerns about economic prosperity with the broader questions of national security. It evaluates how Canada compares—in terms of its capacity both to protect against foreign economic intelligence-gathering and to engage in economic intelligence-gathering itself—to other states and presents a choice of future options for Canadian policymakers.

ACRONYMS

AT&T	American Telephone and Telegraph Co.
BCNet	Business Cooperation Network
BCNI	
BND	Bundesnachrichtendienst
BSIS	British Secret Intelligence Service
BVD	Bundesverteidigungsdienst
CCC	Canadian Chamber of Commerce
CEA	Canadian Exporters Association
CIA	Central Intelligence Agency
CIDA	Canadian International Development Agency
CMA	Canadian Manufacturers Agency
CNN	Cable News Network
COCOM	Coordinating Committee for Multilateral Export Controls
CSE	[Canadian] Communications Security Establishment
CSIS	Canadian Security Intelligence Service
CTOT	Canadian Trade Office in Taipei
CTPL	Center for Trade Policy and Law
CWF	Canada West Foundation
DFAIT	Department of Foreign Affairs and International Trade
ECC	Economic Council of Canada
EDC	Export Development Corporation
EU	European Union
FBI	Federal Bureau of Investigation
FIAS	Foreign Intelligence Assessments Secretariat
FITT	Forum for International Trade Training

G-7	Group of Seven
GATT	General Agreement on Tariffs and Trade
GCHQ	Government Communications Headquarters
GDP	Gross Domestic Product
IAC	Intelligence Advisory Committee
IBEX	International Business Exchange
IBM	International Business Machines
ICSI	Interdepartmental Committee on Security and Intelligence
IIP	Institute for Industrial Protection
IRPP	Institute for Research on Public Policy
JETRO	Japan External Trade Organization
KCIA	Korean Central Intelligence Agency
MITI	Ministry of International Trade and Industry
MNE	Multinational Enterprise
NAFTA	North American Free Trade Agreement
NGO	Non-governmental Organization
NRC	National Research Council
NSA	National Security Agency
NSP	National Security Plan
NSC	[U.S.] National Security Council
OECD	Organization for Economic Cooperation and Development
ONA	[Australian] Office of National Assessments
PMO	Prime Minister's Office
RCMP	Royal Canadian Mounted Police
R&D	Research & Development
RG	Direction de Renseignements Généraux

SCC	Science Council of Canada
SGDN	Secretariat Général de la Defense Nationale
SIGINT	Signals Intelligence
SIRC	Security Intelligence Review Committee
SME	Small and Medium-sized Enterprise
STP	Strategic Trade Policy
TRIP	Trade Related Aspects of Intellectual Property
UN	United Nations
UNIDO	United Nations Development Organization
WTO	World Trade Organization

INTRODUCTION

Evan H. Potter

WHAT ARE THE APPROPRIATE ROLES and mandates for intelligence services in a world in which there is growing competition for market share and a recognition that, more than ever, there is a need for a rules-based system to govern global economic activity? To be sure, gathering economic intelligence is a key priority of any national government and its intelligence community. This community includes all the institutions of the state (of which intelligence services are but one component) that collect, analyze, and distribute information to protect and promote national economic security, whether it be information on a new market for telephone switches in China or reports of impending financial collapse in Mexico. Today, such activity has taken on an added urgency: economic strength rather than military might is becoming the barometer of a nation-state's power. Financial crises can spread across global markets in minutes and the protection of the national investment in enabling or strategic technologies becomes a growing challenge because "knowledge" is difficult to monopolize when globalization is further entrenched by advances in information technologies. At the same time, the international community is in the process of building on the last four decades of negotiations to create a more liberal and transparent international economic system so as to make progress on a set of new, more complex economic policy issues, including intellectual property, labour rights, and foreign direct investment. Such changed circumstances in the post-Cold War international system raise fundamental questions about how economic security should be conceptualized and how governments are responding.

Recent years have witnessed a number of episodes in which economic intelligence-gathering has achieved a high profile. When the U.S.-Japanese auto negotiations reached a climax in 1994, for example, working alongside the American trade negotiators were intelligence officials offering assessments of how far the Japanese side could be pressed. This followed allegations that a year earlier, during the Uruguay Round trade negotiations, the Central Intelligence Agency (CIA) had provided the Clinton administration with accounts of discussions among key members negotiating the worldwide trade accord—notably the French and the European Commission. For intelligence services the transition from a predominant focus on arms control, counter-terrorism, and political (de)stabilization in the name of national security, to one attuned to capital flows, exchange rates, the latest scientific and technological advances, and international trade and investment promotion has not been easy. Nevertheless, the political prominence of trade conflicts, whether between Japan and the United States over autos, Canada and the European Union (EU) over fisheries, or the United States and France over culture, to name just a few, has sent intelligence services an important message: focus more energy on economic security. Together these trends and incidents are significant because for the first time intelligence services realize that trade talks to protect and increase their countries' global trade and investment shares are becoming a major national security issue of the post-Cold War era.

"National security" is a nebulous term that has historically included economic security, but is more associated with the military and political dimensions of security; today, however, it refers increasingly to "national economic security" interests. This has resulted in a greater focus on the economic intelligence systems and legal regimes in place to protect and enhance national standards of living.

It is becoming more and more difficult for policy makers to promote "national" economic security as the borders of their firms are changing with the growing clout of multinationals and consortia. There is a paradox in the process of globalization, however. Although global borders between markets are disappearing, national politics and policies still matter.[1] In fact, the increased competitiveness of firms on a global scale, as they grapple for diminishing shares of world markets, has forced nation-states to reconsider the structures of their national economic intelligence systems, their domestic legal regimes, and the mandates of their intelligence services. The present volume addresses the question of what value-added is brought by intelligence services to the objective of national economic security through either their offensive activities or their defensive actions. Such an investigation raises other questions about the correlations between and among a number of explanatory variables, including the degree of openness in a society and its capacity to share information, how national cultures affect economic competitiveness, the role of intelligence services in enhancing national economic performance, and the causal relationship between a particular combination of defensive and offensive economic intelligence capacities employed by a state and its ability to enhance national economic security. The following specific questions are raised by the contributors to this volume:

- Is there a strong correlation between an intelligence-sharing society and an economically competitive one? How is this related to the success of intelligence services in supporting national economic security? How does Canada compare with other industrialized countries in the context of such questions?

- What type of information are intelligence services best able to supply to the private sector?

- What type of information is the intelligence community best able to supply to governmental decision-makers?

- What are the costs of economic espionage?

- Using the case study of Canada, are the legal regimes in place domestically and internationally sufficiently robust to counteract the effects of economic espionage?

- From the perspective of economic theory, is there a strong or weak rationale for increasing the role of intelligence services in enhancing national economic security?

How are the intelligence services of states reacting to the changes we have been considering? In order to meet the changing needs of policy makers, particularly in the Anglo-Saxon world, they appear to be moving from relative indifference to trade and economic matters to an increased focus on trade negotiations, macroeconomic trends, and the economic impacts of so-called cooperative security concerns, such as population migrations, international crime, communicable diseases, human rights, and environmental crises. It should also be said that such a shift in focus has helped to demonstrate their relevance in the face of budget cuts. But the adaptation is not without its difficulties. All intelligence services are having trouble adjusting to a more subtle world of trade politics, where economic competitors are also political allies, and where a far wider range of players—business leaders, bankers, and politicians concerned about domestic employment rates—are demanding to be consulted. The fundamental question for Ottawa and Washington is whether information gained from economic spying in Tokyo, Bonn, and Paris is worth risking some of their most important alliances. On the other hand, the Japanese, Germans, and the French see few inconsistencies in (and suffer fewer moral qualms about) gathering economic intelligence on each other, either openly or clandestinely, while still maintaining a broad political consensus on such matters as the value of common security arrangements and the need to liberalize global trade and investment.

This book evaluates the political, institutional, legal, and economic rationales for the involvement of intelligence services in collecting, producing, distributing, and protecting economic intelligence. It consists of four chapters written by experts on public policy, security intelligence, law, and economics that are organized around the issues and policy dilemmas facing states and firms as they devise new strategies to protect and appropriate economic intelligence. The common debate running through the analyses is the degree to which intelligence services can enhance national comparative advantage. The study's primary focus is on Canada, although it provides a comparative perspective on the experiences of France, the United States, Britain, Japan, Germany, and Russia.

The first chapter, by Evan Potter, provides a detailed description of the public sector and private sector agents and institutions that make up Canada's economic intelligence-gathering system. Potter evaluates this system's strengths and weaknesses in relation to the economic intelligence systems of a number of Canada's major competitors—Germany, Japan, and the United States. This chapter is followed by Samuel

Porteous's essay, which examines issues arising from the increased activity of Western intelligence services in protecting and pursuing their respective national economic and commercial interests. The author examines the debates surrounding the relative effectiveness of intelligence services in collecting, producing, and ultimately distributing economic intelligence to policymakers and the private sector. Anthony VanDuzer's chapter captures the dilemma faced by Canadian policymakers as they respond to the increased targeting of Canadian know-how by foreign states and their surrogates with agencies such as the Canadian Security Intelligence Service (CSIS) and the Royal Canadian Mounted Police (RCMP), whose legal mandates bind them to an almost exclusively defensive legal posture. The final chapter, by James Brander, provides an economic analysis of economic intelligence. Brander considers whether there is any reasonable economic rationale for the involvement of intelligence services in economic espionage or in economic intelligence more broadly.

CHAPTER SUMMARIES

The System of Economic Intelligence-Gathering in Canada

Evan Potter states that the end of the Cold War, increased globalization, and the integration of Canada into a North American community have all focused attention on a major paradox. Although Canada is the eighth largest trading nation and is a world leader in some high-tech industries, its share of world trade in the last two decades has dropped by 27 percent and its international competitiveness ranking has been slipping since 1989, putting its national economic security increasingly at risk. The chapter starts by explaining how and why the strategic management of economic intelligence is integral to building a competitive national economy for a new global market, and then compares Canada's economic intelligence system with the practices and systems of a number of other industrialized countries.

The analysis points to national culture as the major factor in determining the characteristics of an economic intelligence system. Potter speculates that perhaps because of Canada's shorter history as a nation, its smaller population base, its abundant resources, its greater dependence on government institutions, and a high degree of foreign investment in its economy, Canada has not been forced by circumstances to be more effective in mobilizing national resources into a more coherent and effective system of information exchange and information management. The Canadian case study highlights wasted efforts, lack of coordination between public and private sectors, and under-utilization of Canada's vaunted multilateral networks. With regard to solutions, Potter argues that given Canada's non-corporatist and more confrontational style of national economic and political decision-making, and its generally competitive peak interest groups, there are inherent difficulties in transposing wholesale European and Japanese models onto Canada.

These structural problems are emphasized in the chapter because they lead to a disturbing conclusion: the Canadian economic intelligence-gathering system is confined to being primarily defensive, precisely at a time when competitive world markets are calling for a more offensively oriented system. Potter concludes that without a drastic perceptual change—the creation of a "grand strategy"—in the Canadian public and private sectors with regard to the importance to the bottom line of the systematic processing of economic intelligence, Canada will not see a reversal of its diminishing international competitiveness. For this reason the chapter recommends the revival of a national economic council with the full support of the federal cabinet, the creation of an "information society" through the greater use of public databases and technology consortia, and speculates on a more offensive mandate for Canada's intelligence services.

Economic and Commercial Interests and Intelligence Services

Samuel Porteous examines issues arising from the increased activity of Western intelligence services in protecting and pursuing national economic and commercial interests. Porteous makes two sets of arguments. First, he argues that there is a need for intelligence services to become more effectively integrated into the public policy process on economic matters. Such restructuring, however, raises a number of problems, including turf battles both within and between governments' economic and security intelligence bureaucracies, "quality of analysis" concerns, the future of traditional intelligence-sharing networks, and the extent to which governments should have access to private and commercial communications on the "information highway" to both protect and promote national economic security.

Porteous's second broad argument regarding the use of intelligence services to provide commercially relevant intelligence to the private sector raises a host of equally compelling questions. From a philosophical standpoint, would differing Canadian and American perceptions of the legitimacy of government involvement in the economy naturally extend to the involvement of their respective intelligence services? What role do intelligence services have in providing benefits to commercial actors, including "stateless" multinational corporations? Does economic espionage, because it is sponsored by the state (as opposed to industrial espionage), create an unfair subsidy that will support uncompetitive domestic producers at the expense of consumers and taxpayers? Or, is it legitimate to support strategic trade policy in this way, especially in a world in which national specializations often depend on technological advances?

Porteous foresees five general roles for intelligence services in protecting and pursuing economic and commercial interests in the years ahead. The first two are established and familiar, if not vigorously pursued. The final three will break new ground for many Western intelligence services directed to engage in them.

The first concerns the use of counter-intelligence to prevent foreign intelligence services or their surrogates from engaging in clandestine activities directed at economic and commercial interests. This is an intelligence service's least controversial function, and most Western services have been directed to increase activity in this area. Second, intelligence services will use their unique collection capacity to provide decision-makers with economic intelligence unavailable through other means. For example, Porteous suggests that policy makers will increasingly receive reports on the monetary and fiscal policies of the major economic players in the international system not only from their finance and international trade ministries but also from their intelligence services. Third, these services will more carefully monitor states' adherence to international economic agreements—especially intellectual property conventions—and unfair or "sharp" business practices (bribery, for instance). Fourth, so-called "special activities" designed to influence events, behaviour, or policy formulation in foreign countries, which could range from disinformation campaigns that target third country markets to covert influence on important economic decisions, will be engaged in sparingly, if at all, by most Western intelligence services. The fifth, and possibly the most controversial role from the standpoint of the North American intelligence community, is the pursuit of commercial information and technologies for the express purpose of giving them to favoured domestic firms or consortia. Most Western powers have publicly disavowed any involvement in this activity. Finally, the author raises a caveat: there is distinction between predicting what will occur and predicting that it will be done well.

The Impact of the Legal Regime

The main purpose of Anthony VanDuzer's chapter is to examine both the possibilities and the limits of the statutory mandates of CSIS and the RCMP in relation to economic security. He specifies the gaps in the substantive legal protection, both domestically and abroad, for the Canadian private and public sectors with regard to the appropriation of information and technological data. He raises a number of key questions. How does the Canadian legal system, which includes the international obligations to which Canada is subject, define the kinds of intelligence-gathering behaviour by foreign agents that are subject to legal sanction? What is the permitted scope for CSIS and the RCMP to engage in activities intended to defeat legal and illegal economic intelligence-gathering activities? Where does the Communications Security Establishment (CSE) fit in? VanDuzer points out that one difficult aspect of this question is the extent to which CSIS may disclose information it has in order to permit government institutions or firms to defend themselves against the collection activities of foreign states.

VanDuzer concludes that although there will be more progress on the protection of intellectual property rights through Canada's participation at multilateral trade negotiations at the World Trade Organization (and perhaps also through regional agreements), more enforceable legal sanctions will discourage only the more obvious and open infringements of copyrights, patents, and trade secrets law. Such negotiations will have little ability to curtail the growing problem of economic espionage, which is by definition clandestine and therefore not subject to international "regulation." Indeed, as VanDuzer explains, the only way for Canada to "regulate" economic espionage is through the establishment of a more enforceable and less porous domestic legal framework which would require amendments to the Criminal Code and the largely ineffectual Official Secrets Act. The chapter also considers briefly the legal environment in which Canadian government agencies would carry out the collection of economic intelligence outside of Canada for the purpose of obtaining a positive advantage for Canadian government or business. He notes that the current legal regime in Canada provides very little scope for such activities.

Finally, VanDuzer proposes changes to the legal framework governing Canada's intelligence services, by listing three options: an amendment of the CSIS Act to permit an expanded foreign intelligence-gathering function; the creation of a separate foreign intelligence agency with its own statutory mandate; or the expansion of the CSE into a foreign intelligence-gathering agency with its own statutory mandate.

The Economics of Economic Intelligence

James Brander's chapter, by means of an analysis of three general economic arguments—strategic trade policy, public good, and police—evaluates the role and effectiveness of intelligence services in protecting and providing economic intelligence. According to the strategic trade policy argument, nations might have incentives to use espionage to shift benefits from foreign to domestic firms. Viewed in this way, espionage is much like a subsidy to the latter. He concludes that such activity tends to be harmful to innovative activity as a whole. When one country gains from economic espionage, the damage done to other countries exceeds the benefit to the country that gains. This suggests that there would be a global economic gain if countries could agree not to undertake direct economic espionage.

Brander states that the difficulty in reducing economic espionage is that the roles of different countries are highly asymmetric in the inter-national espionage "game." Most countries have relatively little to lose from industrial espionage, because their domestic firms have few secrets. The largest potential loser from economic espionage is the United States, primarily because it provides a disproportionately large share of the world's innovation and therefore has a lot to protect. The United States's vulnerability is further exacerbated because it is relatively open, both as a society and a business community. The author concludes that Canada's role is not dissimilar to that of the United States, although Canadian firms have somewhat less innovation to protect, even after adjusting for the relative sizes of the countries, than do American firms. According to the author, it is therefore necessary for countries such as the United States and Canada to undertake more vigorous defensive espionage activities.

The public good argument provides a strong case for the existence of national and international statistical and research agencies that provide general economic information to governments and many other users. However, Brander is unconvinced that such economic intelligence can be provided by covert intelligence services.

The third argument, which Brander refers to as the "police" argument, concerns the contributions of intelligence services to the overall security of the system of voluntary exchange that underlies the efficiency of modern market economies. Most such activities—enforcing contracts, protecting private property—are carried out by the domestic justice system, including the police and courts, although the author does see an important residual role for intelligence services. In this way, the author views intelligence services as an extension of domestic police services.

The last section of Brander's chapter considers three important continuing trends in the world economy and their possible impact on intelligence services. The main point of this section is that the world is becoming a more crowded and more integrated place, in which it is increasingly difficult to distinguish between "us" and "them" on a national basis. As a result it will be more difficult for intelligence services to base their activities on an adversarial model of world affairs.

MAIN THEMES AND DEBATES

The agenda for national security strategies has changed dramatically in the last decade. Economics is coming to occupy a more prominent position in determining the capacity of Canada and other nations to maintain their relative positions in the international system. In this study the authors test and examine how the protection and promotion of economic intelligence can profoundly affect national economic and commercial interests. From the chapter outlines we can see at least seven cross-cutting themes. The first theme is that *a country's economic structure and its attitude toward government intervention in the economy are key factors influencing the role of intelligence services in the domain of economic intelligence.* The fact that there are differing "information-sharing cultures" means that their economic intelligence systems will also differ. Potter suggests that those societies with an ease of information exchange will have more effective economic intelligence-gathering networks, including a greater tolerance for the practice of economic espionage. The question that this raises and is explored in this volume is whether, all things being equal, such societies have a competitive edge in the global economy, and whether part of this advantage lies in offensive and, where necessary, clandestine economic intelligence-gathering capacities of intelligence services. Obviously, the competitiveness of a national economy is a function of a host of variables (both qualitative and quantitative), including natural factor endowments, types of industries, levels of research and development, the skills and education of the population, and the like. Indeed, the host of variables seems to expand annually, which may mean that at some point the role of intelligence services may be included.

The second theme, related directly to the first, concerns establishing *the actual costs and benefits to national economies and of protecting and collecting economic intelligence or of failing to do so adequately.* This is the first step in assessing the true value of the intelligence community's contribution to national economic welfare. Here some of the contributors' views diverge most conspicuously. The problem as expressed in all the chapters is two-fold: first, getting an accurate sense of the damage caused by the acquisition of protected economic information, which, as Potter points out, represents only a small fraction of the total amount of economic intelligence; and, secondly, clearly distinguishing between the dollar value-added that can be provided by intelligence services as defensive institutions, that is, by protecting "their" firms from economic espionage either at home or abroad, and their roles as offensive collecters of information on behalf of private sector clients from their national jurisdictions.

A major problem is clearly the paucity of data and empirical studies. Without these, there appears to be significant reliance on anecdotal evidence, which is given great prominence through the media's reporting of spectacular incidents of economic espionage (for example, the alleged bugging of seats on Air France). Porteous reports that the General Accounting Office, the investigative arm of the U.S. Congress, had to abandon its plan to study the extent and impact of foreign government spying on American companies when it became clear that firms had little desire to discuss this matter. That being said, Porteous goes on to conclude that despite "the obstacles to formal calculation," certain prominent American business leaders and government representatives agree that the cost of economic espionage to the U.S. economy is in the billions of dollars, with the White House Office on Science and Technology coming up with a damage estimate of over US$100 billion annually. He cites examples of how cost-effective the CIA's efforts have been in preventing American firms from losing market shares through corrupt practices by foreign firms or governments. Thus intelligence collection to prevent the targeting of national firms is deemed both virtuous and a gain to the U.S. economy.

On the offensive side of the ledger, Porteous discusses the value of low-cost "well-directed [espionage] operations" that have saved some countries (he cites France and Russia as examples) billions of dollars in research and development costs. Apparently, the payback from just one successful French economic intelligence operation exceeded the annual budget of the French secret service itself. He also asserts that economic intelligence is not just about the acquisition of leading-edge technology. Often the simplest form of intelligence (plant layouts and bid information) pays surer and more immediate benefits than the procurement of technology. Porteous concludes that the infrastructure—such as signals intelligence technology—for the collection of protected information is already in place, and comparatively little additional investment would be required to orient some of this capability to commercial areas. He would, however, likely not see the need to create a new, fully fledged foreign intelligence agency for a country such as Canada, which VanDuzer suggests as an option. In sum, then, on the basis of his cost-benefit analysis, Porteous believes that the increased involvement of intelligence services in economic intelligence is supportable.

Brander, using simple game theory, demonstrates how governments would see the advantage of using intelligence services to acquire economic intelligence, but he contends that ultimately such economic espionage has the effect of reducing overall global welfare, although it would have immediate benefits to particular countries and firms in terms of jobs and contracts. In an ideal world if all governments were to renounce economic espionage, everyone would be better off. However, he concedes that with such different levels of economic development in the world, there will always be an incentive for some countries to cheat.

Related to the above discussion on the private sector costs and benefits is the question of the use of economic intelligence acquired by intelligence services for the purpose of improving public policy-making. Porteous contends that despite the "quality of analysis" concerns raised by some, there is growing role for intelligence services in this area. Brander, however, counters that intelligence services should not get into the business of trying to replicate the functions of national statistical agencies, ministries of economics and trade, or the many international agencies and institutions that already provide this information.

Perhaps the problem is to determine at what point intelligence services, particularly in North America, would cross the line between, on the one hand, economic counter-intelligence (say, the monitoring of only the corrupt practices of foreign firms so as to ensure a level playing field for "their" firms) and on the other hand, channelling to their private sectors *any* other commercial intelligence that comes into their possession as part of their regular duties (for example, terrorism, money-laundering, political counter-intelligence), something that may ultimately lead to offensive operations that target sensitive commercial information. For some observers, this is the slippery slope. Brander and VanDuzer can agree that intelligence services do have an important, if perhaps secondary, role in so-called "police" matters at home. And all the authors would agree that potentially they have key roles in the monitoring of corrupt practices abroad and the fulfilment of obligations by signatories to international treaties. Where there appears to be significant disagreement between Brander and the other authors (especially Porteous), however, is on the economic benefits accruing to national economies from the provision to firms of clandestinely acquired commercial information by intelligence services.

The third theme, and perhaps the most controversial issue raised by the authors, *is the clandestine appropriation by intelligence services of commercial information for distribution to individual firms or commercial sectors.* The problem here is "Who is us?" when multinationals are global webs made up of firms from many countries, with products, know-how, and factors of production such as labour and capital flowing around the world. "Who is them?" What is a domestic firm, a foreign firm? Which contributes more to national economic security and should therefore receive more direct support from the state, the domestic firm that produces most of its output outside the country or the foreign firm that invests more locally? Indeed, does government have any business in picking winners and losers? And are strategic industries an exception?

Porteous and Brander see the benefits of the nexus of economic espionage and strategic trade policy in different ways. Here espionage is formally very similar to a subsidy to domestic firms. According to Brander, at the international level such activity tends to be harmful to innovative activity as a whole. In essence, when one country gains from economic espionage, the damage done to other countries exceeds the benefit to the country that gains. Porteous takes a more reality-based approach by pointing out that in a knowledge-based global economy, where comparative advantages can be transferred rapidly from nation to another, governments can, through properly targeted subsidies to domestic firms deemed to have strategic value, lower these firms' costs and theoretically allow them to provide more profits, and thereby benefit the country as a whole.

The provision of clandestinely acquired information to the private sector is also a fundamental issue at the heart of whether—given the resistance to state intervention in some Anglo-Saxon business cultures—North American intelligence services should be in the business of providing such information to firms or sectors. That being said, Porteous asks whether this cultural resistance has not already been broken in light of recent reports and testimony that the CIA has provided American companies with information on corrupt practices of foreign firms.

The fourth theme running throughout the book is that *Canada is not playing on a level playing field*. The fundamental question is what policy actions can realistically be taken by Ottawa and the Canadian private sector to redress this imbalance. From the legal perspective, VanDuzer notes that Canada's domestic legal framework to protect against the gathering of economic intelligence in Canada by foreign agents is not as punitive and restrictive as the legal regimes in place in France and Germany. And with regard to Canada's capacity to gather foreign economic intelligence in a clandestine fashion, as the Potter and VanDuzer chapters point out, because of CSIS's statutory mandate as a security intelligence agency (essentially a spycatcher) these limitations are obviously a handicap. Most of Canada's main economic rivals, because they have foreign intelligence agencies in addition to domestic security intelligence agencies, are active collectors of foreign economic intelligence. They target the strategic industries of their economic rivals (who may also be political allies), and, as Potter points out, have strong private sector and public sector networks to both protect and promote national economic security through cooperation on economic intelligence-gathering.

The fifth theme concerns *whether with greater incentives to appropriate high-tech data and knowledge it is enough for countries to respond through largely defensive means.* As mentioned, all the authors agree on the intelligence community's role in a defensive counter-intelligence capacity to prevent firms from being targeted by foreign intelligence services or their surrogates. Where there is less agreement is on the offensive side. Porteous contends that while there are problems with an offensive mandate this should not be an excuse for doing nothing. He asks rhetorically whether intelligence services would know what to look for. Yet, during the Cold War they did indeed seek and appropriate militarily applicable technology. Nor is he sure that such measures as international agreements that protect intellectual property rights will constrain intelligence services from going after key technologies at the pre-patent stage. Ironically, then, all the authors see a role for intelligence services in monitoring international agreements on the one hand; on the other, these same agencies should, in certain cases, according to some contributors be expected to help their individual firms to break the spirit of, if not the actual obligations in, the very agreements to which their political masters have affixed their signatures.

In the Canadian case, it is to be noted that approximately two dozen countries operate against Canadian interests within Canada and abroad. Most of these operations are directed at economic targets. The question is whether Canada's domestic legal framework, as outlined by VanDuzer, and the existing, but limited, foreign intelligence-gathering capacities of CSIS and the CSE are sufficient to negate the advantages of the more offensively-oriented economic intelligence-gathering activities of its major competitors. As Potter points out in his overviews of the intelligence mandates of some of Canada's major allies, apart from in the United States, such debates over the balance between domestic legal regimes and the need for offensive capacity hardly exist in Japan and some continental European countries.

Do the debatable benefits of offensive intelligence-gathering capacities and the larger defensive benefits justify increasing overall intelligence budgets or creating separate foreign intelligence services in countries such as Canada that now have largely defensive intelligence mandates? As Brander says, "An empirical judgment must be made ... whether economic counter-espionage has sufficiently low costs and sufficiently high benefits that it is worth doing." The same can be said about offensive economic espionage. Again, the problem with making such empirical judgments is that savings (or prevented thefts) are difficult to quantify. Finally, such an issue may never reach the stage of serious public policy debate: how does a government justify rolling back the welfare state while at the same time enlarging its intelligence community?[2]

The sixth theme is *the shift to more cooperative relations between the intelligence service and the private sector since the end of the Cold War.* The Potter, Porteous, and VanDuzer chapters suggest that the American and Canadian intelligence services—but particularly the latter—need to become more aggressive and outward-oriented. Policy makers and business communities in the United States and Canada accept that their respective intelligence services should be focused more on preventive foreign economic intelligence activities such as reporting on "sharp" business practices by foreign companies. However, there is as yet no consensus between the business and government communities nor within them about the highly sensitive issue of whether the intelligence services should use clandestine means to influence external economic developments (such as exchange rates and international trade negotiations), and the profitability of individual firms.

Yet there is clearly a concern. Porteous and VanDuzer refer to the recent amendments to intelligence service legislation and executive branch statements in the United States and Britain to demonstrate that governments are continually trying to incorporate a clearer role for the defensive and offensive uses of economic intelligence. With regard to Canada, VanDuzer spends a considerable part of his chapter discussing the "economic" provisions of the CSIS Act and the Criminal Code, and concludes that there is currently significant ambiguity in the Canadian legislation and that Ottawa may wish to incorporate the type of economic provisions in its enabling legislation that have been completed or are being seriously contemplated in the United States and Britain.

The final theme, highlighted by the Potter and Porteous chapters, is *the philosophical differences between the Anglo-Saxon world and other countries on the legitimate use of intelligence agencies in increasing economic competitiveness.* For some nations—notably the continental Europeans, Japan, and Russia—the use of intelligence services to actively protect and promote economic security is "old hat"; for others, such as Canada and the United States, turning the sights of their respective intelligence services to commercial matters has proved to be more difficult.

Basically, those who advocate a more aggressive foreign economic intelligence mandate for North American intelligence services ask why, if they are willing to do dirty tricks for the defense of traditional conceptions of national security, they are not also able to do dirty tricks for economic gain. On the other side, those more sceptical about the benefits of this orientation ask whether intelligence services should risk the lives of their agents for the sake of private companies, some of which could be majority-owned by foreigners. This is a particularly apt observation in the context of the Canadian economy, where more than half of the country's largest firms (in terms of assets and total sales) are subsidiaries of foreign—primarily U.S.—multinationals, and where the largest Canadian majority-owned firms, such as Northern Telecom, produce most of their sales and benefits abroad.

In short, then, the question is whether North American intelligence services should get into the business of industrial espionage. For those philosophically opposed to allowing a government to spy on behalf of its private sector, the solution to the protection side of the economic intelligence equation appears to be more aggressive counter-intelligence programs and domestic and international legal frameworks to protect commercially sensitive information.

The chapters in this book make clear that there are strong correlations between the collective attitude in nations toward the sharing of information, the domestic legal frameworks in place with regard to the defensive mandates and roles of intelligence services, and the leeway afforded to these services with regard to the collection of foreign economic intelligence both at home and abroad. Those societies that have greater state intervention in the economy and greater public-private information sharing will be more likely to have intelligence services that actively engage in offensive economic intelligence-gathering—including economic espionage. Therefore, in light of these conditions, the attempt to create a significant increase in the foreign economic intelligence-gathering capacity of certain countries—especially in the Anglo-Saxon world, which lacks a history of corporatist political structures, where state intervention in the domestic economy is less prevalent, and where as a result there is less direct information exchange between the public and private sectors—may prove stillborn.

Nevertheless, the intelligence services in the Anglo-Saxon countries can be made more effective in providing their political leaderships and senior bureaucratic levels with strategic information on economic trends and the trade negotiating positions of competitors, or reporting on corrupt business practices. As well, there is increased scope for Canadian and American intelligence services to increase their defensive operations to counter economic espionage by other states. In terms of offensive strategies, it appears that the North American intelligence services now also have more room for manoeuvre to expand their economic intelligence-gathering abroad—but only insofar as it creates a level playing field for their firms in the international market by making sure that all parties adhere to internationally accepted trade rules and practices. However, the American and Canadian intelligence services may be far more prone to failure in supplying commercial intelligence to their respective national business communities and in rewriting their statutes to reduce significantly the targeting of their economies by foreign states and their surrogates. The most problematic issue for the North American intelligence services remains the use of intelligence services (personnel and technology) as a direct means to expand market shares of individual firms and thus national economic growth.

In conclusion, there are four major challenges for Canadian policymakers as they attempt both to defend and to promote Canada's economic and commercial interests in a global economy characterized by "cooperative competition" at its best and "covert economic warfare" at its worst. The first is the creation of an information culture in Canada in which there is a comprehensive effort to manage and exchange strategic information or economic intelligence among the private, the public, and the non-profit sectors. There must be a collective acceptance that the renewal of industrial capacity, of full employment, and of Canada's national competitiveness is contingent on the circulation of information, which may require the creation of a central clearing house of scientific and economic intelligence.

The second challenge is to gain support at the highest political level for such an "information society" in Canada. The Cabinet must collectively accept that the inefficient and uncoordinated manner in which economic intelligence is currently collected, distributed and, when needed, protected, is doing possibly billions of dollars of damage to the Canadian economy annually.

Third, given the general consensus that the "old ways" of responding to the international economy are no longer optimal, the challenge is for the Canadian government to decide whether more efforts and resources should be directed to protecting Canada's economic and commercial interests from targeting by foreign states and their surrogates, or whether there should be more emphasis by the Canadian government on expanding market share abroad by open and clandestine means. Indeed, the protection and promotion of economic intelligence are two sides of the same national economic security coin.

The last major challenge is the means by which Canada will respond to the third challenge: to what extent should the domestic legal framework in Canada be changed to provide increased protection for proprietary information, if it needs to be changed at all? And what overhaul is necessary and feasible in Canada's intelligence community, with specific reference to the increasing role of its intelligence services in the protection and promotion of commercial and economic interests?

All the contributors to this volume would agree that economic security is a broad goal sought by all governments. They would also agree that the intelligence community's role in achieving this goal is secondary to that of the private sector and other government departments, who have purely economic and trade mandates. Yet, as recent legislative changes in the United States, Britain, and Australia indicate, the secondary nature of the intelligence community's role does not render it unimportant. As the international system moves from geopolitics to geoeconomics, the influence of the intelligence communities on the international economic system and on microeconomic interests remains uncertain. What is certain is that for many countries, from the last superpower to the old and emerging middle powers, intelligence services are going to be asked to be more active in warning of threats to national economic interests and in identifying opportunities to advance these interests.

1. Michael Hart, "A Multilateral Agreement on Foreign direct Investment: Why Now?" Occasional Paper No. 37 (Ottawa: Centre for Trade Policy and Law, Carleton University, 1996) mimeo, 7.

2. An exception in the Canadian case is Alistair S. Hensler, "Creating a Canadian Foreign Intelligence Service," *Canadian Foreign Policy* 3, 3 (Winter 1995-96), 15-35. On the budgetary impact on CSIS see Reg Whitaker, "Security and Intelligence in a Cold Climate," in Gene Swimmer, ed., *How Ottawa Spends 1996-97: Life Under the Knife* (Ottawa: Carleton University Press, 1996), 409-41.

I

THE SYSTEM OF ECONOMIC
INTELLIGENCE-GATHERING IN CANADA

Evan H. Potter

THE END OF THE COLD WAR, increased globalization, and the integration of Canada into a North American community have all focused attention on the role and importance of economic security. As well, the Chrétien government's 1994 Foreign Policy Review called for a broadening of the definition of security (referred to as "human security") to include economic prosperity.[1] Canada, perhaps more than any other industrialized nation given its dependence on trade, is redefining its national priorities as the objectives of economic growth and technological innovation are becoming paramount in the face of increasing international competition.

If Canada's foreign policy strategy during the Cold War was anchored in the world of military security, in the 1990s it is led by economic diplomacy. Canadian foreign policy is thus more than ever about achieving and protecting market access.[2] As such, two troubling paradoxes come to light concerning Canada's competitiveness. Canada is the eighth largest trading nation, yet it has a very narrow trading base, which is heavily dependent on resources. As well, Canada's international competitiveness ranking has been slipping since 1989.[3] Compounding this situation is the fact that with the real costs of transportation and communications continuing to decline, as services make up an increasing proportion of global commerce, the United States—by far Canada's most important economic partner—will acquire neighbours that it did not have before, creating even more competitive pressure on Canada. The competitive challenges facing Canada obviously do not strike only at the macro-level of the economy but go to the very heart of how individual Canadian firms operate. At the same time that Canadian firms are increasing their knowledge bases through research and development, they will be forced to increase the offensive and defensive techniques of managing competitive information or economic intelligence. These techniques are not the exclusive responsibility of the individual firm, however. The propensity of a nation's firms to cooperate at a certain level is an important determinant of a country's relative national economic power.

With economic growth the major focus of public policy, this chapter seeks to illuminate the importance of "economic intelligence" and the "economic intelligence system" for the achievement of Canada's national economic security. The chapter is divided into four sections. The first defines economic intelligence and its links to information technology. The second outlines the structure of the economic intelligence system in Canada, examining the role of economic intelligence in the public and private sectors, and highlighting both the system's strengths and its weaknesses. Here there will be emphasis on the pressure, emanating from budgetary deficits and the accumulated national debt, for government to reduce its role in both the creation and distribution of economic intelligence, which in turn may lead to a greater private sector role in the economic intelligence system. To place the Canadian system in context, the third section provides a summary review of practices and systems of selected competitor countries. The final section offers a number of recommendations on improving the structure of the Canadian system. While there is no wish to impose a foreign model on Canada—which would be inappropriate given the unique circumstances of every nation's development—there are certainly lessons to be learned from our competitors.

DEFINING ECONOMIC INTELLIGENCE

One of the first conceptual problems with terms such as "economic intelligence" and "economic intelligence systems" is one of semantics, that is, establishing a commonly accepted definition. As a first cut, how, for example, are "knowledge," "information," and "intelligence" related? Knowledge is not synonymous with either "information" or "intelligence," although one presumably has to have both to have knowledge. And does "system" imply the cumulative knowledge of a society? Should a distinction be made between economic "information" and economic "intelligence"? The national security literature, for example, refers to "economic intelligence"; meanwhile, the management studies literature, business people, and government officials responsible for promoting trade and investment rarely refer to economic intelligence, preferring instead to differentiate between "market information" and "market intelligence" or "strategic research," which, in the private sector, may be located in any one or combination of departments (for example, economics, corporate planning, research and development, marketing).

With such a *mélange* of terms, for the purposes of consistency this chapter does not make a distinction between "information" and "intelligence," and instead proffers the view that there are several levels of intelligence, from the most basic (analogous to "information") to the most processed and potentially confidential ("clandestine"). A narrow definition of economic intelligence is "policy or commercially relevant economic information, including technological data, financial, proprietory commercial [e.g., business plans and bids for major commercial projects, customer survey data, etc.] and government information [e.g., information on trade negotiations, economic plans and strategies], the acquisition of which by foreign interests could, either directly or indirectly, assist the relative productivity or competitive position of the economy of the collecting organization's country."[4]

A comprehensive study of economic intelligence led by Henri Martre of the French government's Commissariat Général du Plan defines it more broadly as

> the combined coordinated actions of research, processing, and distribution with the purpose of its [economic intelligence] exploitation as useful information for economic actors. These diverse actions are engaged in legally with all the necessary protection for the firm, under the most favourable conditions given the considerations of timeliness and cost.[5]

More simply put, it is the provision of useful information to companies so that they can elaborate and implement coherent strategies and tactics necessary to gain market share.

Here the notion of economic intelligence implies going beyond strictly the gathering of information, that is, the gaining of insights into science and technology developments, the strategies of competitors, changing financial, legal, and regulatory regimes—all potentially *passive* exercises—to one of using information *actively* for the protection of competitive position and influence (through "operations" of information-gathering and disinformation).[6] It is the understanding that there are tactical and strategic (or clandestine) components to this information-gathering that take place at a number of levels that are themselves interlinked. This can be summarized as a *four-level function* of economic intelligence. The four levels are:

- the primary level (within the firm);

- an intermediate stage (inter-professional and local networks, such as strategic alliances between the financial services community and information technology developers to liberalize the movement of capital and financial information);

- the national level (linked strategies between different—government, business, labour—decision-making centres, favoured in more corporatist political environments and most apparent in continental Europe and Japan)[7]; and

- the transnational level (through strategic alliances undertaken by firms of all sizes) or the international level (strategic influence pursued by nation-states bilaterally, plurilaterally, and multilaterally, as exemplified by the European Union's support for the transnational research networks of its Member States, or Canada's various bilateral research and development agreements with other states).

The term "economic intelligence system" refers to the cumulative practices and strategies of information use, developed in every country at different levels of organization—the government (federal and sub-federal), industry, firms, education, and the population as a whole. The "economic intelligence community" for its part is a component of the system and encompasses all the institutions of the state that produce and consume economic intelligence.

Economic intelligence passes through four stages: creation, production, distribution, and consumption. There is no lack of the first and no potential lack of the fourth. However, these two stages can be affected only marginally by public policy. The intermediate stages—production and distribution—are the structural layers where public policy can make all the difference at home and abroad. In addition, in discussing economic intelligence the connection between the domestic and the foreign should be amplified. For instance, regulatory policies (transportation, telecommunications, inter-provincial trade barriers, and the like), social welfare programs, and education and training are all domestic public policy concerns that affect national economic performance. Thus, much of what makes Canada competitive internationally is actually domestic.

Adapting Martre's useful typology, there are four types of economic intelligence, as shown in Table 1:

- *Primary* and *Secondary* economic intelligence (the "green" and "yellow" zones respectively) range from data retrieved from open sources such as Statistics Canada, on-line data retrieval systems (Lexis Nexis, Bloomberg, Reuters, and the like), think tanks, university research centres, libraries, trade associations, media, and specialist publications, to still open but perhaps more costly and hard to find information. The basic difference between the two levels is the ease of acquisition of information in the *public* domain.

- *Tactical* economic intelligence (the "red" zone) refers to more sensitive and privileged information sourced from customer surveys, personal contacts (company visits, for example), and less open ways of information such as "invitation only" specialist symposia. Data internal to the firm, including sales and cost analyses, staff reports (R&D reports, for example), project bids, and the like, would be classified as tactical. In intelligence circles this is often referred to as "hidden" information.

- *Clandestine* economic intelligence[8] (the "black" zone) refers to proprietary or classified information—often highly processed—that is obtained illegally through clandestine human or technical means.

A few qualifiers for this typology are in order. First, starting at the secondary level there is more processing of information and less structured and less open ways of obtaining it (for example, the difference between public and "invitation-only" conferences). Second, at the private sector level, most companies do not have a strict security classification, as is the case, for example, in the Canadian federal government (with its classifications such as "protected," "confidential," "classified," and

TABLE 1: TYPOLOGY OF ECONOMIC INTELLIGENCE

Characteristic	Primary	Secondary	Tactical	Clandestine
Colour code	Green zone	Yellow zone	Red zone	Black zone
Access	**Accessibility is greatest**; everyone can observe. Information is available (in hard copy or electronically) through simple procedures that can be undertaken by the non-specialist (e.g., by mail, through the Internet or other electronic bulletin boards, faxlinks, 1-800 numbers, etc.). **Because of differing legal systems and disclosure regimes**, the level of access to information varies from country to country.	Although the availability of economic intelligence is not as widespread because of scarcity of supply, high cost, or the need for specialist know-how (e.g., techniques to access particular databases), it is still freely accessible and in the public domain. This type of information is usually in the form of published text, whether in hard copy or electronic form. An example of this would be some Statistics Canada publications (e.g., *Canadian Economic Observer*) on macro-economic trends, or it can refer to sector studies (e.g., the telecommunications sector in Germany) sold by subscription or by, say, the Canada-German Chamber of Commerce.	Economic intelligence is "tactical" when it concerns information that is *more difficult to acquire and that has a degree of confidentiality*. This type of information, whose acquisition under certain circumstances could be unethical, is usually acquired through primary research (e.g., interviews, oral communications). It can also be acquired from client surveys (formal and informal), industry conventions, and consultants (e.g., *Canadian Corporate R&D Database*). Here, the raw information provided from levels one and two is treated with a higher level of analysis and can be translated into the strategies and tactics used by firms in their industries, their ability	Economic intelligence of a "strategic" nature concerns that information whose accessibility is sophisticated, difficult and delicate. It consists, for example, of identifying the future intentions or capacities of competitors (firms or states). This type of information is frequently sought by managers, intelligence services, and the many professional groups (lawyers, consultants, agents) who act as purveyors of this information to one or more firms or states. The challenge for the initiator of this type of information is to integrate scarce information into a comparative advantage, whether at the level of the firm or the nation-state. Because of the scarcity and hence high value of the information, there is an incentive for the individual, the firm, or the state to overstep the boundaries of ethical standards and use illegal methods, in order to be

TABLE 1 (cont'd)

Characteristic	Primary	Secondary	Tactical	Clandestine
Colour code	Green zone	Yellow zone	Red zone	Black zone
(cont'd) Access			(cont'd) to launch new products, and organizational restructuring (i.e., activities internal to the firm).	(cont'd) more competitive. The compilation of numerous sources of this highly scarce information may thus lead to a "strategic" economic intelligence. An example of this could be the prior knowledge by one firm or state of the intentions of a competitor firm or state during the international rendering of a multi-million dollar contract to, say, overhaul a fleet of aircraft.
Authorized/ unauthorized	Everything that is not prohibited is supposedly allowed. Open access.	Everything that is not prohibited is supposedly allowed. Open access.	Everything that is not prohibited is supposedly allowed. Conditions on access (security personnel or ethical considerations).	Everything that is not authorized is *not* allowed. Access is given only to specific private and state sector personnel. If access is unauthorized it is clandestine.

TABLE 1 *(cont'd)*

Characteristic	Primary	Secondary	Tactical	Clandestine
Colour code	Green zone	Yellow zone	Red zone	Black zone
Type	Open information.	Open information (90 %).	Partially open or sensitive information.	Proprietory/denied information (10 %).
Category of legal infractions		Possibility of intellectual property infraction.	Interpretation of jurisprudence. Trade secret infraction.	Infractions of criminal and commercial law. Physical or electronic penetration of public administration. Physical or electronic penetration of firms.

Source: Adapted and translated from Henri Martre, *Rapport du groupe intelligence économique et stratégie des entreprises* (Paris: Commissariat général du plan, février 1994), 18-19; annex in Jean-Pichot Duclos, "'L'intelligence économique' : pour un modèle français," *Défense nationale* 16 (1990), 86.

"secret"). Thus there is spillover across the typology, depending on the circumstances of information collection and dissemination. And in some cases, putting a firm's internal data into the public domain may be unethical but not illegal, whereas in others, when an employee has signed a secrecy agreement the information source would be in the black zone, and such an act would prompt legal action.

There is a frequently held assumption that the juxtaposition of the word "intelligence" with "economic" makes the economic information confidential. But if one accepts this chapter's schema of different levels of economic intelligence rather than a continuum on which economic "information" passing through various stages of processing becomes "intelligence," then economic intelligence is no longer by definition referring to confidential information. For example, data contained in the Economist Intelligence Unit reports is highly processed, but they are available in most libraries. Indeed, the vast majority—estimated at 90 percent[9]—of economic intelligence gathered by the public and private sectors is derived from open sources in a legal manner involving no clandestine, coercive, or deceptive methods.

Finally, a word about scholarly or policy-oriented research on economic intelligence. Not surprisingly, in the open-source literature, research on comparative economic intelligence systems, as opposed to comparative security intelligence systems, is scarce. This is no doubt due to the difficulty in defining, conceptualizing, and, perhaps most of difficult of all, quantifying economic intelligence. How does one go about quantifying (both present and future) research and development? What about the unknowable percentages of "tactical" and "clandestine" intelligence? Furthermore, how does one quantify "influence"? In the Canadian context, for example, what influence do the myriad private sector-sponsored studies on Canadian competitiveness (undertaken with funding in part from foreign multinationals, including Kodak Canada's sponsorship of a competitiveness study,[10] and the Business Council on National Issues-sponsored study by Michael Porter on Canada's com-petitiveness[11]), have on decision-makers in both the private and public sectors? The reason for seeking to put a dollar value on economic intel-ligence is simply to be able to estimate the loss to Canada's national income and therefore relative competitiveness resulting from foreign (both open and covert; private and state-sponsored) intelligence-gathering (see the chapter by Samuel Porteous).

The Impact of Information Technology

Before examining Canada's economic intelligence system, it would be helpful to describe briefly the link between economic intelligence and the dynamic changes brought about by information technology. According to Kaye, after a 25-year period of advances in information and communications technology, the 1990s have ushered in the information revolution. What separates the information revolution from the communications revolution is that three previously separate streams of technical development, communications, computing, and data storage, have converged. With the cost barriers and technical barriers that had previously prevented the full exploitation of information now being lowered, we have entered into the age of open information capability. Kaye believes that it is this open information capability that has started the information revolution.[12]

The new open information capability will change how society processes and organizes its economic intelligence: intra- and inter-corporate and public sector boundaries or barriers and management hierarchies "need no longer be imposed by the exigencies of information flow and problem solving."[13] The emergence of an information society has had five major effects:

- globalization;

- fragmentation, decentralization, and democratization (for example, proliferation, knowledge-based companies, the increased role of sub-national governments, and the multiplication of players involved in the process of governance);

- as mentioned, the breakdown of the bureaucratic/industrial way of organizing, characterized by downsizing, privatization, delayering, and the creation of more "client driven" organizations;

- less possibility for secrecy; and

- the blurring of boundaries between industries, between public and private sectors, between goods and services, and between states, all of which has led to the need for new alliances and relationships and the need to rethink conceptual categories.[14] In short, the collection and distribution of economic intelligence is being democratized as the result of advances in information technology and the emergence of an information society.

But this is not all. As well as information technology transforming the operational service-delivery and management practices in spheres of activity ranging from government services and financial services to manufacturing, it has also been catalytic in the emergence of new industrial sectors. For instance, the increasing weight of intangible or non-material investment (R&D, software, education and training, marketing, design) makes it clear that the nature of the regulating processes of economic activity are being profoundly altered. In other words, information technology is playing a pivotal role both in the *process* and the *content* of Canada's performance and hence its economic security. Sophisticated communications networks being developed in North America, Europe, and Asia are already delivering vital information to business and industry, wherever it is located. These networks provide exporters and investors with a comparative advantage in the form of high-quality, competitively priced economic intelligence and data links to global markets. Given Canada's dependence on trade, the economic impact of information technology is enormous, both as a growth industry in its own right and as an influence upon overall economic development, job creation, and, increasingly, on export performance.[15] As will be described in this chapter, large and small enterprises are benefiting from electronic data interchange and just-in-time delivery procedures that depend on telecommunications and data links.

But as much as the information revolution and the advances in information technology and communications before it have benefited society by engendering a remarkable explosion of economic intelligence as well as facilitating its transfer, in Canada the cooperation between the public and private domains in this process has been more hesitant than in many other industrialized countries. Canada's production and distribution structures, that is, the intermediate stages of the economic intelligence process, have simply not managed to keep up with the quantity and quality of information being produced.

CHARACTERISTICS OF THE CANADIAN ECONOMIC INTELLIGENCE SYSTEM

The Problem

The examination of the national network of economic intelligence brings few surprises. As Figure 1 and Table 2 both show, the official sources of economic intelligence include departments, departmental corporations, branches designated as departments, special operating agencies, Crown corporations (non-commercial and commercial), exempt Crown corporations, joint enterprises, and other entities, not to mention provincial ministries and agencies.[16] Outside of government there are financial centres, Canadian and foreign-based multinationals, management consulting firms, peak business associations, research institutes or think-tanks, and universities; at the same time, these domestic "Canadian" actors and institutions are influenced by foreign state and non-state actors, especially the U.S. government and the U.S. academic and private sector communities, not to mention Canada's myriad multilateral affiliations.[17] Figure 1 is a picture of a somewhat "anarchic" cross-cutting Canadian economic intelligence system that is not as interconnected as those systems found, for example, in Japan, Germany and France (Figures 2, 4 and 6 respectively); it appears closer in structure to those of the United States and Britain (Figures 3 and 5 respectively), although it is distinctive in that it does not appear as centralized (not surprising given Britain's unitary political system). As this chapter will describe, Canada possesses a highly confederal system of economic intelligence-gathering that is in many respects duplicative, inflexible, and lacking a systematic and structured series of links and channels between and among the major economic actors at the four "functional" levels of economic intelligence interaction described earlier.

In the absence of a corporatist framework at the federal level (Quebec is notable for its corporatist approach at the provincial level), the present Canadian system has a host of troubling characteristics: an absence of national economic security strategy; insufficient distribution within the public and private sectors of economic intelligence sourced from Canada's many multilateral ties (we might as well exploit our traditional "joiner" mentality to the fullest); insufficient exploitation of Canada's multicultural communities; weak transfer of military-industrial (DND, NRC) knowledge to the private sector; the relative lack of active

FIGURE 1: ECONOMIC INTELLIGENCE
IN THE CANADIAN ECONOMY

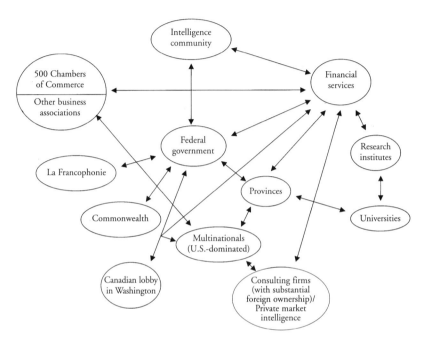

Source: Author

participation of labour in the national economic intelligence system (the exception being perhaps the Canadian Labour Market Productivity Centre); and dominance of foreign firms in the private economic intelligence market (see the listing of consulting firms in Table 2, under the category of "Restricted Public Economic Intelligence").

From the firm's perspective, the function of economic intelligence is not sufficiently integrated into general corporate strategy. For many Canadian firms, economic intelligence means looking at nodes of information (InfoExport/WinExport/Faxlink/Internet, [available from such federal departments as DFAIT], International Trade Centres, provincial government agencies, banks, or consultants, and the like). All these elements taken separately are of course important. The question is whether a more loosely connected system, such as is found in Canada, is superior to one that displays a more integrated approach, as appears to be the case in Japan and Germany.

TABLE 2: TYPOLOGY OF ECONOMIC INTELLIGENCE SOURCES

Public Economic Intelligence[a]	Restricted Public Economic Intelligence	Sensitive Economic Intelligence	Secret Economic Intelligence
Electronic and print media, on-line information retrieval systems, public symposia/conferences, banks, vertical (i.e., industry-specific) and horizontal trade associations (e.g., CCC, Alliance of Manufacturers and Exporters of Canada, BCNI, CMA), university research centres, government-business-university research partnerships (in key technologies), public (including Library of Parliament) and university libraries, and other documentation centres	Specialist information available only by subscription (e.g., newsletters or electronically)	Firms Clients Partners	Confidential consultations in public and private sectors
Federal:	Specialist symposia (by invitation only)	Visits to firms	Illegal/clandestine sources
Agriculture Canada	Law offices (large "full service" operations such as those provided by McLeod Dixon, Ward and Beck, McCarthy Tetrault, and other Canadian law firms with international affiliations)	Targeted information for business association membership only (e.g., Conference Board of Canada, CCC, BCNI)	Electronic and human interception techniques at governmental level through economic espionage (e.g., in Canada allegedly through Communications Security Establishment[c]) or through private means (e.g., industrial espionage)
Bank of Canada			
Canadian Heritage			
Canadian International Development Agency			
Canadian Security Intelligence Service			
Environment Canada			
Finance		Targeted information for labour organization membership only (e.g., Canadian Labour Congress)	
Fisheries and Oceans			
Foreign Affairs and International Trade			
Health Canada			
Industry Canada		Products	
National Defence			
National Research Council			
Natural Resources			
Privy Council Office			
Solicitor General Canada			
Statistics Canada			
Transport Canada			

TABLE 2 (cont'd)

Public Economic Intelligence[a]	Restricted Public Economic Intelligence	Sensitive Economic Intelligence	Secret Economic Intelligence
Treasury Board of Canada National Science and Engineering Research Council, Social Science and Humanities Research Council, International Trade Centres, Royal Commissions **Non-commercial and commercial Crown corporation(s):** Canadian Space Agency, Atomic Energy of Canada Ltd., Export Development Corporation, Canadian Commercial Corporation, Teleglobe Canada, Canadian Wheat Board, Telesat Canada **Other government-funded entities:** Asia-Pacific Foundation, Canadian International Grains Institute, Pulp and Paper Research Institute of Canada, Western Grains Research Foundation, Canadian Intellectual Property Office **Provincial:** Ontario International Trade Corporation, British Columbia Trade and Development Corporation, Department of Economic Development and Trade (Alberta), Ministère des affaires internationales (Québec) **Think Tanks/Research Institutes**[b]: C.D. Howe Institute, Fraser Institute, Canadian Centre for Policy Alternatives, Canada West Foundation, the North-South Institute, Institute for Research on Public Policy, International Development Research Centre **Other:** Public Policy Forum, Canadian Institute for Advanced Research, Conference Board of Canada, World Trade Centres	Management consultants ranging from boutique shops, such as Strategico (Ottawa), to "Big Six" management consulting operations with international affiliations (e.g., Coopers and Lybrand, Peat Marwick Thorne), McKinsey and Co., Baine and Co., Monitor, Anderson Consulting, Phillips Group, Raymond Chabot, etc. Public relations/ lobbying firms (Hill and Knowlton, etc.)	Personal contacts (both deliberate and accidental)	

a This list is by no means complete and reflects only larger public and private sector sources of economic intelligence.
b The Economic Council of Canada and the Science Council of Canada were eliminated in 1992.
c See Mike Frost, *Spyworld: Inside the Canadian and American Intelligence Establishments* (Toronto: Doubleday, 1994), esp. 226-28.
Source: Author

The Causes

While history, geography, language, and culture predispose Canadians to be more collective in outlook in some ways than, say, Americans, it does not does make us as unified in terms of having a national purpose as countries such as Germany and Japan. Canada does not have an information-sharing culture; we are uncomfortable "dealing with" clandestinely-derived information. As this chapter will explain, the best indicator of a nation's approach to economic intelligence is its national culture.

Canada's political history can be characterized as a seesaw between periods of centralization and decentralization: attempts to rationalize the economic intelligence system have often come up against provincial resistance, which in turn has hindered a centralized system of information retrieval. At the same time, it would surprise no one that bureaucracies themselves are full of contradictions that undermine the coordination of economic intelligence. It has been difficult to institute procedures to circulate information from the top down. The hierarchical nature of the public service and the norms and procedures of classification also make it difficult to distribute information. These factors all act as hindrances to the adaptation that is necessary to meet the challenges of the more globalized economy of the 1990s.

At the private sector level, the absence of a culture of economic intelligence translates into a number of outcomes: incomplete use and integration of all levels of economic intelligence, especially the "clandestine" variety; insufficient awareness among some firms and sectors of increased economic competition; a reluctance to compartmentalize sensitive information and the attendant possibilities for economic espionage (see the chapters by Samuel Porteous and Anthony VanDuzer); and the difficulty in sensitizing personnel to how outside agents collect information. In the context of an environment characterized by increasingly fierce economic competition, these errors penalize the private sector—particularly enabling industries that have not adequately integrated the collection and distribution of economic intelligence in their management cultures and practices.

The Collection of Economic Intelligence: The Case of the Canadian State

All state institutions and agencies, as consumers of economic intelligence, are inherently part of the four-stage economic intelligence process (creation, production, distribution, and consumption). What differentiates departments is their participation in the other three stages, which leads to numerous combinations and permutations, as some departments (Statistics Canada) will create, produce, and distribute some types of economic intelligence for example, while others (DFAIT, Industry) will be more focused on the production and distribution stages. This division of labour changes yet again (though less and less with the internationalization of "domestic" departments, as even a cursory examination of the government telephone directory shows) if we distinguish between economic intelligence used for domestic purposes and that being sought from abroad.

Given Canada's trade-dependent status and its characterization as a "trading nation, but not a nation of traders," it would seem that issues of market access and the acquisition and distribution of foreign economic intelligence are vital in any discussion of Canada's economic intelligence system. Canadian consuls and trade commissioners have been collecting economic intelligence for more than a century. In fact, even before the Canadian Trade Commissioner Service (TCS) was established in 1894, Canada had representatives in London and Paris; the province of Nova Scotia had a delegate in Paris as far back as 1780.

Given limitations of space, the reader is invited to consult Hill on the institutional history of Canada's foreign economic intelligence system, the backbone of which is the TCS.[18] A more current treatment of institutional roles and practices as well as the policy dilemmas confronting the system can be found in Griffith.[19] As mentioned earlier, it is difficult enough to estimate the total costs of such a system much less to attempt to arrive at a dollar figure for the contribution it makes to the national economy. That being said, comparisons have been done on the costs of the international business development systems of various OECD countries.[20] For Canada, as much as the approximately $650 million spent by more than 18 federal government departments on international business development[21] is vital to its status as a trading nation, this amount is but a fraction of a much larger national economic intelligence budget that must also take into account Ottawa's support for research in

Science and Technology (S&T) and any provincial spending.[22] Because each country measures its economic intelligence budget differently it becomes very difficult to state definitively whether one country spends more or less than another.

Attempts to Streamline Canada's Foreign Economic Intelligence System

A major improvement to the oft-criticized national system of producing and distributing economic intelligence (characterized by lack of coordination at the federal level and competition between federal and provincial departments) for use by Canada's exporters and foreign investors[23] was evident in DFAIT's international trade business plans in the early 1990s which, for the first time, included references to provincial activities. The Department also undertook a number of initiatives to improve the supply of client-focused market intelligence and information to the export community. Field trials were completed for a market intelligence messaging system, an E-mail-enabled facsimile service that allowed Canadian trade commissioners abroad to communicate market intelligence more quickly and directly to Canadian exporters.

The Chrétien government for its part has recognized that the growth of small and medium-sized enterprises (SMEs) is critical to Canada's economic growth and that this growth will be export-led.[24] As a result, an action plan was prepared in May 1994 by a task force of federal officials, the Canadian Bankers Association, and the Export Development Corporation (EDC) representatives to address three main issues to facilitate the export-readiness of Canadian SMEs: the provision of more timely "market information/intelligence,"[25] and short- and medium-term financing. The reason for the intimate involvement of Canada's chartered banks in this exercise was that in the previous year they had been roundly criticized for their unresponsiveness to the needs of SMEs. The involvement of Canadian banks signalled their recognition that often a firm's first point of contact is a banker and, therefore, in order to better understand the needs of these exporters the banks' staffs had to have more training on trade finance.

Today, there appears to be more team work between the Department of Foreign Affairs and International Trade, CIDA, Industry Canada, EDC, and the Canadian Commercial Corporation. The Corporation draws on market information and market intelligence supplied by Canada's trade commissioners and in turn depends on export financing from EDC and the commercial banks. EDC, meanwhile, has the international expertise that SMEs often have difficulty accessing, such as current information on commercial and political risks—information that EDC provides as part of its "Risks and Opportunities" workshops twice a year.

Other Actors

With regard to cooperation between the government and the private sector on the production and distribution of economic intelligence, the current concern in the business community is that government concentrate on providing intelligence on emerging sectors of business such as services (since this is now the largest component of Canada's economy), as well as providing information on emerging trade policy issues (for instance, labour and social policy, the environment) that may emerge as significant future non-tariff barriers for Canadian business. The business community would like to see the role of government in the economic intelligence field move from that of provider to that of facilitator,[26] something advocated in the Mulroney government's 1992 Prosperity Final Report. In other words, the private sector would like to see government make available economic intelligence that can then be targeted better by the private sector through the programs and services of vertical or horizontal industry associations.

Without the resources of larger firms to gather economic intelligence, Canadian SMEs are at a distinct competitive disadvantage in international markets. The business community has raised its concern about the need for more dissemination of company-specific, reliable, and timely information on market trends and business opportunities abroad. In terms of the appropriate division of labour between government and business in the collection and dissemination of economic intelligence, the private sector has told government that it should deploy its resources (human and capital) where it could expect the greatest return, such as in those markets that have the highest growth rates and are most difficult to penetrate, such as Asia Pacific and Latin America, and that it should let business fend for itself in the more saturated markets of Western Europe and the United States.[27] A private sector review of Canada's international business development system in 1994 [28] made a number of salient recommendations: that all federal and provincial activities relating to international business promotion be better coordinated; that government select, for special attention, high-technology sectors and geographical markets with major export potential for their products and services; that the Trade Commissioner Service strengthen its ability to respond to rapid changes in the international environment, notably by providing more training to officers in priority areas and by increasing the number of short-term executive exchanges with the private sector and International Financial Institutions. The Canadian Chamber of Commerce (CCC), for its part, has been even bolder in suggesting that, on a trial basis, it take over some of the trade promotion functions currently undertaken by government officials in Canada's consulates in the United States.[29]

From an institutional standpoint (see Figure 1), and as the discussion below on the CCC will demonstrate, Canada's business associations are independent from government, unlike the quasi-public sector organizations that one finds in, for example, Germany and France. In the latter countries, regional councils and chambers of commerce play a key role in circulating economic information; therefore, they find themselves halfway between industry and government. Chambers of commerce therefore have a privileged contact with the SMEs, which explains why such organizations in France and Germany give priority to scientific information and technology. Although the Canadian Chamber of Commerce has a Government Affairs and an International Affairs committee, there are no formal institutional connections between the CCC and the federal government (although CCC president Tim Reid has sat on the federal government-run International Trade Advisory Committee). In addition to the national Chamber of Commerce, which is itself affiliated to the International Chamber of Commerce headquarters in Paris, there are ten provincial Chambers and hundreds of local chambers (one in each federal riding!) that to varying degrees distribute and consume economic intelligence. The chambers of commerce in Canada, unlike national chambers in other countries, must rely on the resources of their members (usually larger companies and banks[30]) for the production of economic intelligence that may or may not be distributed to the membership at large. Chambers of commerce in Canada are thus essentially administrative and coordinating organizations rather than production sites.

The Canadian Chamber of Commerce: The Evolution of a Private Sector Approach to Economic Intelligence

The CCC is Canada's largest and most representative business association. It includes 500 community chambers and boards of trade, individual corporations, and over 100 trade and professional associations. The CCC maintains an international orientation through affiliated geographically-oriented business councils (Canada-Arab Business Council, Canada-India Business Council, Canada-Taiwan Business Association, Canada-Korea Business Council, and the ASEAN-Canada Business Council). The Chamber also maintains formal links with independent Canadian Chambers of Commerce in Japan, Hong Kong, and Mexico.

The CCC's international activities began in 1982 through the creation of geographically-oriented business councils that were designed to help promote the visibility of Canadian companies abroad. They acted as a forum for firms of different sizes and from different industries. Each council's activities included seminars, an annual meeting, inward and outward missions, and a newsletter. By the late 1980s, through seed-funding, multiple-year and single-event fee-for-service arrangements with various government departments, both provincial and federal (primarily CIDA and DFAIT), the Chamber's business councils had achieved a considerable national and international profile.

By 1990, however, it was becoming clear that exclusive use of the geographically oriented business council format was not the optimal way of either gathering or disseminating market information or economic intelligence. The dual pressures of government budgetary cutbacks and the increased availability of other sources of market information and intelligence, whether through international business consultants or on-line services and databases to match Canadian exporters and investors with foreign partners, signalled the end of the pre-eminence of the business council format to distribute market information and intelligence within the private sector. The feeling among many in the business community was that "they were being conferenced and luncheoned to death," and that the market information that was being made available through geographically-based councils was neither timely enough nor sector or company-specific enough. This is not surprising, since the CCC's business councils (having one staff member, for example, assigned to cover India, Central and Eastern Europe, the former Soviet Union, and the Arab world) certainly did not have the resources to provide market intelligence (the exception being the Canadian Trade Office in Taipei [CTOT]) for particular members. Obviously, this mattered less for the larger companies than it did for SMEs. In terms of collecting, producing, and disseminating market information and intelligence, the CCC councils were more able to act as door-openers during trade missions outside of Canada than as repositories of economic or market intelligence. Inquiries requiring even the most basic research were usually passed on to Statistics Canada, DFAIT, CIDA, or the Export Development Corporation. In short, the CCC—again with exception of CTOT—while presenting itself as a focal point for private sector inquiries on specific international markets, was in fact in no position to deliver on *a regular basis* sector- or company-specific market intelligence for the members of its business councils, although it did provide some sector information through the council newsletters.

That being said, this does not mean that geographically-based business councils in Canada are ineffective as distributors of economic intelligence. As mentioned, given Canada's "one China" policy, Ottawa does not recognize Taiwan. The Chamber, through a fee-for-service arrangement with DFAIT, has therefore managed the CTOT since 1986. The Office, with a staff of Canadian government officials, functions just like a regular trade mission, apprising interested Canadian exporters and investors on the opportunities and challenges of doing business in this multi-billion dollar market. Another example of an off-shore Chamber-affiliated business council that *did* produce economic intelligence was the Canadian Trade Office in Dubai, which, until it was converted into a Canadian embassy in 1993, was part of the Canada-Arab Business Council. Outside of the Chamber network are a number of other Canadian-based and non-Canadian-based country-specific and geographic business councils of varying sizes and varying capabilities of delivering market information and intelligence. Some of the more prominent councils include the Canada-Russia Business Council, headquarters in Toronto with a full-time Executive Director, the Canada-Japan Business Council, and the Canada-China Business Council (with an office in Beijing).

Returning to the Canadian Chamber's experience, by 1992 it began moving away from the business council format (it divested itself of four councils), and looked for better ways of providing economic intelligence to its members and the Canadian business community at large. Coincidentally, the Conference Board of Canada also decided to close its International Business Research Centre in this year in order to focus on more directed approaches to providing information to its clients. This shift in process also reflected the perception at both the government and business levels that what was needed was a more targeted approach to increasing the capabilities of SMEs to succeed in foreign markets.

The Chamber had in fact indirectly experimented with new approaches to creating an SME network when, in 1989, it started a computer network, *Chambernet*, to link local chambers with the national Chamber in Ottawa. Although at its height the Chamber's head office had 80 local chambers connected, this number was deemed insufficient to make this initiative financially feasible, and *Chambernet* was discontinued in 1992. Since that time (and in the spirit of *Chambernet*), a host of new economic intelligence services, including the Forum for International Trade Training (FITT), BCNet, and the International Business Exchange (IBEX), have been launched.

Forum for International Trade Training (FITT)
In 1992 a consortium of business and labour groups (the Canadian Federation of Labour, the Canadian Manufacturers Association, the Canadian Importers Association, and the Canadian Exporters' Association) in cooperation with the then Department of Employment and Immigration (now Human Resources), created the Forum for International Trade Training (FITT) to teach Canadian companies and employees the skills required to succeed internationally. Part of this training includes a focus on how to understand the dynamics of foreign markets. In short, FITT acts as a way of sensitizing Canadian firms to the utility of economic intelligence in its offensive capacity. This is an example of business and education allying themselves (reflecting the trend toward creating national "networks," mentioned earlier in this chapter), since the FITT is presently available in 30 community colleges with international business programs.[31]

On-line Business Exchange
Another impetus for the evolution in the private sector's (as well as the public sector's) approach to the distribution of economic intelligence has been the information revolution. As a result, the CCC, acting as the

national representative in Canada of a joint venture between Global Business Alliance/Systemhouse Canada and the U.S. Chamber of Commerce, has participated in the International Business Exchange (IBEX) system. The IBEX was designed to allow firms throughout the world to find, qualify, and negotiate with foreign and domestic partners based on the basis of specific offers or requests. With the negotiations between firms on-line, IBEX created a borderless trading floor of transactions.

SME Network

The Chamber's focus on capacity-building in Canada was symbolized by a small business networking program (SME Network), which attempted to develop a new thinking in Canada that small companies cooperating could be more competitive by working together rather than standing alone. Initially envisaged as a way for companies to share administrative services, this joint venture was positioned to eventually encourage these firms to share marketing or R&D expenses. According to CCC executives this type of networking had been successful in Norway, Denmark, and Italy and had also attracted the attention of the Australian government.[32]

Business Cooperation Network (BCNet)

In response to the need to provide Canadian SMEs with increased access to economic intelligence on foreign markets, in July 1993 the CCC began managing the Business Cooperation Network in Canada in partnership with the federal government (through Industry Canada) and the governments of Nova Scotia, Quebec, Ontario, and British Columbia. BCNet, which was initiated by the European Commission in 1988, is a computer matching service designed to help west European companies find the right kind of international partners for a broad range of activities, including technology transfer, cooperative R&D, sales or service representation, co-marketing and co-manufacture, and joint ventures or strategic alliances. The Chamber's involvement in BCNet was shortlived, however. The service was discontinued after little more than a year of operation because of an apparent lack of interest in the Canadian business community. The membership seemed more interested in using this European-based computer matching service to explore the U.S. rather than the European market.

What conclusions can be drawn from the above description of the private sector's activities? First, there is a shift in the corporate world away from conventional sources of economic intelligence (government departments, industry associations) to a broad spectrum of sources, including customized and specialized research services; a shift away from short-term, project-specific use to ongoing, long-term use to define strategic direction.[33] In this environment, and with the leaps in information technology, the use of new external sources of economic intelligence will include national and global databases. In short, what is being developed in Canada and around the world is a system of privately-run (though publicly-financed at the initial stages in Canada) electronic corporate matchmaking.[34] The question this raises is whether the public sector in Canada, which has traditionally been responsible for the dissemination of much of the foreign economic intelligence, should continue to compete with private "customizers" of economic intelligence. The latter group is able to target the SMEs (precisely the public sector's major client base) with lower-cost information products, since, unlike the public sector, they do not have a universal mandate (that is, rather than providing "country profiles" they can opt for much more specialized sector research). In fact, the advent of private sector as opposed to public sector databases (long the government's "ace" when it came to talk of privatizing Canada's international business development) may render government databases such as Winexport obsolete.

Think Tanks/Research Centres as Repositories of Economic Intelligence

Perched between governments and business are the think tanks or research institutes (either university-based or not). Before evaluating their role in, and impact on, Canada's economic intelligence system, we must briefly describe the major Canadian think tanks. Because of space limitations, the discussion in this section seeks only to provide an outline of their place in the economic intelligence system and is not a substitute for institutional histories of each institute; nor is it a substitute for detailed case studies of how research institutes contribute to the policy debate, although as will be noted, "influence" in terms of policy relevance is a criterion of economic intelligence. While several prominent institutes will be discussed (see Table 2), this is for purposes of illustration only—one can find specialized institutes in every business sector (often affiliated with industry associations such as the Canadian Pulp and Paper Institute or with university research centres) as well as more broadly-based think tanks that focus on cross-cutting public policy issues (the C.D. Howe Institute, the Canadian Centre for Policy Alternatives, and the like). When aggregated these research institutes are sure to outnumber those discussed in this article.[35]

Another point that must be made is that not all think tanks and policy institutes are engaged in the same type of behaviour. Some are *information-centred,* that is, they concentrate on generating information and research primarily for publication; others are *convocation-centred,* in the sense that they bring people together to explore issues and exchange views; and a third format is a *consociational* approach, where a balance is struck between information generation and convocation activities.[36]

Although different in organization, the Fraser and C.D. Howe institutes are primarily information-centred economic think tanks, in that they have professional staffs that produce or commission research (often from academic economists) that is turned into monographs, annual reports, or collections of articles running the gamut from taxation policy to the impact of free trade and globalization on the Canadian economy. Each institute also holds one or two symposia each year.

The Canada West Foundation (CWF, founded 1973) and the Institute for Research on Public Policy (IRPP, founded 1971), although information-centred, are altogether different in organization from the C.D. Howe and Fraser institutes, since for the most part they act as holding companies for projects rather than producing the research directly themselves (although the IRPP does have a director for research). Over the years the CWF has become more of a networking organization, producing newsletters and co-sponsoring studies, events, and conferences whose objective it is to air Western concerns. The IRPP, meanwhile, after a period of expansion in the 1980s when it was active in a number of fields with five or six broad research programs (including international economics and the environment), in the early 1990s consolidated its operations in its Montreal office. It no longer has a very prominent public profile, although it publishes *Policy Options,* a well-regarded magazine for the exchange of ideas and commentary. As Lindquist notes, IRPP "was unable to convert an impressive array of activities into an institution larger than the sum of its parts."[37]

Perhaps the best example of a purely convocational institute is the Public Policy Forum. It acts as an elite forum, as a catalyst to explore issues and ideas, and it generally does not sponsor research studies.[38]

The Conference Board of Canada (founded 1972), on the other hand, is a prime example of a consociational strategy. The Board's activity seems to be split fairly evenly between publications and events, in that it has functional councils for senior executives (which sometimes sponsor research studies), and research centres (focusing on such subjects as the environment, tourism, financial services, and international issues), which are funded by additional membership fees and have their own advisory councils, making them in effect into mini-institutes, and it publishes regular reports on national and provincial economic forecasts, regular reports on corporate practices,[39] various "outlook" documents, and research monographs.

Another source of economic intelligence is university-based research centres. With over sixty Canadian universities, many with policy-oriented centres, this would at first glance appear to be a rich vein of economic intelligence.[40] These centres to varying degrees have adopted the characteristics of consociational institutes, in that they organize workshops and symposia, and publish working chapters, monographs, conference proceedings, and annual reviews of policy sectors. But as the next section shows, despite their independence, university research institutes—unlike their non-university-based cousins—for reasons of culture (academic freedom) and low budgets, generally lack access to current information and data and to key decision-makers, and consequently may not be as effective as producers and disseminators of economic intelligence. There are, of course, exceptions. The Centre for International Studies at the University of Toronto, which in recent years has focused on trade policy issues, for example, appears to have an active and well-funded research program. The Centre for Trade Policy and Law in Ottawa, which is jointly run by The Norman Paterson School of International Affairs at Carleton University and the Faculty of Law at the University of Ottawa and is funded mainly through government contracts, has created a critical mass of specialist trade policy research through its well-attended public symposia and regular publications. In recent years, there also appears to be have been substantial private funding to establish centres at various universities for the study of Asia Pacific.

Despite the diversity of research institutes, then, is it possible to identify some patterns across institutes with regard to different categories of economic intelligence? Of all the institutes, only the Conference Board is heavily involved in producing data (rather than repackaging it) not available from other sources as well as providing analysis based on this information.[41] Additionally, what is interesting about the C.D. Howe and Fraser Institutes and the Conference Board is that they disseminate economic intelligence at two different levels. At the primary level of economic intelligence (Table 1), the Howe Institute, for example, through its *Observer, Policy Review,* and *Outlook* and *Policy Commentary* publications, and the Conference Board, through its *Canadian Business Review* and other more specialized reports, disseminate information publicly. And, at the secondary level, these institutes also provide economic intelligence to their members (as opposed to the general public), through initiatives such as the Conference Board's senior executive councils. It can also be conjectured that with the cross-fertilization of contacts between the employees of the financial services industry, the staff of major non-university economic think tanks, and officials in the provincial and federal government departments (primarily the Privy Council Office, Finance, Industry, and Foreign Affairs and International Trade), there would be ample opportunity for the exchange of "tactical" economic intelligence. This is more likely because of the small number of players, in light of the handful of economic research institutes.

How do the research institutes fit into the broader economic intelligence system? A number of conclusions can be drawn from the above discussion. Each government department has one or more favoured external research institutes (sometimes referred to as departmental NGOs) to which it contracts policy studies that produce economic intelligence. For instance, the Finance Department provided contracts to the now defunct Economic Council of Canada (ECC)[42] and regularly contracts out work to the C.D. Howe Institute (of which it is also a member) and the Conference Board of Canada;[43] Industry Canada provided funding through its Science and Technology secretariat to the now defunct Science Council of Canada (SCC) and other research institutes in the private and university sectors; the Department of Foreign Affairs and International Trade provides multi-year funding to, among others, the Centre for Trade Policy and Law at Carleton and Ottawa Universities, the Asia Pacific Foundation, and, as mentioned, on a fee-for-service basis to the Canadian Chamber of Commerce.[44]

Not only do federal and provincial governments contract out to these institutes or fund them directly, in the case of the non-university institutes (particularly the Conference Board, and the C.D. Howe

Institute), federal government departments are also members, along with many of Canada's largest firms. As noted in Figure 1, there is also a close connection between the major financial interests (notably the "Big Six" chartered banks and brokerage firms) and these institutes, with the former's economists often seconded to do research under the auspices of the latter.[45] At the same time, the non-university-based research centres such as the Fraser Institute traditionally contract much of their research to academic economists. Thus what we see is a close, but indirect, relationship among private, non-academic economic research institutes (but which employ academics on contract), the federal and provincial governments, and the major financial centres. It is indirect, since, unlike the ECC and the SCC, the Fraser and C.D. Howe institutes, the Canadian Centre for Policy Alternatives, and the Conference Board are not para-public institutions. In terms of the link between peak interest associations such as the Canadian Chamber of Commerce and the Business Council on National Issues and the university-based and private research institutes, there appears to be no formal mechanism (or desire) for channelling relevant research from the institute community to the larger Canadian private sector through these broad-based business associations.[46]

Another issue that must be addressed is the quality of the economic intelligence being produced by research institutes and think tanks. This becomes a very subjective exercise, given their different mandates and organizational styles; nevertheless, academic analysts such as Tupper complain that the economic intelligence and attendant policy prescriptions from the likes of the C.D. Howe Institute and the Canadian Centre for Policy Alternatives suffer from an inadequate research base and an "overtly political character."[47] Lindquist appears to agree, saying that although institutes in theory should translate empirical data in the social sciences (this applies as well in the applied sciences) into language that is more relevant to a larger number of societal actors, there is no "compelling" evidence that this is actually occurring.[48]

A further conclusion to be drawn is that although there has not been a census of Canadian think tanks, the paucity of Canadian research institutes (perhaps a function of our lamentable R&D record) and think tanks when compared to the plethora of publicly and privately sponsored research centres in the United States,[49] Japan, and larger West European countries points to the difficulty in Canada of having a more even balance of public and private or para-public sector influence in managing the national economic intelligence system. As will be pointed out in the next section, the value-added brought by research institutes and think tanks to the economic intelligence system is their higher degree of independence and their ability therefore to act as a counter-weight in public policy decision-making. The ostensible rationale for the elimination in 1992 (as result of the 1992 budget) of the Economic Council of Canada (ECC) and the Science Council of Canada (SCC), the only organizations with a sufficiently broad economic intelligence vision to be considered central clearing agencies of information as well as applied research, was that the "analytic slack" could be taken up by the host of non-profit institutes and for-profit consulting organizations.[50] However, five years afterward it is not clear that this has indeed tran-spired. To be sure, the C.D. Howe Institute reports now receive more coverage in the print and electronic media; yet few would suggest that this institute alone should be tasked with the responsibility of map-ping out an alternative, non-governmental vision for Canada's future economic security.

Finally, in describing and evaluating research institutes, we have not mentioned the very Canadian habit of striking royal commissions, task forces, and parliamentary committees to analyze all matter of public policy. To this author's knowledge no such committee, task force, or royal commission has been appointed to look at the organization of Canada's economic intelligence. Given the problems outlined above, perhaps it is time.

Canada's Economic Intelligence-Gathering System: A Preliminary Assessment

To reiterate, both a country's strategic development and its development of strategic information depend on the interaction of a number of sub-systems. By exposing and highlighting the interplay of sub-systems or levels, one can formulate better national strategies. A sub-system that is isolated, or the concentration on one sub-system at the expense of others, undermines systemic cohesion. For example, economic intelli-gence users in firms, while having access to streams of data and analysis generated internally (in economics departments, planning departments, and the like), are in fact faced with starkly different levels of availability, relevance, and quality in the economic intelligence produced externally and distributed by management consultants, universities, and research institutes. The factors influencing the attributes of the economic intelligence are also bound to change from country to country.

Given their complexity, the challenge is then to simplify the interplay among economic actors in the economic intelligence system. For this, the public management literature offers some useful typologies and conclusions. For instance, if we use Baer's typology and, instead of evaluating for inter-disciplinary research success, use his "attributes" to evaluate the relative effectiveness of various domestic actors to collect and distribute economic intelligence, some interesting findings come to light. While the general trends noted in Table 3 are, at this preliminary stage of research, based only on anecdotal evidence and should therefore not be accepted as definitive,[51] they nevertheless, as a first cut, offer some flavour of the types of problems that attend the creation of a more interlinked *national* economic intelligence system. (See also Figure 1 and Table 2.)

The multinational management consulting firms such as McKinsey and Co. are rated so highly in terms of information access because their global reach and size enables them to plug into a myriad public and private databases and research sources around the world and, perhaps most potently, because of their often direct access to key political and economic decision-makers.[52] The other factor to consider is that, as is the case in France, many of the larger management consulting firms in Canada are foreign multinationals. This allows them to channel economic intelligence (derived from the analysis of their Canadian clients' competitive strategies) to clients outside of Canada (although obviously there are certain ethical considerations here).

The Baer typology is also useful for other reasons. First, the question of "independence," especially from the influence of the government of the day, suggests that the independent research centres and think tanks discussed in the previous section (irrespective of their ideological orientation) and universities are rated highly.

"Policy orientation" is an important attribute, since it points to the propensity for a particular actor to have an understanding of the overall national economic strategy and be able to feed advice into this process. To reiterate, Canadian universities, unless they are receiving federal or provincial dollars for specific applied research (Centres for International

TABLE 3: THE CAPACITY FOR ECONOMIC INTELLIGENCE-GATHERING IN CANADA

Attribute	University	Independent Research Centre	Firm[a]	Government Department or Agency	Management Consultant
Policy orientation	lowest	intermediate to high[a]	intermediate	highest	high
Access to information	lowest	high	intermediate	highest	very high
Independence	highest	intermediate to high	Intermediate	lowest	moderate
Scale and continuity of effort	lowest	high	high	low	high and persistent
Incentives for interdisciplinary project performance	lowest	high	high	intermediate	high
Incentives for distribution of economic intelligence[b]	intermediate	highest	lowest	intermediate	low

[a] The "firm" as an actor would also include vertical and horizontal business associations, since they represent an agglomeration of firms.

[b] This attribute has been added by this author to Baer's five attributes; it brings in the concept of an information-sharing culture.

Source: Adapted from the typology first developed by W.S. Baer, "Interdisciplinary Policy Research," in Independent Research Centre Report, P-5347 (Santa Monica: Rand, January 1975), 5, and reproduced in Alan Jarman and Alexander Kouzmin, "Public Sector Think Tanks in Inter-agency Policy-making: Designing Enhanced Governance Capacity," Canadian Public Administration 34, 4 (Winter), Tables 1 and 2, 518-19.

Business Studies, for example), with their low access to data, are likely to be able to provide only primary and secondary economic intelligence, and will leave it to the institutes and private information brokers to provide policy-relevant or tailor-made economic information. As we shall see in the next section, the lack of a coordinated transfer of economic or scientific research undertaken in academic departments (as opposed to research institutes at universities, which tend to be more interdisciplinary), and research institutes, government, and the private sector, hurts Canada's competitive position.

Figure 1 shows that in terms of managing Canada's economic intelligence, the economic intelligence community, the business associations, and the multinational sources of economic intelligence (La Francophonie and the Commonwealth) are generally disconnected from the more intensive contacts between Canada's financial services industry, research institutes, universities, and the other federal and provincial governments. By not having, for example, a more integrated network of chambers of commerce, the system at present is far less centralized than, say, the system in Japan or in Germany (to be discussed later in this chapter).

THE ECONOMIC INTELLIGENCE SYSTEMS OF COMPETITOR NATIONS

The above analysis raises a number of issues concerning the improvement of Canada's economic intelligence system. This section looks at how the experience of Canada's economic intelligence system compares to that of its major competitors—specifically Japan, the United States, and Germany. But before drawing some comparisons, it would be useful to clarify whether we can consider the different economic intelligence systems to be "models." According to Martre, economic intelligence systems are models because they satisfy the following three conditions: "The practice of economic intelligence is permanent, continuous in its use of techniques, and perennial in its use of strategies."[53]

Although all economic intelligence is, of course, ultimately aimed at enhancing national economic security, different countries go about achieving this economic security in different ways. Tables 4 and 5, using a taxonomy of economic intelligence systems, attempt to emphasize both the differences and the similarities across the systems.

TABLE 4: FUNCTIONAL TAXONOMY OF NATIONAL ECONOMIC INTELLIGENCE SYSTEMS

(1) an aggressive global program of economic intelligence-collection largely through overt means.

(2) an aggressive global program of economic intelligence-collection including significant covert means.

(3) a more defensive global program of economic intelligence-collection (concentrating on preventing economic espionage).

(4) a high level of cooperation among public sector and private sector users and producers of economic intelligence (that is, using economic intelligence as a lever for national competitiveness).

(5) an intermediate level of cooperation among public sector and private sector users and producers of economic intelligence.

(6) a low level of cooperation among public sector and private sector users and producers of economic intelligence.

(7) an active indigenous private market for economic intelligence.

(8) an active private market for economic intelligence with a high degree of foreign control.

(9) a high-level of awareness regarding the importance of economic intelligence at the level of the individual firm.

(10) a low-level of awareness regarding the importance of economic intelligence at the level of the individual firm.

TABLE 5: COMPARISON OF NATIONAL ECONOMIC INTELLIGENCE SYSTEMS
(Using Categories from Table 4)

Country	Public/Private Organization	Focus
Canada	Highly decentralized economic intelligence system, with 30 federal government departments and agencies with 128 missions abroad; provincial governments with offices abroad; competitive national business association environment (Canadian Chamber of Commerce, Alliance of Manufacturers and Exporters of Canada, Business Council on National Issues).	3, 6, 8, 10
France	Ministère des Finances acts as super-ministry for other government departments.	2, 5, 8, 10
Britain	Department of Trade and Industry plays key role, as does the City.	1, 5, 7, 9
United States	Decentralized economic intelligence system; recent attempts at executive level to better organize the flow of strategic information.	2, 5, 7, 10
Germany	The private sector, through chambers of commerce (whose membership is mandatory), is the hub of the economic intelligence system; also playing leading roles are the Länder.	2, 4, 7, 9
Japan	Collective culture is important, especially in binding government departments with conglomerates.	1, 4, 7, 9

Source: Author

These structures can be further coalesced into three more or less disparate clusters:

- In some countries, with a more individualist and less information-sharing ethos, government acts more as a facilitator in the market-place than as a player in its own right, and focuses on creating a level playing field (business transparency) and the right macro-economic conditions to facilitate the achievement of economic growth.

- In other countries, with a more collectivist or statist approach, government aims to protect and build national industries ("national champions") and to participate directly in the market-place as well as to provide the private sector through regular and formal channels with extensive services and information.

- Finally, some national economic intelligence systems are character-ized by a greater complementarity between the public and the private sectors, with no one actor having the leading role in the provision of economic intelligence.

Before we go on to look at specific countries, a few general comments are in order. The nature of the economic intelligence system in place in a particular country will depend on the structure of state-societal rela-tions. For example, Griffith points out that the more an economy is market-based, the more likely it is to have open sources of information. There is a more open regulatory environment, few market access bar-riers, and transparent business practices. Most OECD countries would fit this description, and consequently in these countries private sector eco-nomic intelligence services are likely to be effective and widespread. He points out that although market failure in itself does not provide a ratio-nale for increased government services, since the cost of privately distributed economic information is becoming less and less prohibitive, in the case of Japan, with its attendant institutional, linguistic, and cul-tural barriers, there is greater reason for those outside of Japan to rely on public sector-led economic intelligence-gathering. In general, then, the larger the role of government in a particular economy, the less effective will be private sector services and the more important will be interme-diaries or agents,[54] which in turn increases the likelihood of illegal or unethical acts to acquire economic intelligence, since the proportion of information classified as "tactical" will be greater.

Japan

Japan was the first industrialized country that made "information" a fundamental lever of its development. Unlike the Anglo-Saxon countries, however, it made information a collective resource rather than an individual resource. The Japanese economic intelligence system can be differentiated from the Anglo-Saxon models in that it is based on a synergy of technological, industrial, and commercial strategies that are inextricable from an offensive-oriented economic intelligence system. Martre outlines the five major characteristics of Japan's strategic use of information: a global and local approach to world markets; an approach tailored to the unique characteristics of every country that Japanese firms are trying to penetrate; a long-term strategy; an approach that is integrated with the strategies of Japanese multinationals; and the selective dissemination of knowledge.[55] According to Peter Schweizer, the Japanese since 1962 have had in place a formalized system of foreign economic intelligence-gathering under the auspices of the Institute for Industrial Protection (IIP), which is funded by MITI, and whose mandate would be located in the "red" zone in terms of the type of economic intelligence that is being collected.

Perhaps the most difficult, and potentially the most forceful, aspect of the Japanese economic system from a Western perspective, is the culture of collective information (see Figure 2, page 59). (Because it is customary to share rather than "buy" or "sell" information, Japanese businesses are reluctant to purchase open economic intelligence from consulting firms either in Japan or abroad.) This information culture permeates all the major institutions, including the Information Research Office (tasked with sending weekly reports from around the world directly to the prime minister's office), MITI, JETRO, and larger Japanese firms with overseas operations. There is also a tacit understanding, again linked to culture, among Japanese conglomerates (keiretsu) not to destroy each other through domestic competition, but rather to think of economic competition in the long term, which creates a certain solidarity (Japan Inc.?) that is channelled outward.

What the Japanese model shows is a remarkable consensus and cooperation among the society's major economic actors in relation to the steps—clearly both overt and covert—necessary to enhance national economic strength. In the Canadian context this would be akin to having the presidents of the Canadian Chamber of Commerce and the Business Council on National Issues along with the president of the Canadian Labour Congress agree with Canada's chief trade commissioner (the deputy minister for international trade) and the minister for international trade that it is the ends of economic intelligence not the means that is the major issue. So, under this scenario, if Canadian officials covertly acquired "strategic" economic intelligence this would be tacitly, if not explicitly, accepted.

The United States

Unlike the German and Japanese economic intelligence systems, the United States system (Figure 3) is decentralized, a fact that can be attributed to a political and economic system that reveres the individual as opposed to the group. That being said, in the face of overwhelming threat (Nazi Germany, the Soviet Union), American economic actors have, during times of national crisis, also been able to mobilize their resources. As is the case in Japan, this has translated into a certain amount of offensive economic intelligence capacity by U.S. economic actors. However, because American conglomerates do not have the tradition of Japanese *keiretsu*, alliances have been more short-lived. Nevertheless, as Martre points out, whatever losses are suffered by the United States because of its uncoordinated economic intelligence effort are made up by the sheer financial power of the largest American companies to gather information. For instance, General Motors' budget for "competitive intelligence" alone exceeds the entire budget for the French foreign intelligence service.[56] A paradox of the private economic intelligence system is that although the United States has the largest business intelligence market, it has succeeded in making itself grow more rapidly than the U.S. economy.

Over the last two years, in the face of predictions that the United States was losing the competitiveness war to, in particular, the Japanese, the Clinton administration has attempted if not to exert more control over, then to gain more understanding of, the economic challenges facing the United States, by having three committees (national security,

FIGURE 2: THE ROLE OF CULTURE IN THE JAPANESE ECONOMIC INTELLIGENCE SYSTEM

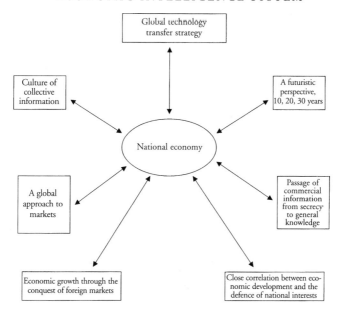

FIGURE 3: ECONOMIC INTELLIGENCE IN THE U.S. ECONOMY

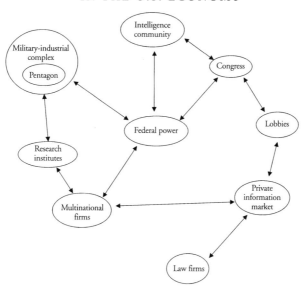

Source: Intelco, in Henri Martre, *Rapport du groupe intelligence économique et stratégie des entreprises* (Paris: Commissariat général du plan, février 1994), 45, 49.

economics, and the interior), all with equal power, reporting directly to the president. The objective of this new institutional structure (before Clinton, the world revolved around geopolitics rather than geoeconomics) reflects a desire at the level of the executive to better organize the disparate channels and sources of economic intelligence in the federal bureaucracy.

In fact, some elements of the debate on economic intelligence in the United States revolving around, for example, the ability of U.S. multinationals to manage their global information networks, how much influence should be exerted by lobbyists and business intelligence specialists, and the duplication of economic intelligence within government, sound familiar in the Canadian context. The crisis of confidence at IBM in 1993 was, according to Martre, only the tip of the iceberg, and may have prompted a change of attitude toward the structure of economic intelligence in the United States. It questioned the ability of U.S. firms to prosper if they continued to focus on short-term business cycles, if they failed to pool strategic resources, and if they continued to ignore the benefits both to themselves and to the national economy of a more collective economic intelligence system. Although one would not expect to transpose the Japanese or European system to the United States, there is evidence of an increasing willingness in the American private sector (in spite of its mistrust of government) to cooperate with the federal government in fashioning an international business strategy (for example, as it enters the newly open economies of Central and Eastern Europe).

The apparent change in the U.S. attitude serves notice to Canada that it will face a new, more coordinated economic intelligence threat. It is interesting to note that both the United States and Canada appear to be moving to more "partnerships" between the private and the public sector in managing strategic information.

Germany

In contrast to the U.S. and the Canadian systems, but similar to Japan's, the German system is characterized by the sheer volume of information flowing from various actors (the state apparatus, populations of German ancestry, 6000 chambers of commerce, unions, provinces, and the private information market) in the German economic intelligence system (see Figure 4) toward a tightly interwoven and powerful centre domi-nated by banks, insurance companies, and large industrial groups. The centre, however, is not really a "place" but rather a web of relations between an extraordinarily small number of decision-makers (said to be fewer than 100) at the federal, sub-federal, and industrial levels.[57] The German economy (like that of Japan) has been constructed on the prin-ciple of a common national strategic goal recognized by all the major economic actors.

One of the most powerful elements of the German economic intel-ligence system is its tradition (dating back to the Hanseatic League) of having the private sector, through a system of chambers of commerce, intimately involved in all facets of governance. Through the structure of local chambers, the German private sector is intimately involved in every aspect of local, provincial, and federal policy-making, a system that, carried over to the economic intelligence system, sets the German model apart from the other systems that have been outlined. Perhaps most distinctively, the German private sector, rather than the govern-ment, is the hub of the economic intelligence system.[58] In the Canadian, British, and French models, with the tradition of professional public services, there is a measured distance between the public and private domains; there is a tendency for the state to attempt to "control" information flow (an increasingly untenable position) in order to retain its power. In Canada, where there is a much less cohesive private sector than, say, in France, with its *conseil du patronat* and Britain, with the very influential Confederation of British Industries, there is a greater reliance on both the federal and provincial governments for economic intelligence. What *is* similar between the Canadian and the German sys-tems is that sub-federal units—the provinces in Canada and the Länder in Germany—are very aggressive in making firms from their jurisdic-tions more competitive (sometimes to the disadvantage of firms from other areas of their countries).

With respect to the type of economic intelligence being sought by the German private and public sectors, it is significant, given the long track record of German economic espionage dating from immediately after the Second World War, that the German state has had no com-punction about creating (in three phases over the last 45 years) an economic intelligence system whose objective has been both to system-atically penetrate foreign firms and governments, with emphasis on

France, Britain, the United States, and Eastern Europe, and to protect
Germany from the intelligence systems of these same countries.[59] One
would assume that if the German state were engaged in sourcing
"strategic" economic intelligence in the United States it would be doing
the same in Canada.

In light of our discussion of the structure of Canada's research and
think tank community, it is noteworthy that since the early 1980s there
has been a transfer of knowledge and personnel between the German EIC
and private foundations financed by the German business community.
So important is the collection of foreign economic intelligence in the
minds of Germany's business leaders that they hired the former top officials of the Bundesnachtrichtendienst (BND), the foreign intelligence
service, and the Bundeskriminalamt (equivalent to the RCMP) to manage
this collection. The equivalent in the Canadian context would have been
for Reid Morden, former Director of CSIS, and Norman Inkster, former
Commissioner of the RCMP, to have been either hired by the Business
Council on National Issues or tasked by a consortium of Canadian business leaders to head up a new research foundation. (As it happens,
Morden went on to become the chief executive officer of Atomic Energy
Canada Ltd., a Crown corporation.)

Finally, the one major weakness of the German intelligence
system—and an important one given this chapter's prediction that there
will be increased reliance by firms on global databases (thus possibly cir-
cumventing the need for public sector assistance)—is the tendency by
the German companies to under-utilize databases and to continue to
rely on the network of research institutes, private information brokers,
and German commercial networks abroad.[60] In this area, the Canadian
private sector—led by the Canadian Chamber—seems to be ahead.

In conclusion, Table 5 summarizes the broad differences and similarities between Canada's economic intelligence system and those of its
competitors. It should be noted that Canada, France, and the United
States are similar in that their firms either have not yet realized the
importance of "tactical" economic intelligence for their competitiveness,
or are either too reluctant, or have not yet put in place the appropriate
mechanisms, to exploit this level more fully. For a majority of Canadian
and American business people, but perhaps not a majority of French
business people, there may be a cultural resistance to the regular use of
unethical and potentially illegal methods of obtaining economic intelligence. This is not to mention the difficulty from a North American

FIGURE 4: ECONOMIC INTELLIGENCE
IN THE GERMAN ECONOMY

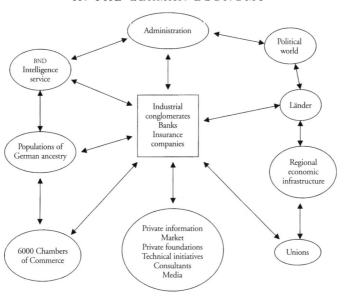

Source: Intelco, in Martre, *Intelligence économique*, 59.

standpoint of having the state "pick" the beneficiaries of micro-economic intelligence collected by the state whether through covert or overt means. Another striking difference between the systems in the United States, Canada, Britain, and France (see Figures 5, 6, page 65), on the one hand, and Japan and Germany on the other, is the predilection in the latter to present a unified and national approach to economic intelligence. Martre frequently comments on the "synergies" that are exploited among domestic organizations in these countries both in terms of the production and distribution of information.

Since 1994, Canada (and also the United States) has been approaching this more collective approach. The process was tentative at first. This was no doubt due to the competitive nature of Canada's peak industry associations and the suspicion of federal officials that these associations were going to try to "steal" the public sector's historical monopoly of foreign economic intelligence-gathering. Today, however, the "Team Canada" slogan is being trumpeted by both private[61] and public sectors. It is hard to determine the origins of the slogan; it would certainly not strike the Japanese or Germans as corny—although for most Americans "Team U.S.A." would connote athletic rather than commercial prowess. Whatever its origins, to some extent "Team Canada" has been taken up by the public sector with its emphasis on a "team" approach in its 1994 International Trade Business Plan (for example, Prime Minister Chrétien's frequent trips to promote Canadian business abroad starting with a trip to China in November of that year). The call by the private sector for a national International Commerce Board received a more lukewarm response by Ottawa's trade mandarins, especially at DFAIT. No doubt the senior officials cited the existence of the International Trade Advisory Committees and the Sector Advisory Groups on International Trade as rendering any new oversight body duplicative. Nevertheless, the pressure for change emanating from the Canadian business community motivated the then International Trade Minister, Roy MacLaren, to agree to the idea of high-level private sector input into how the foreign dimension of Canada's economic intelligence system could be reformed. This was translated into a committee of "12 eminent Canadian business people" led by L.R. Wilson, CEO of Bell Canada Enterprises, which in September 1994 submitted a report of recommendations. The report, which addressed only the international dimension of Canada's economic intelligence system, pointed out that Canada should take heed of the fact that its main competitors (the United States, Japan, Britain, France, and Germany) were reorienting their economic intelligence systems to specific industrial sectors. It recommended that Ottawa target six sectors: advanced materials, bio-technologies, information technologies, medical, education, and health-care products, and environmental industries.[62]

FUTURE DIRECTIONS

It has now become almost a cliché to talk about a post-Cold War era in which ideology has been replaced by trade as the source of greatest friction and competition among nations. Analysts have even used the oxymoron "competitive cooperation" to describe relations among industrialized states in the 1990s.

FIGURE 5: ECONOMIC INTELLIGENCE IN THE BRITISH ECONOMY

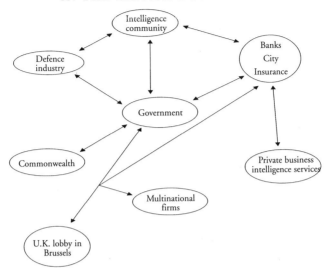

FIGURE 6: ECONOMIC INTELLIGENCE IN THE FRENCH ECONOMY

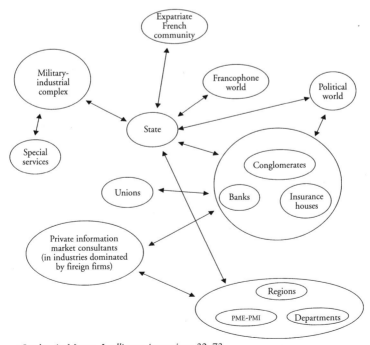

Source: Intelco, in Martre, *Intelligence économique*, 32, 73.

Returning to our definitions of economic intelligence, the idea of a competitive national economy is multi-leveled. It encompasses the following:

- technological innovation and management of information at the level of the firm (for example, the move away from conventional sources of economic intelligence).

- increased capacity of the industrial base (for instance, the move toward increased SME networking within, and functionally across, business sectors).

- competitive relations between firms (for instance, the Japanese trend to compete nationally but to cooperate internationally).

- decisions by governments concerning the degree to which they would engage in "tactical" and "strategic" collection of economic intelligence (Canada and the United States are reluctant, Britain less so; the practice is considered normal operating procedure in Japan, Germany, France).

- nature of state-societal relations and national culture (that is, collectivist versus more individualist approaches to the economic intelligence process).

- the dual impact of domestic fiscal conditions (high public debt in industrialized countries) and international competition on the propensity of national economic actors to cooperate.

What this chapter has shown is that the strategic management of economic information has become an integral facet of the new global market. As national economics vie for diminishing markets, the methods of production and distribution will become more competitive. The brief sketches of the economic intelligence systems of some of Canada's major competitors point to national culture as an over-whelming and major independent variable in determining the characteristics of an economic intelligence system. A nation's culture (defined here as its citizens' sense of themselves and the national purpose) is thus at the heart of national economic intelligence systems. One could conclude that the more there exists a commonly accepted national purpose, the more actors will "accept" the moral dilemmas of "tactical" and "strategic" economic intelligence, and the more the objective of enhanced competitiveness (with the tangibles of jobs, growth, and increased standards of living) will supersede the means to achieve it.

Japan, which is poor in resources, and Germany, which has centuries-long trading traditions, stand out for their use of economic intelligence (especially the higher levels) as motors for their strategic development. In this vein, careful national economic planning models were set in place in which all the economic actors (industry, academia, labour, and the public administration) understood their respective roles and participated in an intuitive national plan (as distinguished from the rationalized plans of the communist states) of cooperation to maximize national economic welfare.

The Canadian economic intelligence system, in contrast—perhaps because of Canada's shorter history as a nation, its small population and abundant resources, and the predominance of U.S. investment—has not been forced by circumstances to be more effective in mobilizing national economic resources into a coherent system. The Canadian case-study highlights wasted efforts, lack of coordination (especially between provincial and federal governments), under-utilization of Canada's vaunted multilateral networks (how much economic intelligence is gathered, for example, from Canada's memberships in the Commonwealth and La Francophonie?), and mismanagement of economic intelligence within the individual firm. As well, the fact that a non-corporatist and more confrontational style of national economic and political decision-making[63] is the setting for generally competitive peak interest groups,[64] demonstrates the inherent difficulty of a wholesale transposition of European and Japanese models onto Canada.

Where does Canada go from here? Returning to our multi-leveled conception of Canada's economic intelligence system, two broad recommendations can be made.

First, an effective Canadian economic intelligence system will not be realized without a fundamental review of how the federal government collects economic intelligence and to whom it communicates it. An examination across Canadian government departments would reveal tremendous ad hockery in the economic intelligence-gathering process, something far less apparent in the German and Japanese systems.

For this reason, the federal government should seriously consider the re-creation of national councils in economics and science (as it has said it will do on the foreign policy front[65]). At present, Canada has a broad economic intelligence collection capacity through a number of key federal government departments, such as Industry Canada, Finance, and DFAIT. Departmental information is processed and channeled to the Privy Council Office where it is digested by various cabinet committees.

In the meantime, until the national economic and scientific think tanks have been recreated, a second-best solution may be to create a more publicly-connected National Economic Council modelled on Clinton's secretariat. Since 1992, Canada has been forced to rely on a series of competitiveness secretariats (e.g., the "Prosperity Secretariat") and agencies such as the Canadian Institute for Advanced Research. To protect key industries (energy, telecommunications, transport, biotechnology) from economic espionage, an awareness program has been initiated by the Canadian Security Intelligence Service. However, it is clear that whatever efforts do exist to enhance the effectiveness of Canada's economic intelligence system, they are isolated and unconnected to a broader strategy.

As is the case in France,[66] there are two major obstacles that undermine the effective dissemination of economic intelligence in Canada. First, collectively the national actors have not entirely accepted that full employment, the renewal of industries, and Canada's competitive position internationally are contingent on the strategic management of information. Second, the reason that there is only a partial appreciation of the value and role of economic intelligence is that Canadian companies concentrate their efforts upon combatting industrial espionage. What this means is that the Canadian system is confined to being primarily defensive precisely at a time when competitive world markets are calling for an economic intelligence system that is coordinated to be more offensive.

The second broad recommendation is to look at the ability of firms to coordinate, collect, and disseminate their know-how. Unlike France, which in 1992 created an association for the promotion of economic intelligence and competitiveness ("l'Association pour la promotion de l'intelligence économique et concurrentielle"),[67] the Canadian private sector is only now looking at the value of databases to enhance the dissemination of economic intelligence.

Related to this is the question whether it is the government's or the private sector's role to create an organizational structure allied to "industrial sectors" that would work across existing stakeholders, pulling together the strengths Canada has in certain key industries.[68] In other words, before we reconfigure Canada's foreign economic intelligence-gathering network, it would be both naive and counterproductive not to address the domestic situation. For example, it is foolish to expect Canadian industry to be active and aggressive abroad when it spends so little on its domestic intelligence-gathering operations and cooperation. So, returning to "culture," enhancing national economic power must begin domestically with a structured program (already begun through FITT, although this is designed for potential exporters only), as opposed to "speechifying" and exhortations to improve the economic intelligence-gathering techniques and practices of individual firms. Only when there is a perceptual revolution concerning the importance to the bottom line of the systematic processing of economic intelligence, will Canada see improvements in its international competitiveness.

Together the above recommendations highlight the fundamental debate on whether an intelligence-gathering system necessarily has to be centralized to be effective. In other words, highly tailored market information (as distinguished from the collection of general macro-economic information for use by governmental decision-makers), may not require a central clearing house; indeed, most Canadian business people (despite the government-funded practices of the past), rely on agents and consultants rather than trade commissioners once they have made the initial entry into a foreign market. As a result, one has be clear as to what type of information should be centralized and what type of information can be more effectively used if it less centralized. What remains clear, however, is the need for a greater sharing of information, within both the public and the private sector, and between the two.

How is this "revolution" going to be created? It should be acknowledged that Canada stands at a considerable disadvantage at the starting gate of the competitiveness race. Part of this is structural, in that we do not have an established elite network that would bridge the public and private sectors to facilitate greater cooperation between the two. For example, Canada's competitors in France have l'École Polytechnique, Britain has the "old boy" system, and the United States has the Ivy League. These training grounds, combined with very effective government-industry executive exchange programs, create bridges and networks that work to the benefit of all. What comparative advantage Canada *does* have it does not however use. Here I am referring to the federal government's extensive support of multiculturalism. Canada, unlike Germany, with its tentacles reaching out to Germanic communities around the world, does not make optimum use of its ethnic communities; Canada should be able to draw on people's contacts in their native countries to further our economic intelligence needs. Of course, while encouraging the private sector (especially SMEs) to use publicly available databases and participate in export or technology consortia, the public sector will have to think of new roles for itself in the provision of added value to the system.

These broad recommendations may be supplemented by a series of more practical ones.

The Political Level

One way of encouraging more public-private cooperation would be to create an Economic Intelligence Strategies Committee. This would include representatives from the relevant ministries (Foreign Affairs, Industry, CSIS), and the heads of key agencies (NRC, CANARIE, Centre for Advanced Research). Such a committee should be essentially political. It should not work from briefing books and complex agendas generated by ministerial sub-committees. Nor should it include consultants or more than one or two academics to cover educational matters. Unlike a national council, its purpose would not be administrative. Nor would it attempt to be executive. Rather it could gather twice a year, for example, over a weekend, to attempt to make sense of what economic intelligence policy is doing and what it is not but should be doing. It would serve the purpose of clarifying, exposing weaknesses, developing strengths, and encouraging a general national economic intelligence strategy. In other words, it would serve as an informal coordinating and idea-generating committee, linking government and the private sector.

Building an Economic Intelligence Society

Although it is unlikely that Canadians could, or would want to, emulate the Japanese system of rigid conformity, we nevertheless need to deliberately identify key economic intelligence sources around the world and the appropriate techniques for Canadians to exploit them. One method would be to build greater links with researchers in Canadian universities—perhaps to set up a program on economic intelligence as has been done in Sweden. Universities, notorious for maintaining impermeable disciplinary walls, may be encouraged to establish a centre for the study of economic intelligence to pool expertise on the gathering and dissemination of economic intelligence. Neither federal nor provincial governments make more than perfunctory efforts to tap academic resources (for example, business school analyses of the changing nature of corporate intelligence-gathering; schools of public administration on the best way for the public service to organize economic intelligence; departments of political science on the mutually-reinforcing natures of economic intelligence and national security; and departments of economics on building models that could estimate the losses to GDP arising from industrial espionage).

Another tactic, as the Japanese model shows, would be to send Canadians "unofficially" to foreign countries for the purpose of insinuating themselves into the local environments, whether as students, academics, researchers, or business people. After a predetermined period they would then report back to the federal government, presumably with primary, secondary, "tactical," and "strategic" intelligence in hand. As a means of gathering fresh intelligence this may be appealing to some in the intelligence services. However, it is highly unlikely that many private citizens would be willing to become economic spies for Canada.

The Role of the Intelligence Services in Providing Tailor-made Commercial Intelligence

The use of intelligence services to provide firms with clandestinely-collected, tailor-made commercial intelligence, although widely practiced in Germany and France, has been an uncommon practice in Canada's economic intelligence community. That is not to say that Canadian policymakers, as the following chapters by Porteous and VanDuzer detail, are not exploring the costs and benefits of such aggressive offensive actions. Indeed, the revelations of former CSE officials suggest that Canada itself has not been completely immune to the attractions of using its world-class communications expertise in a clandestine fashion (through the Communications Security Establishment) to snare contracts. Yet these activities raise important questions about the shifting priorities of the intelligence services within their respective economic communities, especially those such as the United States, which has vast resources and fewer traditional targets. Here a host of ethical, legal, and practical issues (Who gets the information? Who chooses? How can domestic and international legal frameworks be radically overhauled in a short period of time? Will firms the get the "right" intelligence?) arise that are beyond the purview of this more general and comparative treatment of the economic intelligence system in Canada. They are the subject of detailed analysis in the following chapters.

NOTES

1. Report of the Special Joint Committee Reviewing Canadian Foreign Policy, *Canada's Foreign Policy: Principles and Priorities* (Ottawa: Parliament of Canada, November 1994), 11.
2. In the words of Rodney de C. Grey, Canada's former ambassador to the Tokyo Round of the GATT, "For a small country surrounded by larger countries and heavily dependent on trade with one of them, foreign policy should, in major part, be trade relations policy."
3. The World Competitiveness Report for 1994 placed Canada fourteenth out of twenty-three industrial countries in the study; Canada was eleventh in 1993, and fourth in 1989.
4. Samuel D. Porteous, "Economic Espionage," *Commentary*, No. 32 (hereafter, Porteous, "Economic Espionage," I); see also Porteous, "Economic Espionage:

New Target for CSIS," *Canadian Business Review* 20, 4 (Winter 1993), 32-34; S.D. Porteous, "Economic-Commercial Interest and the World's Intelligence Services: A Canadian Perspective, "*International Journal of Intelligence and Counter-Intelligence*,", 8, 3 (Fall 1995), 275-302.

5. Henri Martre, *Rapport du groupe intelligence économique et stratégie des entreprises* (Paris: Commissariat général du plan, février 1994), 16. This author's translation.

6. Martre says that "influence" is a part of the British concept of economic intelligence, and is much richer in nuance than simply talking about "information" and "intelligence."

7. The need to engage in "influence" explains the importance of the plethora of interest group representatives and government relations consultants in Ottawa and in the capitals of the provinces.

8. What Martre refers to as "strategic" intelligence.

9. Jean Pichot-Duclos, "L'intelligence économique: pour un modèle français," *Defense nationale* (1993), 86-87, Tables 1 and 2.

10. Alan M. Rugman and Joseph D'Cruz, *New Compacts for Canadian Competitiveness* (Toronto: Kodak Canada Inc., and University of Toronto Press, 1992); Rugman and D'Cruz, *Fast Forward: Improving Canada's International Competitiveness* (Toronto: Kodak Canada Inc., 1991); Rugman and D'Cruz, *New Visions for Canadian Business: Strategies for Competing in the Global Economy* (Toronto: Kodak Canada Inc., and University of Toronto Press, 1990).

11. Michael E. Porter, *Canada at the Crossroads: The Reality of a New Competitive Environment* (Ottawa: Business Council on National Issues, 1992).

12. David Kaye, "Managing the Information Revolution: Lessons for Business from the French Revolution," *Futures* 26, 4 (1994), 420.

13. *Ibid.*, 423.

14. From an unpublished chapter presented by Steven A. Rosell, president of the Meridian International Institute, at a symposium on "Information Technologies and International Relations," held in Ottawa on 13 January 1995.

15. André LeBel, president and CEO, Teleglobe Canada Inc., quoted in *Worldbusiness* (December 1994), 34.

16. Compilation by author.

17. I mention the Commonwealth and La Francophonie in Figure 1 only because rarely are they thought of as economic intelligence sources for Canada. The Organization of American States may also be useful in this regard in the coming years. Usually organizations such as the IMF, IBRD, OECD, G-7, multilateral development banks, and the UN family of agencies are highlighted as key sources of information for Canada's private and public sectors.

18. O. Mary Hill, *Canada's Salesmen to the World: The Department of Trade and Commerce, 1892-1939* (Montreal: McGill-Queen's University Press, 1977).
19. Andrew Griffith, "From a Trading Nation to a Nation of Traders: Toward A Second Century of Canadian Trade Development," *Policy Planning Staff Paper* No. 92/5 (Ottawa: Department of External Affairs and International Trade, 1992).
20. *Ibid.*, esp. Ch. 5. Griffith drew on studies by F.H. Rolf Seringhaus and Philip J. Rosson, *Government Export Promotion: A Global Perspective* (London: Routledge, 1990); Diddy R.M. Hitchines, *Canadian Trade Promotion Policies in Comparative Perspective* (unpublished draft, 1991); and a report of the U.S. and Foreign Commercial Service, *International Trade Administration, Export Promotion Activities of Major Competitor Nations* (unpublished, September 1988).
21. Griffith, "Trading Nation," 4. International business development is defined as "comprising 'ministerial missions,' 'trade fairs and missions,' 'market intelligence,' and 'market access' issues."
22. Tables 1.1 and 1.3, Secretariat for Science and Technology Review, Resource Book for Science and Technology Consultations, Vol. 1 (Ottawa: Industry Canada, 1994).
23. For a critique, see Tim Reid, "Challenging Canada's International Business Paradox: A Private Sector Perspective," *Canadian Foreign Policy* 1, 1 (Winter 1992/93), 87-102; Jock Finlayson, "Directions for Canadian Trade Policy: A Private Sector View," *Canadian Foreign Policy* 1, 3 (Fall 1993), 115-20.
24. On November 2, 1994, Roy McLaren released a report entitled "Servicing SME Exporters: Government and Banks Working Towards Better Support," which marked the greater expansion of involvement of Canadian financial institutions in responding to the export interests of SMEs.
25. The *SME Exporter Action Plan* (started in May 1994 and the basis for the minister's report) proposed four ventures to address the information deficit: a guide developed by bank/financial institution trade specialists, DFAIT, and other interested parties to assist the exporter in locating key contacts; a series of fact sheets on the most frequently used services; an InfoCentre Bulletin Board that is an electronic data bank of international market opportunities and export finance information that can be accessed via telephone using a personal computer and a modem; and training through the Institute of Canadian Bankers, the training arm of the Canadian Bankers Association, that will educate a broad base of bankers and financial institution specialists on the importance of exports.
26. "The Chamber's International Affairs Committee," *Worldbusiness* (October 1994), 28.

27. Finlayson, "Directions," 116.

28. International Business Development Report, Submitted to the Hon. Roy MacLaren, Minister for International Trade, September 30, 1994.

29. Tim Reid, "Challenging Canada's International Business Paradox: A Private Sector Perspective," *Canadian Foreign Policy* 1, 1 (Winter 1992/93), 87.

30. As an example of how the CCC's members can be tapped, it is instructive to note that the senior executives of the major Canadian banks would, at various times, be members of the CCC's banking or taxation committees and can thus make available to the CCC the resources to their respective organizations.

31. Author interview with David Hecnar, a manager of the Canadian Chamber of Commerce, December 1994.

32. "The Chamber's International Affairs Committee," *Worldbusiness* (October 1994), 30.

33. Eva E. Kiess-Moser and James G. Barnes, "Emerging Trends in Marketing Research," *Organizational Effectiveness Research*, Report 82-92 (Ottawa: Conference Board of Canada), 5, 15.

34. See Tyson Macaulay, "The Development of Electronic Commerce in Canada," *Policy Options* 15, 7 (September 1994), 40-43.

35. Evert A. Lindquist, building on the research of Doern and Phidd and Pal, provides a useful overview of the literature in Canada on Canadian think tanks, a description of a select number of institutes, and an evaluation of their effectiveness in the public policy process. See E.A. Lindquist, "Think Tanks or Clubs? Assessing the Influence and Role of Canadian Policy Institutes," *Canadian Public Administration* 36, 4 (Winter 1993), 547-79; G.B. Doern and R.W. Phidd, *Canadian Public Policy: Ideas, Structure, and Process* (Toronto: Methuen, 1983); L.A. Pal, *Public Policy Analysis: An Introduction* (Toronto: Methuen, 1987).

36. Lindquist, "Think Tanks," 557.

37. *Ibid.*, 562.

38. The PPF seeks to be a catalyst for action. It assembles background date to inform round table discussions and issues summaries of the proceedings, but generally does not sponsor research studies.

39. These split into five divisions: *Economic Forecasting and Analysis, Organizational Effectiveness Research, Public Policy Analysis, International Business Research*, and *Business Sectors Research*.

40. Lindquist observes that it is difficult to offer a complete portrait of university-based research institutes, since no study has reviewed academic centres at Canadian universities. See Lindquist, "Think Tanks," 568.

41. *Ibid.*, 562.

42. Although it was rumoured that there was no love lost between the two organizations and that Finance was not saddened at the closing of the ECC.

43. Lindquist, "Think Tanks," 554.

44. Foreign Affairs and International Trade Canada, *1994-95 Estimates, Part III Expenditure Plan* (Ottawa: Ministry of Supply and Services Canada, 1994), 112-III, A-115, 116-III. Although DFAIT funding to the CCC is for international business development rather than research, because the CCC-administered CTOT is the only "official" Canadian institution in Taiwan, it also has a research mandate.

45. Allan Tupper, "Think Tanks, Public Debt, and the Politics of Expertise in Canada," *Canadian Public Administration* 36, 4 (Winter 1993), 545. Tupper notes that the 1985 Royal Commission on Canada's Economic Development produced far more valuable economic intelligence than is evident in the current output of Canada's think tanks.

46. This is understandable, since under current budgetary realities an association executive would be hard pressed to attempt to justify the salary of an employee whose sole job it would be to keep track of the more broadly applicable economic intelligence being produced by Canada's think tanks and research institutes. At present, this is done somewhat sporadically through informal and personal contacts between association employees and think tanks.

47. Tupper, "Think Tanks," 535.

48. Lindquist, "Think Tanks," 552.

49. It has been estimated that there are over 1000 think tanks throughout the United States and about 100 in the Washington, D.C. area alone. See J.A. Smith, *The Idea Brokers: Think Tanks and the Rise of the New Policy Elite* (New York: Free Press, 1991), xiv.

50. Lindquist, "Think Tanks."

51. This is based on the author's knowledge of the various actors' orientations and is not based on any survey results.

52. Presentation by a partner with McKinsey and Co. (Toronto), at a seminar held at the Department of Foreign Affairs and International Trade, Ottawa, 25 May 1994. The author was the rapporteur for this seminar.

53. This author's translation of Martre, *Intelligence économique*, 28.

54. Griffith, "Trading Nations," 22.

55. Martre, *Intelligence économique*, 44.

56. *Ibid.*, 48.

57. *Ibid.*, 57.

58. Martre reports that the Germans seem to be world experts at disseminating information both to each other and to foreigners about German products and

services. He notes that there are 3400 professional publications with a circulation of about 60 million, which has created the world's greatest concentration of information exchange.

59. See diagram 6 in Martre, *Intelligence économique*, 61.

60. *Ibid.*, 62.

61. Reid "Business Paradox," 95. In 1993 the president of the Canadian Chamber proposed the creation of a Canadian International Commerce Board and a "Team Canada" to Canada's international business development.

62. See "International Business Development Review Report," submitted to the Hon. Roy MacLaren, Minister for International Trade, September 30, 1994, 5.

63. The examples in recent years are legion: increased diplomacy of Aboriginal peoples, provinces pursuing individual trade diplomacies, labour refusing to participate in formal consultations over national issues such as Canada-U.S. free trade, constitutional debates, questions about Quebec's separation, etc.

64. Although the Canadian Chamber is Canada's most representative horizontal business association, it cannot be said that it is more influential than the Business Council on National Issues, which represents 150 of the largest "Canadian" firms (over 20 percent of which are subsidiaries of U.S. multinationals).

65. The Liberal government has repeatedly stated the view that the previous government destroyed Canada's breadth and depth in public policy analysis. It will thus support the creation of new national institutes such as a Canadian Foreign Policy Development Centre. See Lloyd Axworthy and Christine Stewart, "Democratization," Liberal Foreign Policy Handbook (May 1993); *Canada's Foreign Policy: Principles and Priorities for the Future*, Canada, Report of the Special Joint Committee of the Senate and the House of Commons Reviewing Canadian Foreign Policy (Ottawa: Publications Service, Parliamentary Publications Directorate, 1994), 87.

66. Martre, *Intelligence économique*, 118.

67. The fact that this new association, designed to develop competitive intelligence in French firms, is a branch of the U.S.-based Society of Competitive Intelligence Professionals is indicative of how late the French are in realizing the need for a national strategy.

68. Barry Eccleston, president and CEO, Rolls-Royce Industries Canada Inc., at the 1994 Annual Meeting of the Canadian Exporters Association, as quoted in *Worldbusiness* (December 1994), 32.

II

ECONOMIC AND COMMERCIAL INTERESTS AND INTELLIGENCE SERVICES

Samuel D. Porteous

THE 1990S IS A DECADE OF FUNDAMENTAL political and economic change. The collapse of the Soviet Union and all its repercussions, coupled with a rapidly changing and increasingly interdependent world economy, have resulted in the relative ascendance of economic concerns. In a world free from the constraints of a close to all-consuming military and ideological conflict, low politics has become high, and the concept of "economic security" has gained significant ground on its military and political counterparts. This chapter examines the implications of these changes for Western intelligence services. More specifically, it considers current and potential roles for intelligence services in an economic environment characterized by both dramatically increased international competition and a recognition of the need to build a rules-based system to govern international trade, covering everything from intellectual property to foreign direct investment.

The chapter is divided into two main parts. The first considers economic intelligence support to government and focuses on the relative capacities of intelligence services in the collection and the analysis of economic intelligence. The second major part of the chapter examines the more topical but ultimately less important issue of direct intelligence support to commercial actors, including, but not limited to, the much-discussed issue of using intelligence services to obtain and pass on commercial proprietary information to favoured firms.

ECONOMIC INTELLIGENCE SUPPORT TO GOVERNMENT

As in the military and political spheres, government decision-making in the economic sphere is sometimes supported by intelligence service activity. This is nothing new. What we are seeing now is an increased focus on this activity by Western nations. In fact, in the wake of the Cold War most countries in the habit of publicly discussing their intelligence activities at all have indicated that they are using or will be more actively using their intelligence resources to support their economic and commercial interests.

In its most basic form, intelligence of this nature aims simply to assist government leaders to better discharge their economic management responsibilities. Services provided can range from acquisition of economic information unavailable through open sources regarding major economic decisions, such as currency devaluations, to intelligence regarding one country's clandestine attempts to influence another nation's economic interests. The defensive activity outlined in the latter example is the most widely understood and accepted form of intelligence involvement in the economic sphere. For this reason the section focuses primarily on offensive intelligence activity in support of government decision-making. The section examines issues that arise from this activity, including communication and coordination difficulties and questions concerning the quality of analysis to be expected from intelligence services in this area. Also discussed is the potential impact this activity may have on a country's foreign relations and traditional military and political alliances.

Intelligence Support to Government Decision-makers: The Public Record

The United States, Britain, Australia,[1] South Africa[2] and even G-7 adjunct Russia,[3] are among those states that have in the past made official statements regarding their desire to see their intelligence services increase their activity in this area.

The Americans, as is usually the case, have been the most open on the issue. In a presidential statement signed in 1994, President Clinton of the United States went into great detail concerning just what his administration expected from U.S. intelligence with regard to protecting or pursuing American economic interests: "In order to adequately forecast dangers to democracy and to U.S. *economic well-being*, the intelligence community must track political, economic, social and military developments in those parts of the world where U.S. interests are most heavily engaged and where overt collection of information from open sources is inadequate" [emphasis added]. The White House document signed by President Clinton goes on to say that "economic intelligence will play an increasingly important role in helping policy makers understand economic trends. Economic intelligence can support U.S. trade negotiators and help level the economic playing field by identifying threats to U.S. companies from foreign intelligence services and unfair trading practices."[4] It is important to note that the presidential statement, by its recognition that intelligence services will be utilized where "overt collection ... from open sources is inadquate," clearly envisages the utilization of clandestine methods to obtain this intelligence. Even in the era of the Internet and CNN there are still secrets. When the goal is obtaining and analyzing information unavailable from open sources there is no danger of overlap with other government actors. Clinton clearly understands what differentiates intelligence services from other government collectors of economic intelligence. Only intelligence services have a mandate encompassing clandestine collection and analysis. This is not a service provided by the numerous private sector economic intelligence firms such as Oxford Analytica or the Economist Intelligence Unit.

The U.S. statement is also of interest because of its considered use of the term "economic well-being," the heart of a subtle but seemingly important development in the Western approach to economic and commercial interests and intelligence. Britain's Intelligence Services Act of 1994 also makes use of the term, and its placement in that Act is instructive. The Act discloses for the first time the functions of the British Secret Intelligence Service (BSIS) and the Government Communications Headquarters (GCHQ) with regard to Britain's economic and commercial interests. According to the Act, under the authority of the British secretary of state, the functions of the BSIS include obtaining and providing information as well as performing "other tasks" relating to the actions or intentions of "persons outside the British Isles." These functions of the BSIS, like those of the GCHQ, both foreign intelligence organizations, are to be exercisable only in the interests of national security, prevention or detection of serious crime, and, most importantly from the point of view of this chapter, "in the interests of the economic well-being of the U.K."[5]

Of essential importance here, particularly with respect to intelligence service involvement in the economic arena, is the Act's use of terms. By introducing the concept of economic well-being as a standard for BSIS and GCHQ engagement and setting it apart from national security, the British indicate that while some economic and commercial interests issues may not directly threaten the national security interests in the traditional sense, they are, nonetheless, important enough to be supported through the use of the intrusive and considerable powers of the British intelligence community. The American use of the term seems intended to achieve the same result.

The term "economic well-being," therefore, is not to be construed narrowly within the confines of traditional views of national security, that is, strictly tied to the defence and foreign policies of Britain or the United States. This narrow interpretation might for example have limited intelligence service interests to issues like security of supply of certain critical materials or technologies. As a threshold requirement, the need to establish an impact on a country's economic well-being is substantially easier to meet than establishing an economic threat to a country's national security. The use of this term clearly indicates that the British government, like its American counterpart, wants its intelligence community involved in the broadest way practicable in furthering and protecting the economic and commercial interests of the state.[6] It must also be noted that these are two of the governments most often noted for encouraging less, not more, government involvement in the economy.

The Canadian government has made no official statements concerning intelligence community involvement in the provision of economic intelligence to support government decision-making beyond statements relating to its defensive posture. CSIS, as the government's security intelligence agency, primarily concerned with defensive intelligence, has publicly acknowledged its role in reporting on and analysing the threat of economic espionage engaged in by foreign powers. While the Service recognizes this as an important role, it has made it clear that counter-terrorism is its primary responsibility and that defending against economic espionage is just one component of its counter-intelligence function. There has been, however, no Canadian equivalent to the public American and British embrace of offensive intelligence activity in support of the seemingly broad concept of "economic well-being." In fact, the Canadian minister for Foreign Affairs has reaffirmed the long-standing government policy that Canada does not require a foreign intelligence service capable of recruiting agents and running covert operations abroad to pursue economic or other information.[7] Nonetheless, there have been indications from parts of the Canadian intelligence community of a more aggressive posture in this area. In early 1995, the Communications Security Establishment (CSE), Canada's agency responsible for signals intelligence (SIGINT), which includes activities such as the collection of foreign intelligence from telecommunication interception, advertised for applications from university graduates for analyst positions, noting that "graduation in fields such as economics, international business, commerce ... would be an asset."[8] The head of the CSE has also been reported as stating that demands on his organization are increasing as the agency moves into economic intelligence and computer support.[9]

It is clear from this discussion that those who continue to examine the issue of economic and commercial interests and intelligence from the sole perspective of what amounts to a massive economic threat to national security, for example, the debt crisis of the 1980s and the threat it posed to Western banking structures, are examining only part of the puzzle. Many Western intelligence services have now been directed by their governments to operate in this area to support their state's "economic well-being"—a much lower threshold.

Provision of Economic Intelligence and Related Services to Government Officials: Problems and Issues

The practice of having the intelligence service provide economic intelligence and related services to government decision-makers, be it for offensive or defensive purposes, raises several issues. An analysis of these problems, particularly in the North American context, reveals the importance of defining just what the government requests of its intelligence services and the methods used to meet these requests.

Tension Between Economic Departments and Intelligence: Coordination, Quality of Analysis, and Other Issues

In North America, unlike some other regions, economic departments tend to be considered peripheral or secondary members of the intelligence community.[10] Until quite recently, in fact, North American intelligence services, partially because the relative prosperity enjoyed by North America since the end of the Second World War, perceived the economic and commercial elements of their work as decidedly secondary in importance to military and political concerns. This perception was not always shared by those states with longer memories, less preoccupation with the Cold War, and keener senses of economic security. Consequently, communications between intelligence services and the economic departments in Canada and the United States have been described as uncertain, informal, and characterized by ad hockery. One expert has described intelligence policy in this area as "largely a matter of collection requirements, which are voluminous but too unfocused. Intelligence agencies are left to do what they feel is appropriate."[11]

Communication and Coordination: One of the major problems stemming from this ad hockery is poor coordination between intelligence services and economic departments. Again the U.S. system provides an instructive example. Intelligence expert Ernest May has analyzed issues surrounding intelligence involvement in economic issues. May argues that despite the existence of liaison offices located within American departments such as Treasury, Commerce, and the Office of the Special Trade Representative,[12] the U.S. National Security Council (NSC) does not have a history of dealing well with economic issues.[13] He cites as an example the treatment of the Latin American debt crisis of the early 1980s which, at the time, was considered to be one of the greatest current threats to U.S. national security.

According to May, faced with the prospect of the U.S. financial sector being thrown into chaos by defaulting Latin American banks, the NSC's senior director of economic affairs set out to warn the president.[14] The problem was, however, that "neither the Treasury nor the Federal Reserve had seen the NSC as a natural venue for a problem in their domains and neither agency had a comfortable relationship with the intelligence community." The result was "they succeeded in keeping their worries to themselves." May's account of the intelligence treatment of the debt crisis, while instructive, omits any reference to the alleged role of American intelligence in distributing "bugged" software to various international financial institutions involved in the debt crisis to better monitor the situation.[15]

It is not known, if this did indeed occur, to whom this information went or whether they found it useful. This points to a very important difficulty in analyzing the impact of intelligence activity of any kind. Typically, intelligence product is provided only to the highest levels of government or to specific clients. Because of the tendency of intelligence services to operate on a "need to know" and containment basis to protect sources and methods, even senior officials of major departments may not be able to speak with authority on what exactly intelligence services provided to whom and its value. This argument applies equally to some members of the intelligence bureaucracy who, despite their years of experience within the community, actually have minimal experience with economic intelligence issues.

Communication and coordination difficulties apparently remain an issue for the Americans. The presidential statement on the U.S. intelligence community and U.S. economic and commercial interests cited earlier clearly communicates a desire on the part of the White House to "develop new strategies for collection, production and dissemination (including closer relationships between intelligence producers and consumers) to make intelligence products more responsive to consumer needs.... Revise long-standing security restrictions where possible to make intelligence data more useful to intelligence consumers."[16] The document also calls for better coordination between overt and covert collection. Similar conclusions were provided by the congressionally mandated bipartisan presidential Aspin-Brown commission when it tabled its report on the future of the American intelligence community.[17]

It remains to be seen what impact these calls for improved coordination between overt and covert collection could have on intelligence participation in new Clinton administration projects such as the "Advocacy Centre"—a situation room in the U.S. Commerce Department. Reportedly the centre is "staffed by specialists who track, minute by minute, the status of thousands of giant projects around the world that American firms are vying to win."[18] Competitor progress is also followed. One unnamed official is quoted as saying of the centre, "the idea is to bring the whole force of the Government together to press the case for American business."[19]

Other Western powers are also searching for new policies and structures. In March of 1995 France announced the creation of what appears to be an organization similar in function to and to an extent modelled on the U.S. Advocacy Centre—the Committee for Economic Competitivity and Security. The committee, to be chaired by the French prime minister, will "research, analyze, process and distribute information" with the goal of protecting economic secrets and advising French firms and the government on trade strategy.[20] Its work is to be coordinated by the Secretariat Général de la Défense Nationale (SGDN), which analyzes intelligence for the French prime minister.[21] Such centres clearly would provide excellent locales for better coordination between overt and covert collection.

In Canada, coordination between various departments and the intelligence community is sought through an interdepartmental committee structure directed out of the Privy Council Office—a central government agency. This committee structure includes the deputy level Interdepartmental Committee on Security and Intelligence (ICSI), chaired by the Clerk of the Privy Council and its intelligence subcommittee, the Intelligence Advisory Committee (IAC), established in 1993. The IAC is supported in its work by its own Foreign Intelligence Assessments Secretariat (FIAS), which draws on intelligence community and other government expertise through the intelligence expert groups.[22] It would seem this structure, similar to the British model, could be used to better match economic department interests with Canadian intelligence service capabilities and production.

The increasingly seamless nature of military, political, and economic influences in determining threats and opportunities for a nation's citizenry is pushing Western intelligence services and economic departments to work more closely together to improve their product. In the near future, however, prospects for dramatically improved communication and coordination are not bright. Despite attempts to address this problem, traditional divisions between Western intelligence services and economic departments, coupled with ambivalent attitudes toward government involvement in the economy, ensure that proper communication and coordination in this area will remain a challenge.

Quality of Analysis Concerns: Apart from communication and coordination concerns, the value of intelligence service involvement in this area depends largely on the quality of the economic intelligence that is gathered and analysis that is provided. Ideally, intelligence services would provide government decision-makers with either valuable economic intelligence unavailable from any overt source or a value-added analysis of the issue, or both.

It is generally conceded that intelligence services, if properly tasked by those who needed the information, would be able to collect economic intelligence of use to decision-makers clandestinely. For example, in testimony before a U.S. Senate committee, FBI Director Louis Freeh stated that foreign governments had been targeting, among other subjects, prepublication data on U.S. economic, trade, and financial agreements, tax and monetary policies, foreign aid programs, and commodity policies.[23] In addition, French operatives have been quoted as saying that just a few economic espionage operations relating to currency markets netted benefits for France that more than paid the cost of running the French intelligence service.[24] Finally, only a few years ago, former chief U.S. trade negotiator Mickey Kantor publicly praised the CIA for the information it provided during tense auto negotiations with the Japanese.[25] While the clandestine collection of otherwise unavailable information remains an intelligence community niche, the added value provided by intelligence analysis is a more contentious issue. Many policy-making entities jealously guard the analytical function and see intelligence service analysis as an uninformed and unwanted intrusion into their territory.[26]

This view ignores the traditionally accepted need to maintain some distance between those whose task is to provide objective information and those who make policy. The goal of course is to avoid intelligence being perceived to "sell" policy rather than "inform" it.[27] This policy-neutral approach of intelligence services toward information is a further reason for conflict between economic departments charged with policy formulation and intelligence services, who may provide intelligence that complicates their policy process. Former U.S. Director of Central Intelligence during President Carter's administration, Stansfield Turner, describes this as the conflict between "fresh intelligence" and "established policy."[28] The need for this separation has, however, been challenged by those who argue that it simply replaces policy makers' biases in intelligence analysis with intelligence community biases.[29] Still, it seems that the clandestine techniques required for collection and some analysis of non-open source information would be unwelcome and awkward additions to many economic departments with broad policy-making mandates. Many of these departments would simply prefer the option of using or not using intelligence analysis made available to them.

The experience of the Australian Office of National Assessments (ONA), as coordinator of the relatively small intelligence community of a Western middle power, is instructive in this area. In fulfilling its role, the ONA initially found it hard to engage the interest of Australian economic departments. The latter were "unconvinced intelligence advice or resources had much to offer in the formulation of sound economic policy."[30] The Department of Trade in particular was leery of too close a relationship with intelligence. The department reportedly feared that any association with intelligence, even if it were only in analysis, could send the wrong message to foreign governments and companies with whom they were negotiating. They also did not want Australian businesspeople to think they engaged in spying. Partially in response to this and with a desire to avoid overlap, the ONA focused its economic intelligence product on illuminating "capabilities and intentions that competitors and adversaries seek to conceal."[31] One example of a subject matter given this treatment was the impact of sanctions on the South African economy, a clear perspective of which could not be drawn from solely open sources.

It seems that the existing overlap, duplication, and quality concerns could be addressed if intelligence services analyzing economic or commercial issues built their analysis around information unobtainable from open sources or information that while unclassified or proprietary would be difficult for economic policy-making departments to locate either from private sector or public sector sources. This, coupled with a focus on "capabilities and intentions that competitors seek to conceal," would ensure that intelligence analysis would be a value-added product distinct from standard foreign affairs or trade analysis or something reasonably obtainable from private sector sources. Even with this sort of approach, however, intelligence analysis of economic and commercial issues would remain a minor but occasionally important contributor to a government's analytical capacity. The value-added for intelligence services in this area will continue to rest largely in their unique capacity to collect information clandestinely that would otherwise be unavailable.

Alienating Allies and Troubling Trade Blocs

A further problem with economic espionage and related activities for many countries is that economic competitors are often "friends," and since the end of the Cold War there are fewer and fewer countries that can be considered "enemies." In the absence of the great rivalry of the past fifty years the concept of friendship may have broadened and at the same time become more shallow.

In the diplomatically difficult realm of economic espionage, comfortable distinctions between adversaries and allies do not always apply. On the field of economic espionage one's potential adversaries could well be one's military and political allies. In the absence of the discipline imposed by the Cold War, nations, like modern corporations, feel freer to both compete and cooperate at the same time.[32] Pierre Marion, the former head of the French intelligence service, summed up the attitude of countries that engage in economic espionage against their military and political allies: "We are really allied. But in the economic competition, in the technological competition, we are competitors; we are not allied."[33] This view is echoed by Stansfield Turner. "If economic strength should be now recognized as a vital component of national security, parallel with military power, why should America be concerned about stealing and employing economic secrets?"[34]

Rethinking and realigning potential adversaries in this manner has the potential to undermine traditional intelligence-sharing networks. In a world where business must no longer take a back seat to Cold War ideology and unfair trade practices are seen by some as the economic equivalent of an act of war, economically and commercially valuable intelligence may be shared much less freely within military and political alliances.

It is interesting to speculate whether the traditional intelligence-sharing networks that deal in military and political matters will soon find their parallels in economic intelligence-sharing networks. Given that it is the most mature and comprehensive of these regional agreements it is likely that pressures for any changes of this nature would likely first arise within the European Union (EU) structure.[35] Certainly in the area of international trade negotiations, since the EU often negotiates trade issues as a bloc, this intelligence-sharing split between North America and the EU on trade negotiation intelligence is already present. This is not to suggest, however, that the relatively narrowly focused North American Free Trade Agreement (NAFTA) would present the same opportunities for intelligence integration as the EU, or that individual states will not pursue their individual interests within the trade blocs as well.[36]

The clearest public acknowledgement of this growing linkage of economic and security interests with trading blocs can be found in a French global military review. The document, with which France hopes to influence the European security agenda, recognizes both that security is now defined less in terms of territory than in terms of economic and industrial interests and that France's vital interests, particularly at the economic and industrial level, are "barely dissociable" from those of fellow EU members.[37] The paper calls for the development of common intelligence structures and a consequent reduction of Europe's dependence on American intelligence resources. According to some reports, the British view is that despite some concerns about maintaining an independent British capability, "it is absurd to weaken the Anglo-U.S. intelligence link even at the risk of being accused by Britain's EU partners of being a Trojan horse."[38]

As time passes, however, even economic intelligence-sharing networks based on regional trade groupings may seem too rigid. Nation-states, and perhaps even some discrete economic zones within these states, may turn to more time-limited, goal-oriented tactical alliances necessitating more fluid economic intelligence alliances. In either case, new and strengthened alliances driven by economic interests will test the durability of older military and political alliances such as NATO and the communications interception or SIGINT agreements such as that between Canada, Britain, the United States, and Australia.[39] It seems inconceivable that military or political alliances would not be weakened if the countries involved were members of separate competing economic intelligence-sharing networks representing rival trade groups.

INTELLIGENCE SERVICE SUPPORT
TO COMMERCIAL ACTORS

The previous section dealt with the issue of intelligence service provision of economic intelligence and related services to government decision-makers. This section's topic, economic espionage and related services of more direct interest to commercial actors, ranging from economic espionage in support of national champions to monitoring major international deals for bribery, is more controversial. As such the problems and issues raised by this practice have drawn significant interest and attention. The section's focus is on what is actually happening in these areas and the views of both corporations and countries on this matter.

Intelligence Activity of Direct Interest to Commercial Actors: The Public Record

Amid estimates of billions of dollars in losses and press accounts of foreign intelligence services spying on companies, the heads of the FBI and CIA in a joint address to a congressional committee warned in 1992 that about 20 nations were suspected of engaging in economic espionage in the United States.[40] Other officials identified these countries as including Russia, China, North Korea, and Vietnam, and admitted that some countries otherwise considered "friendly" were also engaged in these activities. Similar conclusions have been drawn about economic espionage activity in Canada and other developed countries.[41] Reports of this activity in recent years demonstrate the extent of the problem:

- In April 1993, Hughes Aircraft decided not to participate in the Bourget Air Show after being warned by the CIA that the company was being spied on by the French intelligence service. The president of Hughes Aircraft had been informed that his company was on a list of 49 American companies targeted by the French.[42]

- China is reported to be using some members of visiting delegations and exchanges to conduct economic espionage in the United States, Canada, and other developed countries."[43]

- In Montreal, two members of the Stasi, the former East German secret police, explained how they used phony work records from "sympathetic companies" to gain employment at targeted Canadian companies.[44]

- Business travellers were warned in 1992 not to fly Air France after it was discovered that the French intelligence service was bugging airline seats and using undercover agents to pose as airline passengers and flight attendants.[45]

- In 1991, the West German intelligence service was accused of intercepting a foreign company's telecommunications and passing the information to the company's German competitors.[46]

- In the 1980s Japanese intelligence agents were suspected, in conjunction with Japanese multinationals, of running secret operations against high-tech firms in California.[47]

- A South Korean company reportedly paid an employee of General Electric $1 million a year for trade secrets concerning synthetic diamond production.[48]

Interest in economic espionage is not limited to North America. Many other countries express concern about the practice and predictably portray themselves as victims rather than practitioners:[49]

- German articles talk of American or French use of SIGINT capacity to eavesdrop on sensitive commercial transactions.[50]

- Reuters stories coming out of Britain make similar claims involving a multi-billion dollar arms deal with a Middle-Eastern power that Britain was bidding on.[51]

- China has warned its people about foreigners seeking economic intelligence. In this instance it was the thousand year-old remedies and ancient healing techniques that the Chinese government felt required protection.[52]

- Russian authorities have expressed their concern in an edition of *Izvestiya* about the increasing amount of economic espionage being conducted in their country.[53] Presidential aide Yuriy Baturin accused Asian countries, particularly China and North Korea, of engaging in the practice.

- Finally, even much-abused France was able to put together a major story on economic espionage, the title of which may be translated as "The Pillage of France."[54]

What is of particular interest in examining the foreign analysis of this issue is the blasé manner with which accusations against other countries, often allies, are made. This, despite most countries' repeated and vocal denials that they engage in economic espionage.[55]

Impact

Although some spectacular incidents have found their way into media reports, analysis of the overall economic impact of economic espionage has been impeded by industry's reluctance to discuss the issue in detail. In fact, the General Accounting Office—the investigative arm of the U.S. Congress—had to abandon its plan to study the extent and impact of foreign government spying on U.S. companies when it became clear that firms had little desire to discuss the matter.[56] There are a number of reasons for this corporate reticence. Apart from an instinctive aversion to discussing problems with outsiders, firms fear that disclosure could result in retaliation by foreign governments. They also have to consider the possibility that any information revealed might be leaked and might thereby undermine shareholders' confidence.

Despite these obstacles to a formal calculation, the cost of economic espionage activities to individual firms and the economies that host them is generally agreed by business and government representatives to be in the billions. The White House Office on Science and Technology came up with a damage estimate for just the U.S. economy of over US$100 billion per year.[57] This view is supported by Marshall Phelps, a vice-president of IBM, one of the few companies to estimate publicly the financial damage it has suffered from economic espionage. Speaking for his company before a committee of the U.S. Congress that was investigating the issue, he stated that "governments seeking to bolster national industrial champions" have contributed in a significant way to the billions of dollars in losses IBM has calculated it suffered as a result of the theft of proprietary information.[58]

The extent of these losses can be further demonstrated through an additional example of economic espionage. In 1985, it was reported that the French government clandestinely obtained information on military procurement from the Indian government. They supposedly obtained the details of a rival American firm's offer during the final phase of negotiations on the sale of new jet fighters. This information, once it was transferred to a French firm, was said to give it the edge needed to win the deal on the jet fighters. In the process the U.S. firm lost a billion-dollar contract.[59] Clearly, it would not take too many incidents of this nature to convince a country of the threat posed by economic espionage.[60]

The potential threats posed by the activities of foreign entities engaged in economic espionage lead most observers to agree that intelligence services have a legitimate role in defending against economic espionage. Even a defensive role for intelligence services, however, raises several difficult issues.

Issues Arising from a Defensive Position

Defending Against What?
If intelligence services are to play an increased role in defending private sector entities against economic espionage targeting commercial interests they will require a clear mandate as to what they are defending against. A key question is whether a foreign government must be involved in either conducting or facilitating the economic espionage before the domestic intelligence service would be justified in acting. This would be a comfortable requirement from the point of view of intelligence services, since they typically conceptualize and direct their activities in terms of nation-states. The alternative is to regard the conducting of economic espionage by any foreign entity from either government or the private sector as sufficient cause for intelligence service involvement.

Those who favour requiring foreign government involvement as a necessary condition for intelligence service action argue that the primary justification for intelligence services involvement is the destabilizing effect a foreign intelligence service, with all its resources, brings to the competition between businesses.[61] In this view the damage foreign government economic espionage does to the level playing field merits bringing in the domestic intelligence service to even the odds.[62] Jim Royer, of Chicago's FMC Corp., producer of the M-3 Bradley fighting vehicle as well as industrial chemicals, mirrors the view of many large corporations when he makes the case for government intervention to support domestic industry in these situations: "We can handle the ordinary industrial spy, but we don't have the technology or know-how to combat the type of advanced technologies governments can throw at us. For example, spy satellites and sophisticated strategic espionage ... only government can combat that."[63] These concerns were echoed by James E. Riesback, executive vice-president of Corning, Inc. In testimony before a U.S. congressional committee, Riesback stated that "the resources of a corporation—even a large one such as Corning—are no match for economic espionage activities that are sanctioned and supported by foreign governments. Our intelligence agencies must become partners with U.S. industry in providing secure, enhanced telecommunications services on an international basis." Riesback's concern was such that he proposed that government agencies consider "establishing a secure overseas pipeline for use by businesses seeking to communicate proprietary information to their foreign operations" as a "short-term option."[64]

This, however, may be easier said than done. While theoretically tidy, the strict requirement of foreign government involvement becomes rather messy in practice. In many cases it is very difficult to determine whether the principals involved in an economic espionage operation are being directed or facilitated by a foreign government.

Another problem with a strict focus on foreign government involvement is that it ignores the important issue of the potential impact of the particular economic espionage operation involved. Arguably, the activities of large multinational corporations, rich in intelligence resources, may be more of a threat to a country's economic security than clumsy attempts by tiny under-resourced entities that happen to be nation-states. The growing influence and global reach of some of these organizations puts them on a par with all but the most powerful nations.

The case for the prerequisite of foreign government involvement is further weakened by the fact that intelligence services already involve themselves in certain matters, regardless of the presence of government.

In most cases terrorists are neither directed nor supported by foreign governments. Yet governments feel no qualms about involving their intelligence services in this area. The impact of terrorist activities is deemed significant enough to warrant attention by domestic intelligence services. Governments struggling with this issue will have to determine whether potential economic losses and their ramifications are to be equated in priority with the physical security of their citizens.[65]

Why Defend Stateless Multinationals?
Another issue raised in examining a defensive role for governments in this area is the logic of defending "stateless" multinationals. Almost every analysis of economic espionage raises this issue and questions intelligence service involvement in defending entities with no real "loyalty" to the country within which they operate. Adherents of this view see no logic in a nation-state assisting MNEs, because they have no commitment to any particular country and will simply use any defence with which they are provided or any information they are given to optimize the productivity of their global network.[66] Consequently, any benefits derived by the nation-state providing intelligence or protection to MNEs will be purely incidental.

These observations, however, miss the point that enterprises striving after profit were never expected to put the interests of their investment jurisdiction above their own. In the view of the adherents of a defensive role for intelligence services in economic espionage, a company that provides jobs and adds value to the domestic economy is worth protecting, regardless of its stateless character. Further, in protecting these companies it could be argued that the nation is also protecting its investment climate, which could be injured if it became known that the country was relatively lax in its vigilance against economic espionage and thus posed a greater risk for investors with something to lose.

Issues Arising From an Offensive Position on Economic Espionage

Wasteful Market Intervention by the Government?
While admittedly raising some interesting conceptual issues, the case for defending a nation-state's economic security from the threats presented by economic espionage directed against the private sector seems, at least, grudgingly accepted. Views on the desirability of offensive economic

espionage to assist the private sector, however, are much more fervently divided.

To many, particularly in North America, government intervention to assist domestic industry is invariably ill-advised. Under traditional economic analysis, opponents of offensive economic espionage targeted to benefit the private sector would describe the "intelligence" that is provided to the firm or firms as analogous to a subsidy.[67] This analogy having been drawn, the litany of what is wrong and inefficient about subsidies in general could be used to criticize the practice of economic espionage.

Some would argue that government-sponsored espionage at the level of the firm is undesirable. Governments participating in this activity can be accused of creating market imperfections instead of correcting them, rewarding duplicity instead of innovation, favouring inefficient producers over consumers, and wrongly perceiving international competition as a threat to national security rather than a necessary and welcome component of economic development.[68]

This new form of government aid—economic espionage—would be welcomed by declining industries and uncompetitive businesses. Just as these industries readily accepted government subsidies and other forms of protection, they would welcome, and form pressure groups to obtain, government acquired information and other services available from the intelligence community. The long-term result for the national economy is likely to be the same as those of other failed attempts at industrial policy: uncompetitive domestic producers would gain at the expense of consumers and taxpayers. Scarce resources would be misallocated and weakened uncompetitive industries would become even more dependent on the state. Competitive industries that would normally neither need nor desire this type of assistance would ordinarily request only that government provide a fair, stable, and predictable environment in which to do business.

On a more technical level an argument often presented in North American analysis against economic espionage is that intelligence obtained through this method would be "tactically useless" for a number of reasons. Lack of direct knowledge of a certain business or its technology by intelligence officers is often posited as a significant obstacle to the effective engagement of intelligence services in economic espionage. Yet during the Cold War, intelligence services spent significant amounts of time and energy, with some success, trying to obtain intelligence on various complex military technologies of which the relevant case officers would not have had a profound knowledge. If intelligence services were trusted to go after complex military technologies, often not directly but through the judicious use of agents or other methods, a shift to complex commercial technologies and intelligence applying similar methods would not be unthinkable. The same techniques used to obtain nuclear secrets could be turned to complex commercial technologies or strategies without too much difficulty.

The Strategic Trade Policy Argument

Not everyone views government-sponsored economic espionage as a wasteful allocation of resources. In fact, drawing on strategic trade policy (STP), a relatively new and increasingly popular view of economic relations,[69] it could be argued that the case against economic espionage is based on an antiquated and simplistic view of the world economy and how it operates.

According to STP the patterns of international trade as they exist today reflect temporary advantages as much as, or more than, any permanent underlying advantage of the exporting countries. These temporary advantages include those stemming from imperfect competition, economies of scale, and advantages in cumulative experience or technological advances. Given that many of these advantages are knowledge-based they are therefore, to a certain extent, transferable from one nation to another.

In a world where country specializations often depend on technological advances and certain industries can earn excess profits and generate positive externalities, proponents of STP argue that governments can and should act to take advantage of these strategic environments. According to STP, this can be done by providing government assistance through properly targeted subsidies to domestic firms deemed strategic. By lowering their costs in this manner governments theoretically allow these firms to provide more of these excess profits or externalities that benefit the country as a whole. The European consortium Airbus is often presented as a successful example of strategic trade policy.

It should be noted that while strategic trade policy can be used to present the theoretical case for the use of economic espionage as part of a country's strategic trade policy, there are in practice complicating factors. It has been recognized that when several countries engage in strategic trade policy or by extension economic espionage in competition with one another, they all might end up worse off. A "prisoner's dilemma" scenario exists where interests of governments partly conflict and partly coincide and the pursuit of self-interest under free competition does not result in a collectively optimal result. In this sort of situation it is in the interests of all countries to agree not to undertake economic espionage, although it remains in their individual interests to do so—as long as others do not.

Divergent Economic Structures and Cultures
The European approach to the aerospace industry as evidenced by Airbus is a useful reminder that not all countries even within the Western sphere agree on the proper role of government in the economy. As noted in the chapter by Potter in this study, cultural factors loom large in a state's determination of the role of its intelligence services in supporting its economic and commercial interests. North Americans tend to assume, particularly since the failure of the former Soviet Union, that all countries share their stated views on the proper role for government in the economy. They do not.

The collapse of communism has not left in its wake a uniform approach to capitalism. Western Europeans have their own views about government involvement in the market, and the governments of the so-called "economies in transition" of Eastern Europe and Russia plan to play a large role in the commercial activities within their region for some time to come. Meanwhile, the extensive involvement of the Japanese government in its economy through departments such as Ministry of International Trade and Industry (MITI) and Japan External Trade Organization (JETRO) is well known, and the Chinese continue to speak of their goal of a "socialist market economy." Many of the other burgeoning economies of Asia also feel the need for relatively more government in the economy than is generally stated as desirable in North America.

Even in the United States, adherents of such doctrines as strategic trade policy, many of whom are senior advisers in the Clinton administration, are beginning to question whether there is not a more active role for the American government to play in its economy. Manifestations of this change could be seen in President Clinton's creation of a National Economic Council, U.S. government plans to support the creation of a "flat-panel display industry," the use of government-sponsored consortia such as Sematech and U.S. Car to encourage industries deemed strategic,[70] and the Commerce Department advocacy centre discussed earlier.

Clearly states differ on the legitimate level of government involvement in the economy, and this naturally extends to their view of the legitimate role of their intelligence services. A state's economic structure and its attitude toward government involvement in the economy have a decisive impact on its approach to intelligence service involvement in the provision of economic intelligence or services of more direct interest to commercial actors. In Canada and the United States, provision of most types of information of this kind or related intelligence services directly to commercial actors is seen as improper or as a misallocation of resources. Other countries have different views. A country with a long tradition of state involvement in industry is not likely to view the sanctity of the free market as too great an impediment to economic espionage or related activities with direct impacts on commercial actors. A government policy that embraced these practices to support commercial actors would most likely be adopted in a country where companies could be considered "national champions,"[71] or government and industry links are so close that disentangling state and commercial interests is difficult. In today's world there is no shortage of countries that fit this description.[72]

This line between support to government decision-makers and direct support to commercial actors is admittedly a hazy one. The difficulty of disentangling state from commercial interests in some cases has been recognized even in the North American context. It has been observed that "when the U.S. government sets priorities with respect to trade or technological issues, particular segments and companies of the American economy will inevitably benefit more than others. In such instances, 'economic' intelligence in support of policy or decisions or trade negotiations will in the end have the results which appear from one perspective to have the same results as that provided directly by 'commercial' espionage."[73]

An additional complication arises with the so-called economies in transition, including Eastern Europe, Russia, and China. In many of these countries, particularly the latter two, government and military officials are developing large stakes in the companies and commercial interests surfacing in the wake of central planning. For example, it has been reported with regard to the Russian military, "The MO has become a serious economic actor, with its own bank and investment arms, and thus with its own interests to protect and advance. It has begun to press for a voice in economic policy-making while simultaneously acquiring a significant market role. The scope for conflict of interest here [is] enormous."[74] The question arises as to what happens when the same entity that controls much of a state's intelligence community also controls a good deal of its country's commercial sectors?

A country's economic structure and attitude toward government involvement in the private sector would be key factors in the successful planning of any policy advocating economic espionage. A strategic trade policy that embraced economic espionage would most likely be adopted in a country where government and industry have close links and where there are companies that could be considered national champions and therefore possible recipients of intelligence.[75]

The Risk of Alienating Allies

Apart from wastefully misallocating resources it has been argued that nations engaging in economic espionage run the risk of seriously disturbing relations with their allies. This becomes an even greater concern with the end of the Cold War. Reports argue that while at one time the United States would put up with economic espionage by its allies in the interests of solidarity in the face of the Soviet threat, its willingness to put up passively and quietly with this sort of activity has disappeared along with the Soviet Union.[76] This may explain to a certain extent the willingness of American authorities to name or leak the names of some offending friendly states.

Further evidence of an increasingly hostile environment for practitioners of economic espionage can be drawn from the international trading regime. The intellectual property rules administered by the World Trade Organization (WTO) seek to ensure the adherence of member states to intellectual property provisions that, among other things, enshrine the protection of trade secrets—often the target of economic espionage. Significantly, public authorities and officials will be exempt from liability to appropriate remedial measures for some breach of the agreement only if their actions were taken in "good faith."[77] Economic espionage is rarely conducted in good faith.

While WTO intellectual property provisions may present a new risk to a nation engaging in offensive economic espionage, its potential impact on the activity is uncertain. The WTO is a trade organization and the Uruguay Round's purpose was to deal with trade issues. The sensitive nature of the subject and the extralegal nature of much espionage activity may make countries reluctant to engage intellectual property provisions to address economic espionage issues. If the international community wished to deal explicitly with the issue of economic espionage in support of private sector actors it might be preferable to negotiate a code dealing directly with the subject at the OECD, where for example the issue of bribery is currently being examined.[78] Furthermore, the national security exemption found in most trade agreements would complicate any attempt to bring offenders to task under these agreements.

What is a Canadian or American Firm?

The difficulties surrounding the determination of what is or is not a Canadian or U.S. company in the era of the multinational are sometimes exaggerated.[79] While admittedly a difficult question in some instances, it is nonetheless one that is dealt with daily in myriad other contexts. Many high-tech government-supported consortia, like those mentioned above, have strict nationality requirements, which a corporation must meet if it wishes to join. Tax authorities are also quite familiar with techniques to determine corporate nationality. Clearly, therefore, there are mechanisms in place to determine corporate nationality even for sensitive purposes in the era of multinationals. It will be difficult in some instances, but to suggest it is impossible is naïve or mischievous.

Where national champions are not available, however, a government wishing to engage in offensive economic espionage may be able to rely on consortia to provide a suitable substitute for national champions. Intelligence, like subsidies and lucrative procurement deals, can be channelled through consortia, thus avoiding difficult distributional problems that would plague any government program having to determine which company among many should receive intelligence derived from offensive economic espionage.[80]

Cost Effective?

Another perceived advantage of economic espionage is its potential cost effectiveness. A few well-directed operations could allow cash-strapped nations to achieve the same effect as a large cash subsidy for the relatively low cost of an economic espionage operation. There is some evidence to support this argument. In published reports officials have claimed economic espionage has saved Russia and its companies billions of dollars in research and development costs.[81] French operatives have also been quoted as saying that just a few economic espionage operations netted benefits for France that more than paid the cost of running the French intelligence service.[82] In addition, the CIA, with support from other U.S. government actors, including the President and former Secretary of State Warren Christopher, has claimed that CIA monitoring of the corrupt practices of foreign firms has saved U.S. corporations "billions of dollars" in deals that would otherwise have been lost to foreign sharp practices. Former CIA Director James Woolsey stated in response to questions on this issue:

> We collect intelligence on those efforts to bribe foreign companies and foreign governments into, for example, awarding an airport contract to a European firm rather than an American firm.... And when we find out about those, and we do a fair amount of the time, we go not to the American corporation that's competing, but the Secretary of State, and he sends an American ambassador to see a president or a king, and he—that ambassador says, "Mr. President," or "Your Majesty," your minister in charge of construction is on the take, and you have a lot going on with the United States, and we don't really take kindly to your operating that way.... Frequently but not always the contract is rebid and American firm gets a share of it.... Sometimes the whole thing is done right, sometimes not. But we calculate, really very conservatively, that *several billion dollars a year* in contracts are saved for American firms by our conducting that type of intelligence collection. We intend to continue to do it. It is relatively new. We are very—frankly good at it, and we have had some very positive effects on contracts for American businesses. I sometimes smile as I read the newspaper because some of the very same corporations for whom we have saved very, very large contracts by operating this way will have officials or executives go public and say, "We don't need any help from the American intelligence community." That's fine, that's the way the intelligence business goes [emphasis added].[83]

Although such claims are difficult to evaluate, they do indicate a perception within some intelligence services and the governments that direct them of the benefits to be derived from economic espionage. If these views are an accurate analysis, espionage in support of commercial actors would seem, strictly on a cost-benefit analysis, to be supportable. This would be particularly the case given that the infrastructure required for the collection of this information, such as signals intelligence technology, is already and will remain in place to deal with more traditional security concerns.

In this context it must be remembered that economic espionage is not just about complex leading-edge technology. It also concerns subjects as seemingly mundane as efficient plant layouts and bid information. Often this simpler form of intelligence pays surer and more immediate dividends than the procurement of a technology one may or may not understand and may or may not be able to use. Obtaining information on a competitor's bid, for example, would provide a company with a definitive advantage over its competitors that would provide a certain short-term benefit without any of the difficulties associated with trying to integrate a new form of technology. For these reasons countries may recognize that economic espionage is unlikely to contribute to a sustained competitive advantage and may still engage in the practice for its potential short-run benefits.

The Relative Priority of Economic Intelligence Support to Commerical Actors Within the Intelligence Mandate

On the Defensive Side
Despite any evaluation of the abstract importance of intelligence activity with regard to economic and commercial interests it is important to note that while this is an important and growing focus of intelligence services it remains, in North America at least, a secondary priority. There is general agreement in both Canada and the United States that the bulk of domestic security intelligence service resources, traditionally focused on defensive measures, will be directed to counter-terrorism and traditional counter-intelligence issues such as proliferation. For example, in Canada, CSIS's 1993 *Public Report* indicated that 56 percent of the Service's resources are now devoted to counter-terrorism, with the remaining 44 percent being allocated among counter-intelligence issues, including foreign-influenced activities, proliferation, and economic espionage.[84] Counter-intelligence activity directed toward foreign interests engaging in economic espionage or related activities with more direct

impacts on commercial actors will, therefore, remain an important, but relatively tertiary function. Defending against this activity consequently follows counter-terrorism and traditional counter-intelligence issues in importance.[85]

On the Offensive Side
On the offensive side, both Canadian and U.S. intelligence services have stated that they will not soon be providing intelligence service support directly to commercial actors. As discussed earlier, this was the point stressed by the Americans in their dispute with the French. It should be emphasized, however, that each country's denial of involvement in this type of activity must be examined closely for nuance. Even the British government, which is one of the most similar in economic philosophy to those of North America, while denying it will engage in economic espionage to directly support commercial actors, will reportedly continue to use businesspersons either as paid "agents" or unpaid "alongsides," who will continue to receive "commercially sensitive intelligence for services rendered."[86] This quid pro quo relationship with the private sector and whoever else could provide valuable information is extant throughout the international intelligence community. Much intelligence has the potential to be exchanged in this manner. Also, U.S. practice with regard to the CIA and its monitoring of foreign companies' bribery practices could be strongly argued to be an example of direct intelligence support to U.S. industry.

THE FUTURE OF INTELLIGENCE AND ECONOMIC AND COMMERCIAL INTERESTS

The Post-Cold War Role for Intelligence Services in Protecting or Pursuing a State's Economic and Commercial Interests

As a synthesis of the material discussed earlier, one can establish five general roles for intelligence services in protecting and pursuing economic and commercial interests. The first two are established and familiar, if not vigorously pursued. The final three will break new ground for many Western intelligence services directed to engage in them.

- *Providing counter-intelligence support* is the least controversial function. In this capacity a nation's counter-intelligence service simply

seeks to advise government about and report on the activities
of foreign intelligence services or their surrogates engaging in
clandestine activities directed against their state's economic and
commercial interests.[87] Most Western intelligence services have
been directed to increase activity in this area.

- *Providing economic intelligence to government decision-makers.*
  Here intelligence services through their unique collection capacity
  would provide decision-makers valuable economic intelligence
  unavailable through other means and value-added analysis on issues
  deemed important. This would include intelligence on macro-
  economic policies and significant upcoming decisions of major
  economic actors, for example, in the area of monetary or fiscal
  policy. Again, indications are that most Western intelligence
  services seem to have received direction to increase their activity
  in fulfilling this role as well.

- *Monitoring trade agreements and collecting information on unfair
  trade practices and other sharp practices.* This is a much more narrow
  task. The intelligence provided would support not just major economic decisions but direct responses to activities contrary to the
  economic interests of the state in question. Here intelligence services, among other activities, assist in monitoring member state
  adherence to international agreements affecting national economic
  and commercial interests. Examples of the CIA's pursuit of foreign
  corrupt practices are discussed in the appendix to this chapter.[88]
  The intelligence role in this area is precisely what the Australians
  described as illuminating "capabilities and intentions that competitors and adversaries seek to conceal." This will be a new activity
  for Western intelligence services, given the fact most of the trade
  agreements and understandings they will be monitoring are
  themselves relatively new. Adherence to intellectual property
  conventions will likely take a significant amount of intelligence
  resources devoted to this area.

- *Special activities designed to influence events, behaviour, or policy formulation in foreign lands.* These highly controversial types of covert activities could range from disinformation campaigns targeting third country markets to covert influence on important economic decisions. This will be an area engaged in sparingly, if at all, by most Western intelligence services.

- *The pursuit of commercial information and technologies for ultimate transmittal to favoured commercial actors or consortia.* This, of course, is the much discussed issue of economic espionage to support commercial actors. Most Western powers have openly disavowed any involvement in this activity.

Economic security[89] is a broad goal sought by all governments. Clearly, the intelligence community's role in achieving this goal is secondary to that of the private sector, and even that of government actors responsible for commercial and economic policy. Yet the secondary nature of the intelligence community's role does not render it unimportant. In recent years, American, British, Australian, and South African intentions to increase intelligence community involvement in pursuing a state's economic and commercial interests, both of a commercial and broader macroeconomic nature, appear indicative of approaches already taken or changes being made in the orientation of intelligence services elsewhere. The impact of this increased focus by the intelligence community on economic and commercial interests on international relations, the trading system, and more micro-commercial interests is uncertain. What is certain is that for many countries, from the last remaining superpower to second-tier middle powers, intelligence services are going to be playing an increasingly important role in warning of threats to their economic and commercial interests and identifying opportunities to advance these interests.

Increased involvement in economic security and consequent interaction with the private sector would present intelligence services with many new challenges. The decision as to whether this involvement and interaction is desirable, however, will be made outside the intelligence community. While most governments can be expected to favour some form of economic counter-espionage, attitudes toward offensive economic espionage are more ambiguous. Participation in this controversial activity will probably be determined less by a defensive reflex than by the government's attitude toward international economic competition. Governments that view international trading relationships as adversarial, akin to a military contest, where one party wins and another loses, could be attracted, despite its attendant complexities and pitfalls, to the practice of offensive economic espionage. Those who see international economic competition as just another, albeit necessary, component of economic development that both benefits consumers and keeps domestic producers competitive would be less likely to engage in this practice.

APPENDIX

ECONOMIC INTELLIGENCE SERVICES.
GOVERNMENT AS CLIENT

Reported Incidents: Offensive[90]

It is instructive to examine reported incidents of intelligence support to economic decision-makers within government. These examples indicate that the provision of economic intelligence and related services to government decision-makers is not limited to superpowers or former colonial powers. Those incidents derived from media and other open sources can be divided roughly into three categories: trade negotiation intelligence, macroeconomic intelligence, and covert action. An important distinction between the first two and the last is that the former involve merely the collection of intelligence, while the third involves an actual clandestine intervention into a process designed to affect the outcome.

Trade Negotiation Intelligence

• A European Union member state was suspected of hacking into computer networks linking the European Union to the General Agreement on Tariffs and Trade in order to monitor the communications and thus ensure that its trade interests were not being undercut in the course of negotiations between the two organizations.[91]

• In the early 1980s the Japanese reportedly had a high-level source in the U.S. State Department who was supplying Tokyo with point-by-point information on American positions even before other American departments who were to be consulted on these issues received the information.[92]

• An operator of the Canadian Communications Security Establishment (CSE) reportedly intercepted a conversation between American officials concerning a wheat deal with China for which Canada and the United States were competing. The CSE operator obtained the American's "bottom line" price to obtain the sale.[93]

- According to a CIA agent posted to Japan in the late 1970s and early 1980s, the CIA had then penetrated all the Japanese cabinet agencies. The agency's contacts were reportedly so good in the agriculture ministry that it knew beforehand what Japanese representatives would say in trade talks, their fallback positions, and when they would walk out.[94]

- In February 1995, the French broke intelligence protocol by publicly accusing U.S. intelligence of attempting to bribe French government officials in order to obtain details of France's position in the audio-visual portion of the GATT negotiations.

- The Soviets allegedly used communications intercepts to negotiate very favourable terms on large wheat purchases made from U.S. suppliers in the early 1970s.[95]

Macro-economic Intelligence

- Allegations have been put forward that in the early 1980s American intelligence services introduced "bugged" software into the World Bank and other financial institutions to enable them to provide an early warning to government decision-makers regarding the failure of some Latin American banks. At that time the potential default of those banks was considered a very serious U.S. economic and national security policy problem.[96]

- BSIS, the British foreign intelligence service, has created a new department called "Global Issues" to deal with the threat to British economic interests from the increasing amount of transnational organized crime from former Eastern Europe.[97] The rationale for this move has been explained as partially due to the impact of this activity on the British economy.

Covert Action: Security of Supply

- In the 1950s Western intelligence services reportedly assisted the overthrow of the government of Prime Minister Mohammed Mossadeqh, who had nationalized the Anglo-Iranian Oil

Company. After the coup the Iranian oil industry was reorganized, with the result that American interests controlled 40 percent of the new oil consortium. British and American interests may have conflicted in some areas of this case, but they both shared the desire to pre-empt a pro-communist coup, thus preventing Soviet control of a strategic oil supply.[98]

Reported Incidents: Defensive Concerns

Security intelligence, or defensive activities, engaged in within a state's own jurisdiction to counter or report on the activities of foreign entities engaging in the activities described above is far less controversial.[99] Most states recognize the need to engage in counter-intelligence and many have commented on the increasingly economic nature of this role.

- The 1993 *Public Report* of the Canadian Security Intelligence Service (CSIS) stated that the focus of foreign intelligence services operating in its territory were "increasingly economic in nature."[100]

- In July 1993, the head of the Dutch internal security service, the BVD, stated that its counter-espionage role is geared nowadays to combating Russian desire for intelligence in the economic and technological fields: "We still don't trust the Russians because they state time and time again that they are continuing to gather intelligence."[101]

- In June 1994, Vladimir Tsekhanov, chief of the Russian Federal Counter-intelligence Service's Economic Counter-intelligence Directorate, stated: "It will seem strange to some people, but it is a fact that, with the end of the Cold War, the intelligence activity of foreign services in relation to the Russian economy has been stepped up. Countries of the former socialist camp and the Baltic have gotten in on the act. There is a clear tendency for priorities to shift from military to economic confrontation, with the aim of making Russia a raw materials adjunct of the economically developed countries, to do everything to prevent its access to the world high technologies markets, and to exclude Russia from the list of potential economic rivals."[102]

- Developing countries have also expressed concern regarding their inability to secure their strategic economic data both from unauthorized computer intrusions and devices such as spatial imaging sensors. In one case, Ghanaian officials were concerned about the inclusion of modems linking personal computers in one of their technology transfer centres to United Nations International Development Organization (UNIDO) computers in New York. They were concerned that "sensitive economic data" could be transmitted out of Ghana without detection.[103]

INTELLIGENCE SERVICE SUPPORT
TO COMMERCIAL ACTORS

- Studies conducted by CSIS in 1990-91 led to the observation that a small group of leading-edge companies in Canada had been targeted by foreign intelligence services between 1980 and 1990. In 1992, the Service instituted an awareness liaison program to deal with issues surrounding economic espionage.[104]

- German Chancellor Helmut Kohl surprised American journalists when, in response to questions concerning French economic intelligence activities that had led to a boycott by American companies of the Paris Airshow, "he replied philosophically that what surprised him was not that some countries did engage in such intelligence, but that some others supposedly did not."[105]

- The German intelligence service (BND) is reportedly involved in a "serious debate" regarding the provision of economic intelligence of more direct interest to commercial actors. BND operations chief Volker Foertsch has apparently signed a document stating that BND should "begin furnishing German companies with operational intelligence." An adviser to Chancellor Helmut Kohl responsible for intelligence denied, however, that the BND is involved in competitive intelligence operations. As of early 1994, head of BND Konrad Porzner reportedly has not made his mind up on the question.[106]

- According to German authorities, "Getting an economic edge over their Western competitors, particularly in the international arms trade, still so important to many Eastern European countries, is apparently the main reason for cloak-and-dagger activities these days."[107] This would seem reasonable, since the arms industry is one of the few business sectors where Russia and some Eastern European countries remain even remotely competitive.[108]

- Direction de Renseignements Généraux (RG), an Interior Ministry agency that handles domestic intelligence, has a special unit that specifically targets French employees of foreign firms located in France.[109]

- A Romanian engineer with German citizenship who worked for Mercedes Benz was arrested on July 13, 1994 in Stuttgart and charged with having committed industrial espionage for Romania since 1980. A spokesman for Romania's domestic intelligence service said the RIS was created in 1990 and works solely within Romania and that any foreign activities are conducted by other services. The Romanian Foreign Ministry spokesman had no comments except to say his Ministry does not cooperate in such activities.[110]

- Germany's counter-intelligence agency has reported that, "Most present-day Russian intelligence activity against the Germans is concentrated on prying out industrial and economic secrets.... Western companies, banks, think tanks and economic journals enjoy the status of top priority targets." The report added that Russia's goal was to acquire "information that could be used to modernize Russian enterprises and improve their ability to compete on world markets." In pursuit of this goal Russian intelligence officers allegedly "leave" the service and establish themselves in private enterprise in Germany or Russia without truly having broken with their former employers.[111]

- In June of 1994, *Izvestiya* carried a story quoting Yeltsin's presidential aide Yuriy Baturin expressing the Russian government's concern regarding the increasing amount of economic espionage being conducted in their country. According to Baturin, the theft of technological and commercial secrets from Russia has been exacerbated by Russian economic conditions, which make partici-pation in the practice appealing to increasingly impoverished state and private sector employees.[112]

- Recent reports out of Britain indicate that while British intelli-gence services are forbidden to "take action" furthering the interests of any British commercial firm, MI6 will continue to use businessmen either as paid "agents" or unpaid "alongsides," who will continue to receive "commercially sensitive intelligence for services rendered."[113] It seems that much information could be transmitted to British industry in this manner.

- In 1990, the Indonesian government announced plans to award a $100 million telecommunications contract to either Japan's NEC or America's AT&T. U.S. SIGINT intercepts reportedly indicated that Indonesia was going to award the entire contract to NEC. Forewarned by this information, President Bush allegedly intervened, and as a result the contract award was split between NEC and AT&T.[114]

- In July 1982, National Security Agency (NSA) intercepts of a Japanese company's communications being transmitted from Washington D.C. to Japan revealed that Mitsubishi was transmit-ting information to Tokyo derived from the top secret National Intelligence Daily reports obtained from an American intelligence official contacted by consultants employed by the Japanese company.[115]

NOTES

1. See A.D. McLennan, "National Intelligence Assessment: Australia's Experience," paper presented at the Canadian Association for Security and Intelligence Studies Conference, 28 October 1994, Ottawa, Ontario, 8.
2. The South Africans have also made it quite clear that the skills of their intelli-gence services are to be brought to bear in the economic arena. In late 1994 the South African government released its "White Paper on Intelligence," wherein one of the "purposes" of intelligence enunciated was "to identify opportunities in the international environment, through assessing real or potential competitors'

intentions and capabilities. This competition may involve the ... technological,
scientific and economic spheres, particularly the field of trade." See "White Paper
on Intelligence," South African Government, 21 October 1994, 2.

3. In 1993, the Russian parliament passed a law dealing with intelligence that made
   the collection of economic intelligence a top priority of its foreign intelligence
   services. See Ralph Vartabedian, "The Enemy Within," *Los Angeles Times*,
   13 July 1993, A1.

4. "A National Security Strategy of Engagement and Enlargement," *The White
   House*, Washington D.C., July 1994, 1, 14.

5. Richard Norton-Taylor, "Goal Posts Keep Moving in the Spying Game,"
   Guardian Weekly, 1 January 1995. The concept of "economic well-being" is also
   earlier seen in legislation outlining the responsibilities of MI5, Britain's domestic
   intelligence service.

6. In a similar move, the new French criminal law on espionage effective March 1,
   1994 expands the definition of spying from just military and political matters to
   include industrial and commercial matters. Significantly, the description of what
   the espionage law sought to protect was change from "national defence interests"
   to "fundamental interests of the nation." See Jacques Isnard, "France Seeking to
   Boost the Fight Against Modern Forms of Espionage," *Le Monde*, 1 March
   1995, 8.

7. Jeff Sallot, "Canada Urged to Set Up Foreign Spy Service," *Globe and Mail*,
   15 May 1996, A5.

8. Careers Section, *Ottawa Citizen*, 21 January 1995, E7-8.

9. Jim Bronskill, "Canada's Spies Open Cloak of Secrecy," *Montreal Gazette*, 3 May
   1995, A9.

10. For example, in South Korea government influence and direction in the commer-
    cial sectors is pervasive. The government not only regulates the commercial
    sectors but plays a significant role in their strategic planning. One of the Korean
    government's most powerful tools in maintaining this control is the requirement
    that the government grant approval for the import of foreign technology. The
    government has used the rule to control which businesses are conducted by
    which large Korean commercial interests (*chaebol*). The relatively tight links
    between business and government found in South Korea facilitate the use of
    its intelligence services to support its commercial actors and, not surprisingly,
    intelligence services in South Korea tend to be geared more directly to benefiting
    commercial actors than is the practice in North America. The involvement of
    South Korean intelligence services in this area is clearly set out in reports ema-
    nating from Korean newspapers themselves. A Korean newspaper reported that

the Agency for National Security Planning (NSP), South Korea's national intelligence agency and successor to the KCIA, is moving to put more emphasis on the collection of foreign technology. See *Foreign Broadcasting Information Service-S&T Perspectives* 8, 7 (30 July 1993), translation of Chunggang Ilbo, 6 May 1993. The article notes that despite a hiring freeze, the agency intends to employ more science and technology experts and "specialists in industrial intelligence." Attempts will be made to employ "professionals" with advanced academic degrees capable of both collecting and evaluating "economic and industrial intelligence." The article also states, "The NSP plans in late May or the beginning of June to augment the proportion of this type of personnel it sends abroad." Because of the role of government in the Korean economy, the dissemination of information obtained in this manner does not present as much difficulty as it would in North America.

11. Denis DeConcini, "The Role of U.S. Intelligence in Promoting Economic Interests," *Journal of International Affairs* 48, 1 (Summer 1994), 57.

12. Ernest R. May, "Intelligence: Backing into the Future," *Foreign Affairs* 71, 3 (1992), 70. May notes that these liaison offices are often little more than mailboxes. See also Jeffrey T. Richelson and Desmond Ball, *The Ties that Bind* (Boston: Unwin Hyman, 1990), 128. The authors note that there is an "Office of Intelligence Liaison" in the Commerce Department that is designed to serve "as the departmental link to the intelligence community," and that the Treasury Department has an Office of Intelligence Support, which "provides economic information and analysis to the Secretary of the Treasury."

13. *Ibid.*, 65.

14. Interestingly, this very same threat was alleged to be the primary motivation for the reported "bugging" of software supplied to the World Bank and other financial institutions by American intelligence services.

15. For more on the PROMIS software case see the discussion in Samuel D. Porteous, "Economic Espionage (II)," *CSIS Commentary* 46 (July 1994), 9.

16. "A National Security Strategy," *The White House*, 14.

17. Walter Pincus, "Woolsey Resigns from CIA After Troubled Tenure," *Washington Post*, 29 December 1994, A1.

18. David E. Sanger, "War. Peace. Aid. All Issues Are Trade Issues," *New York Times*, 15 January 1995, E1, 4.

19. *Ibid.*

20. "France Sets Up Trade Intelligence Body," *Reuters*, Paris, 22 March 1995.

21. "Economic War as Seen by France," *Intelligence Newsletter* 262 (13 April 1995), 1.

22. For a thorough discussion of the Canadian intelligence community, see Christopher O. Spencer, "Intelligence Analysis Under Pressure Rapid Change: The Canadian Challenge," *The Journal of Conflict Studies* 16, 1 (Spring 1996), 57-74.

23. "Statement of Louis J. Freeh, Director Federal Bureau of Investigation, Before the Senate Select Committee on Intelligence and Senate Committee on the Judiciary, Subcommittee on Terrorism, Technology and Government Information Hearing on Economic Espionage," February 28, 1996, 4.

24. In his autobiography, *The Evil Empire* (London: Sidgwick and Jackson, 1986), Count Henri de Marenches, the former head of the French secret service (1970-81) makes this claim. See also Peter Schweizer's *Friendly Spies* (New York: Atlantic Monthly Press, 1993), 13, where, in relation to economic espionage, Schweizer quotes Marenches as saying, "In any intelligence service worthy of the name you would easily come across cases where the whole year's budget has been paid for in full by a single operation. Naturally, Intelligence does not receive actual payment, but the country's industry profits."

25. See "CIA Shifts Focus to Trade, Report Says," Reuters, 24 July 1995, *Globe and Mail*, B3.

26. For example, much of the criticism directed toward the CIA's analytical function has come from its reported failure to warn of the collapse of the Soviet economy (although the CIA was not alone in being caught off-guard by events in Russia). Given that the U.S. State Department was also surprised by events in the former Soviet Union, folding CIA analytical resources into the State Department, an idea put forward by some, seems a less than perfect solution. Interestingly, the CIA was limited to doing economic analysis of China and Russia until an agreement signed between the State Department and the CIA in the 1950s allowed them to cover worldwide economic intelligence. See Walter Laqueur, *A World of Secrets* (New York: Basic Books, 1985), 349. Herbert Meyers argues that the idea of the CIA is perfectly sound, and that government needs an ageny or unit charged with "scanning the external environment and assuring decision-makers they are getting the right information and the best possible analysis at the right time. This is a centralized responsibility." Furthermore, "as for Moynihan's suggestion to transfer much of the CIA's analytical responsibilities to the State Department, one can only assume that the Senator has never troubled to read State Department cables other than the (very literate) ones he wrote during his own diplomatic assignments. God knows the CIA's analyses can be improved. But at their worst they stand head and shoulders above the turgid blather that comes out of Foggy Bottom." See Herbert Meyers, "Reinventing the CIA," *Global Affairs* 7, 2 (1992), 9.

27. David L. Boren, "The Intelligence Community: How Crucial?" *Foreign Affairs* 71, 3 (1992), 54. Of course intelligence services may also be tempted to shape intelligence to meet their own needs.

28. Stansfield Turner, "Intelligence for a New World Order," *Foreign Affairs* 70, 4 (Fall 1991), 163.

29. Angelo Codevilla, "Get Smart—Eliminate the CIA," *Wall Street Journal*, 18 January 1995, A14.

30. A.D. McLennan, "National Intelligence Assessment," 8.

31. *Ibid.*, 14.

32. Among competitors who have decided to cooperate on certain projects or are considering the possibility of doing so are Toyota and General Motors, and Airbus and Boeing. See Joseph B. White, "Toyota GM Link May Widen," *Globe and Mail*, 23 December 1992, B2; "Airbus, Boeing Pact," *Globe and Mail*, 7 January 1993, B2.

33. "French Spy," *Security Management*, November 1991.

34. "Economic Espionage: A Limited Role," *Government Executive*, March 1992.

35. Evidence of the currency of this issue as a matter of debate within the EU came in 1992, when a Green Party European parliamentarian posed 65 questions to the EC Council of Ministers about the development of inter-European intelligence networks. The only response was, "The Council is not able to reply to the Honourable Member's questions." Indication of these pressures is also clear from the words of Claude Imbert, editor of *Le Point*, an important French weekly, "I want simply to limit our continent's vulnerability. Protectionism on a national level is evidently condemned to end in catastrophe. By contrast, a Europe-wide system of economic defence would have every chance of success." See the *Financial Times*, 1 June 1993, 14.

36. Recent recruiting ads for the GCHQ indicated a need for graduates with knowledge of Spanish, Portuguese, Dutch, German, and Italian. See Richard Norton-Taylor, "Goal Posts."

37. "French Try to Set European Security Agenda," *Globe and Mail*, 10 May 1994, A11. An interesting discussion of the security implications of a regionalization of world trade can be found in G. Allison and G. Treverton, eds., *Rethinking America's Security* (New York, 1992), 159-64.

38. Norton-Taylor, "Goal Posts."

39. For an excellent discussion of these agreements, see Richelson and Ball, *Ties That Bind*, 27.

40. John Burgess and John Mintz, "CIA, FBI Chiefs Warn Panel Over Economic Espionage," *Washington Post*, 30 April 1992, B11.

41. Randy Newell, "On the Trail of International Spies," *Ottawa Citizen*, 17 April 1993, H2.

42. Paul Quinn-Judge, "U.S. Sends Warning on Corporate Spying," *Boston Globe*, 30 April 1993, 2.

43. Gerald P. Burke "Espionage and More Benign Forms of Economic Intelligence: A Tour d'Horizon," *International Security Forum* (Spring 1992).

44. Randy Newell, "Economic Espionage: Corporate Spying Becoming a Growth Industry," *Montreal Gazette*, 15 April 1993, F1.

45. James F. McCarty, "Cold War II Spies Target Trade Secrets," *Plain Dealer*, 21 March 1993.

46. Peter Schweizer, "Our Thieving Allies," *New York Times*, 23 June 1993.

47. *Ibid.*

48. Schweizer, *Friendly Spies*, 176-85.

49. While North American coverage has remained steadfast in its views of the victims of economic espionage, the perception of primary practitioners is beginning to change. Early on, the French and the Russians were presented in most North American analysis as the primary practitioners of economic espionage. Now, in a realignment perhaps more attuned to today's geopolitical realities, this dubious status is being transferred to the Japanese and emerging Asian economies. In an article in the *Far Eastern Economic Review*, FBI officials stated that 57 countries are running operations to obtain information out of Silicon Valley. These same officials were quoted as labeling Asian governments and multinationals, particularly Japan, Taiwan, and South Korea, as the chief culprits in the attempts to obtain Silicon Valley's secrets. Michael J. Yamaguchi, identified as the American government's top prosecutor in San Francisco, stated that "the biggest fear we have is the Pacific Rim countries." See John Berthelsen, "Friendly Spies," *Far Eastern Economic Review* 157, 7 (17 February 1994), 28-30. Statements over the last five years on perceived origins of incidents of both industrial and economic espionage released by CSIS mirror these concerns. See Samuel D. Porteous, "Economic Espionage: New Target for CSIS," *Canadian Business Review* 20, 4 (Winter 1993), 32-34.

50. David Gow, "Siemens Cries Foul Play But Retracts," *Guardian*, 11 September 1993, 36. Siemens, the Munich-based engineering group, accused competitor GEC Alstrom, an Anglo-French consortium, of engaging in communication interception to obtain a major transportation project contract from the South Korean government that otherwise would have gone to Siemens. Threatened with legal action, Siemens withdrew the claim while the German press speculated about the involvement of French intelligence in the affair. Siemens, however, continued to claim to have received "internal indications from Korea on probable interceptions by third-parties of our communications channel" ("Industry Suspects Espionage

by French Service," *Foreign Broadcasting Information Service-WEU*-93-175,
13 September 1993, 16). A German report claimed that the CIA readily supplies
to U.S. industry data that it has collected. It stated, "U.S. intelligence satellites
record telephone conversations between firms that are competitors of U.S. companies and convey their material to the National Security Agency." From there
the reports were reported to make their way to the desks of U.S. companies.

51. "U.S. Spied on British Defence Projects," *Reuters*, 5 October 1993. A British
documentary reported that a former official with the National Security Council
(NSC) claimed that U.S. monitoring bases in Britain were used to monitor
telecommunications traffic concerning a multi-billion dollar sale of weapons to
Saudi Arabia in hopes of securing an advantage for American economic interests.
While these allegations were rejected by the CIA, British Aerospace, which led the
sales project, stated that it would not be surprised if the claims were true.

52. "Tibet Daily Urges Citizens to Guard Secrets," BBC *Summary of World Broadcasts*,
16 November 1993. According to the broadcast, the daily warned that "China
is a country with an ancient civilization. It has many traditional processing technologies unparalleled in the world. Even some friendly countries and groups are
carrying out activities to steal technological secrets from us. Therefore every
Chinese citizen must always maintain high vigilance."

53. "Russia: Exotic Espionage Centre," *Izvestiya* 8 (9 June 1994). Baturin described it
as a relatively recent problem that must be resolved. According to him, the theft
of technological and commercial secrets from Russia has been exacerbated by
Russian economic conditions, which make participation in the practice appealing
to increasingly impoverished state and private sector employees.

54. Jean-Marie Pontaut, "Espionage: Le grand pillage de la France," *Le Point* 1103
(6 November 1993). The article tells the now-familiar tale of how their innocent
country's economic interests are being injured by spies facilitated or directed by
foreign governments with lower ethical standards.

55. These denials by intelligence services have met with some cynicism. "This week's
'I don't beat my wife award' goes to none other than James Woolsey, director of
the U.S. Central Intelligence Agency, who yesterday denied the CIA conducts
industrial espionage outside the U.S. Of course not. Never in a million years.
No way." "See my way," *Financial Times*, 20 July 1994.

56. Ruth Sinai, "Economic Espionage: Rising Concern for U.S. Intelligence Agency,"
Journal of Intelligence and National Security, Associated Press, 21 February 1993.

57. "Statement of Louis J. Freeh," February 28, 1996, 5.

58. "The Threat of Foreign Economic Espionage to U.S. Corporations," *Hearings Before the Subcommittee on Economic and Commercial Law*, 102nd Congress, 2nd Session, 29 April, 7 May 1992, Serial No. 65, 130.

59. Daniel Scuro, "Votre Secrets, Monsieur?" *Security Management* 36 (October 1992), 75.

60. An analogy can also be drawn between the impact of economic espionage on a country's economic interests and the impact of more familiar espionage on its military, security, or political interests. In this way, economic espionage could be said to be as important to a country's economic interests as more familiar types of espionage are to its more traditional political and security interests. Clearly, espionage plays a minor role in the great volume of relations conducted between nations. The impacts of espionage-related activities on a country's political or security interests are almost never acknowledged and rarely disclosed. This, however, is not the same as saying that they are either exceptionally rare or insignificant. Media reports concerning alleged assistance provided by the American intelligence community to Boris Yeltsin on orders from then President George Bush during the 1991 Soviet coup demonstrates dramatically the potential impact and significance of some espionage activity. In this instance the alleged assistance was reportedly a crucial element of Yeltsin's ascension to power. See Patrick Cockburn, "U.S. Agents Aided Yeltsin During Coup," *Ottawa Citizen*, 17 May 1994, A4. In much the same manner, economic espionage, while not influencing the vast bulk of economic exchanges, has the potential for dramatic impact in some cases, such as influencing the award of a major contract.

61. Perhaps the most important comparative advantage developed governments hold in the practice of economic espionage is their signals intelligence (SIGINT) ability. Their considerable capacity to target, intercept, and decode private and confidential communications poses a serious threat to the communications security of both government and business. The same technical infrastructure that was used to collect military and political information about hostile nations during the Cold War can be focused just as easily on important telephone conversations between executives or transatlantic transmissions of data between subsidiaries. With characteristic reticence, Pierre Marion has described the unsurpassed SIGINT capacity of the United States as the "atomic bomb" of economic espionage. See Alasdair Palmer, "When Spies Mean Business," *Spectator*, 9 April 1994, 18-19. The importance of ensuring this same ease of access to communications darting across the much-discussed information super-highway has been, and will continue to be, the subject of much debate.

62. Corning Inc., the U.S. material manufacturer, a self-described target of state-sponsored industrial espionage, stated that its worldwide operations made it difficult to deal with the threat. Executive vice-president J.E. Riesbeck told a congressional hearing that Corning's attempts to protect itself "are no match for industrial espionage activities that are sanctioned and supported by foreign governments." Jim Wolf, "Industrial Spying Comes in from the Cold," *Reuters*, 3 August 1992.

63. Ronald E. Yates, "Cold War: Part II," *Chicago Tribune*, 30 August 1993, 1. Chicago's FCM Corp. has operated a corporate intelligence unit for eight years.

64. Jim Wolfe, "Industrial Spying Comes in From the Cold," Reuters, August 3, 1992. See also, "The Threat of Foreign Economic Espionage to U.S. Corporations," Hearings Before the Sub-Committee on Economic and Commercial Law, 102nd Congress, 2nd Session (29 April-7 May 1992), Serial 65, 126-28.

65. In their recent amendments to their penal code, the French seem to have decided in favour of the impact over form argument. The new French criminal law, which came into force on March 1, 1994, has several articles whose enactment was encouraged by French counter-intelligence. The law expands the definition of spying from just military and political matters to include industrial and commercial matters. Significantly, the description of what the espionage law sought to protect was changed from "national defence interests" to "fundamental interest of the nation." The coverage of the law was also expanded from just "foreign powers and their agents" to include organizations such as the Mafia, and foreign businesses. "The New Criminal Law and Intelligence," *Intelligence Newsletter*, 24 March 1994.

66. This concern is most often expressed by the question, "What is a Canadian or American company?"

67. The analogy between subsidies and economic intelligence derived from economic espionage and transmitted to commercial actors by government was first made in Porteous, "Economic Espionage."

68. The distributional elements of this question should not be ignored. Like recipients of subsidies, companies that receive "intelligence" will consider the practice beneficial. Whether these sorts of practices provide a net benefit to the country as a whole or the community of nations involved is the question. Stanley Kobor discusses this point at length in his paper "The CIA as Economic Spy: The Misuse of U.S. Intelligence After the Cold War," *Policy Analysis*, The CATO Institute, 185 (8 December 1992).

69. For detailed discussions of strategic trade policy see the following articles by James A. Brander and Barbara J. Spencer, "Tariffs and the Extraction of Foreign

Monopoly Rents and Potential Entry," *Canadian Journal of Economics* 14, 3
(14 August 1981), 371-89; "Trade Warfare: Tariffs and Cartels," *Journal of
International Economics* 16 (16 May 1984), 227-42; "Export Subsidies and
International Market Share Rivalry," *Journal of International Economics* 18, 3-4
(18 February 1985), 83-100; and "International R&D Rivalry and Industrial
Strategy," *Review of Economic Studies* 50 (October 1983), 707-22. Laura
D'Andrea Tyson, one of President Clinton's chief economic advisers, has also
written extensively on STP.

70. In 1987, largely in response to the argument that the poor U.S. competitive
position in semiconductors represented a threat both to national and economic
security, the Reagan administration agreed to a five-year $500 million subsidy to
Sematech, a research consortium of 14 large U.S. semiconductor and electronics
companies. The Clinton administration's push toward industrial policy and
picking winners is discussed in a negative light in "An Industrial Debacle," *The
World & I* (December 1994), 70-75. A more positive view can be seen in the
coverage of Sematech's move toward self-sufficiency. See Louise Kehoe, "Chip
Research Group to Shun Federal Funding," *Financial Times* (London), 4 October
1994, 28. In this report Sematech announced that it will pay its own way and
no longer accept direct federal funding after fiscal 1996.

71. The relative ease of relations between state-owned enterprises and intelligence
services is well demonstrated by the French situation. According to a study
conducted for the French government on the issue of overt economic intelligence-gathering, the government intelligence structure was said to have good
links only with the state-owned segment of France's commercial sector. See Henri
Martre, *Rapport du groupe intelligence économique et strategie des entreprises*
(Paris: Commissariat général du plan, fevrier 1994), 27.

72. In November of 1994 Chinese vice-premier Zhu Rongii reaffirmed the centrality
of state enterprises to China's development. According to Rongii, the Chinese
government remains committed to maintaining a significant level of state owner-
ship in the economy and opposed to large-scale privatization. See "China: State
Enterprises," *Oxford Analytica Daily Brief*, 28 November 1994. Interestingly, the
Chinese government has pleaded difficulties with obtaining cooperation from
Chinese municipal government officials, who are also part-owners of many
Chinese government businesses, as the reason they have been unable to crack
down on intellectual piracy the way the United States wishes them to. See Nancy
Dunne, "China Shifts Factory after U.S. Threat," *Financial Times* (London),
4 January 1994. The Indonesian government has also been chided for its exten-
sive involvement in the country's private sector. In December 1994, the GATT

secretariat released an unusually critical report on Indonesia, criticizing wide-spread cronyism ("close ties exist between the government and large business groups or conglomerates"), and noting that "details of government assistance to strategic industries 'remain obscure' while 'transparency is undermined.'" See Frances Williams, "Indonesia Trade Policies Chided in GATT Report," *Financial Times* (London), 1 December 1994, 7.

73. Randall M. Fort, "Economic Espionage: Problems and Prospects," Consortium for the Study of Intelligence, 1993.

74. See "Russia: Entrepreneurial Army," *Oxford Analytica Daily Brief*, 26 October 1994.

75. David L. Boren, "The Intelligence Community: How Crucial?" *Foreign Affairs* 71, 3 (1992), 58; Ernest R. May, "Intelligence: Backing Into the Future," *Foreign Affairs* 71, 3 (1992), 72; Bruce D. Berkowitz and Allan E. Goodman, *Strategic Intelligence for American National Security* (Princeton: Princeton University Press, 1989), 111. While all these writers discuss the dissemination problem affecting economic intelligence of use to private industry, they do not address government or private sector-led consortia as potential means to disseminate this information. Apart from their obvious role of national champion, the United States and other countries have a history of establishing consortia to achieve various goals. The most recent is "U.S. Car," which brings the Big Three automakers of Detroit together to pool their resources for developing pre-commercial technology and benefit from access to government research stemming from the "Star Wars" program.

76. Quinn-Judge, "U.S. Sends Warnings," 2.

77. Article 48(2) of the draft Agreement on Trade-Related Aspects of Intellectual Property Rights, Including Trade in Counterfeit Goods states, "In respect of the administration of any law pertaining to the protection or enforcement of intellectual property rights, parties shall only exempt both public authorities and officials from liability to appropriate remedial measures where actions are taken or intended in good faith in the course of the administration of such laws."

78. The understandable difficulty of assessing the financial impact of economic espionage has encouraged an unfortunate tendency among some media and government officials. Unable to produce concrete figures, they resort to equating costs due to economic espionage with costs relating to all incidents of intellectual property (IP) infringement. Articles on economic espionage cite global estimates of costs due to IP infringement as evidence of the severity of the economic espionage problem. This is not a good measure. IP infringement costs, such as those due to copyright or trademark infringement, can easily be projected into the billions, but in the vast majority of cases these infringements have nothing to do

with economic espionage. The use of these highly subjective estimates needs to be examined closely. Economic espionage is not the trademark or copyright infringement engaged in by private-sector entities—activities from which the bulk of these costs derive. Private-sector copyright or trademark infringement would, however, qualify as part of the broad "sharp practices" category. If these figures are to be used in future, some effort should be made to tease out which components actually relate to economic espionage.

79. It is interesting to note that the proposition that multinational corporations are truly transnational actors, owing allegiance to no nation states, and locating wherever market advantage dictates, is being challenged. Three-quarters of the value-added by multinationals is still produced in their home countries, and a study by John Cantwell of Reading University found that U.S. multinationals conduct the vast majority of their technological activity at home. See Christopher Lorenz, "'Global Web' still not Free of Tangles," *Financial Times* (London), 15 July 1994, 12; Martin Wolf, "The Global Economy Myth," *Financial Times* (London), 13 March 1996.

80. Furthermore, the existence of numerous high-tech research consortia who limit membership according to company nationality indicates that another often-raised issue—the difficulty of determining the nationality of corporations—may not be the problem some think it is. On the other hand, the existence of means to reduce dissemination difficulties will not erase them. Problems will inevitably arise. Countries considering engaging in or expanding their practice of economic espionage would be well-advised to consider the alleged experience of France. It has been suggested that the embarrassing release of information indicating French intelligence service targeting of American companies, that triggered an American boycott of the Paris Airshow, was the work of disgruntled French firms. The companies responsible for releasing material to the press were apparently unhappy with what they saw as the DBSE's tendency to favour some French firms over others when distributing information obtained through economic espionage. This incident reportedly cooled relations between the DGSE and certain elements of French industry. See Jacques Isnard, "Services secrets et industriel français de l'armement ont des difficultes à coopérer sur les marches étrangers," *Le Monde*, 20 January 1994, 22.

81. Former U.S. Defense Secretary Caspar Weinberger has claimed that the Soviet Union saved between 12 and 15 billion dollars in research and development costs by stealing Western technology, and between five and seven years in research and development lead time. John Picton, "New Role for Canada's Spy Agency," *Toronto Star*, 18 October 1991, A21.

82. In *The Evil Empire*, Count de Marenches makes this claim and refers by way of example to one instance where information on a planned devaluation of the American dollar obtained by French intelligence in 1971 saved the French government a figure that would have "financed the Service for years."

83. James Woolsey, "The Future Direction of Intelligence," paper presented at the Centre for Strategic and International Studies, 18 July 1994, 29.

84. *CSIS Public Report* 1993, 4-9.

85. For a detailed discussion of issues surrounding the counter-intelligence response to economic espionage, see Samuel D. Porteous, "Economic Espionage: Issues Arising from Increased Government Involvement with the Private Sector," *Intelligence and National Security* 9, 4 (October 1994), 735-52.

86. *Intelligence Newsletter*, 230 (9 December 1993), 1. In 1993, *Aviation and Space Technology* reported that U.S. Rep. Dan Glickman, then chief of the Permanent Select Committee on Intelligence, said that "the U.S. is conducting extensive industrial intelligence, but that government stops short of passing propriety data to business." See "Washington Outlook," *Aviation and Space Technology*, 26 April 1993, 19.

87. The defensive element of the counter-intelligence function is relatively uncontroversial here. Clearly, in the course of engaging in this sort of activity much "positive" intelligence may be collected and analyzed. The process of determining how this intelligence should be dealt with remains the same whether it was obtained incidentally through counter-intelligence activities or directly through foreign intelligence collection.

88. According to Toby Gati, U.S. Assistant Secretary of State for Intelligence, U.S. intelligence is monitoring the trade and investment policies and practices of foreign governments, including compliance with international agreements in areas such as intellectual property protection, foreign investment, and market access. See "U.S. Outlines Future Security Threats," National Security Institute, *Advisory*, February 1995.

89. "Economic security" is defined as the maintenance of conditions necessary to encourage sustained, long-term, relative improvement in labour and capital productivity, thus ensuring a high and rising standard of living for citizens. This definition includes the maintenance of a fair, secure, and dynamic business environment conducive to innovation, domestic and foreign investment, and sustainable economic growth.

90. It would be incorrect to infer that the frequency of any country's mention in either incident list presented indicates that country's relative predilection for engaging in these activities. Countries with open democracies and aggressive

media will always provide more examples of aggression than closed countries that may, in fact, be much more active in this area. Also, this author's use of open source examples is not an endorsement by myself or CSIS of their veracity. They serve to illustrate the type of information sought and methods employed to obtain it.

91. Wayne Masden, "Intelligence Agency Threats to Computer Security," *International Journal of Intelligence and Counterintelligence* 6, 4 (Winter 1993), 422.

92. Bob Woodward, *Veil: The Secret Wars of the cia 1981-1987* (New York: Simon and Schuster, 1987), 388.

93. See Mike Frost and Michel Gratton, *Spyworld: Inside the Canadian and American Intelligence Establishments* (Toronto: Doubleday, 1994), 224-27.

94. Tim Weiner, "CIA Spent Millions to Support Japanese Right in 50's and 60's," *New York Times*, 9 October 1994, 1, 14.

95. Fort, "Economic Espionage," 3.

96. "U.S. Spy Agency May Be Tapping Foreign Bank's Computer Data: World Bank Searches for Software with Eavesdropping Bug Planted in It," *Thomson's International Banking Regulator* 6, 2 (17 January 1994), 1.

97. *Intelligence Newsletter,* 230 (9 December 1993), 3.

98. Anthony Cavendish, *Inside Intelligence* (London: Collins, 1990), 139.

99. For a detailed discussion of the government's role in defending against this sort of activity and the issues it raises, see the discussion in Porteous, "Economic Espionage," 735-52.

100. *CSIS Public Report* 1993, 7.

101. "Intelligence Service Chiefs Are Coping with Post-Cold War World," *Financial Times* (London), 30 July 1993.

102. "Economic Counterintelligence Tasks Viewed," *Rossiyskaya Gazeta*, 26 May 1994, Moscow, 1-2, in *Foreign Broadcasting Information Service-USR*-94-061, 10 June 1994, 41-42. See also Chrystia Freeland, "Western Investors Accused of Sabotaging Russian Economy," *Financial Times* (London), 25 January 1995, 3, wherein Russian security documents are quoted arguing "the hidden intervention of foreign capital aimed at undermining the weapons-building capacity and economy of the country." The Chinese government also appears ambivalent about the economic intentions of the West. Sabotage by envious developed countries has been cited as a possible reason for the failures of the Chinese satellite launch program. See Tony Walker, "China Blames U.S. Satellite for Launch Failure," *Financial Times* (London), 9 February 1995, 4.

103. Madsen, "Intelligence Agency Threats," 441.

104. *CSIS Public Report* 1993, 8.

105. Jean Marie Bonthous, "Understanding Intelligence Across Cultures: Transcending Biases and Building an Intelligent Nation/Organization," *JMB International*, New York, 2.

106. "Intelligence New Gray Zones," *Intelligence Newsletter,* 233 (27 January 1994), 1.

107. Craig Whitney, "Germany Finds That Spies Are Still Doing Business," *New York Times,* 12 September 1993.

108. Many have concluded that with the collapse of the Soviet Union, Russia's technological development was even more dependent on technology acquired from abroad: "Britain and Russia are also rivals in the international arms trade. The disintegration of the Soviet Union meant that Britain moved into second place as an international arms seller. Arms sales are one of Russia's principal sources of hard currency. Intelligence on British defence exports and future exports would be of particular at the moment." See Christopher Bellamy, "Spy Affair Shows MI5 Still 'On Guard,'" *The Independent,* 11 January 1995, 2.

109. Madsen, "Intelligence Agency Threats," 423.

110. "Romanian Engineer Arrested for Spying," *Romania Libera,* 15 July 1994.

111. See Craig Whitney, "Germany Finds That Spies Are Still Doing Business," *New York Times,* 12 September 1993, 1, 18. This view is supported by reports that, unlike the KGB, the GRU, Russia's military intelligence service, survived the end of the Cold War at close to full strength. While the GRU has traditionally been tasked with collecting intelligence on sensitive military technologies, this specialty has likely been broadened to included commercially valuable Western technologies. *Intelligence Newsletter* 230 (9 December 1993), 4.

112. "Russia: Exotic Espionage Centre," *Izvestiya,* 8, 9 June 1994.

113. *Intelligence Newsletter* 230 (9 December 1993), 1.

114. Madsen, "Intelligence Agency Threats," 427.

115. Woodward, *Veil,* 368-69.

III

THE IMPACT OF THE LEGAL REGIME

J. Anthony VanDuzer

INFORMATION AND TECHNOLOGY are critical assets for businesses and governments in the global economy of the 1990s. Businesses in Canada and elsewhere require continuous access to the best available information and technologies in order to become competitive. Once a competitive advantage has been attained, however, maintaining it often depends as much on a business's ability to protect its information and technology from appropriation as on its access to new information and technology. As a consequence, access and protection have become important issues of business strategy and organization. The chapter by Evan Potter in this study suggests that this is an especially pressing concern for Canada. Our exports of raw materials and low value-added manufactured goods, historically the foundations of our prosperity, are increasingly threatened by new low-cost competitors. At the same time our transition to new bases of competitive advantage in a knowledge-based economy appears to be faltering. As a result, a high priority in national policy-making must be given to ensuring that the Canadian legal regime provides appropriate levels of both access and protection.[1]

In order to respond to this policy challenge the Canadian government itself requires substantial information. It must have up-to-the-minute information on both threats to competitiveness and opportunities to promote competitiveness. More generally, government needs to have access to the best available information and to be able to protect its information in order to develop and implement economic policies that will facilitate the development and maintenance of Canadian economic security.

While there are many aspects of the problem of access to and protection of information and technology for business and for government, one important question is to what extent agencies of the federal government engaged in intelligence-gathering, particularly the Canadian Security Intelligence Service (CSIS), the Canadian Security Establishment (CSE), and law enforcement agencies, such as the RCMP, should assist government and business? More specifically, how can these agencies best protect government and private sector information and technology from appropriation and how can they promote Canadian economic security by gathering economic intelligence?[2] Finally, what information gathered by these agencies can and should be distributed to the private sector?

The other chapters in this study address these questions in different ways. The main purpose of this chapter is to describe how existing national and multilateral legal rules operate in relation to the gathering of economic intelligence by foreign agents, both government and private sector, in Canada. Samuel Porteous has demonstrated the pervasiveness of foreign intelligence-gathering activity in his chapter for this study. As a result of this pervasiveness the effectiveness of the governing legal framework for defending Canadian interests is an issue of significant concern. In this regard there are several questions that I will seek to answer. How does the Canadian legal framework, which includes the international obligations to which Canada is subject, define the kinds of intelligence-gathering behaviour by foreign agents that are subject to legal sanction? What is the permitted scope for CSIS and the RCMP to engage in activities intended to defeat legal and illegal intelligence-gathering activities? One difficult aspect of this last question is the extent to which CSIS may disclose information it has in order to facilitate actions by government and private sector actors to defend themselves against foreign intelligence-gathering efforts. Some reference will also be made to the CSE, though in the context of an analysis of the legal framework for intelligence-gathering the scope for discussing CSE is limited: at the time of writing this highly secret signals intelligence-gathering unit has no statutory mandate.[3]

The chapter will not focus on the multiple complex issues associated with the policy bases for the legal rules discussed, but rather will concentrate on describing the legal framework and on drawing some conclusions about its nature and characteristics. The analysis will suggest both the possibilities and the limits of the statutory mandates of CSIS and the RCMP in relation to economic security. Then, through a review of Canadian laws regarding intellectual property protection, criminal activities, and export controls I will sketch out the gaps in the substantive legal protection for Canadian business and government information and technology and describe how these gaps limit the effectiveness of CSIS and the RCMP.

The chapter will consider briefly the legal environment in which Canadian government agencies would carry out the collection of economic intelligence outside of Canada for the purpose of obtaining a positive advantage for Canadian government or business. The scope of this enquiry will be limited to identifying some of the kinds of issues that may arise in connection with such activities. In part this is because the current legal regime provides very little scope for such activities. Also a thorough canvassing of the international legal environment is far beyond the scope of this chapter.

Before beginning this enquiry into the legal rules governing economic intelligence-gathering activities, however, this chapter will address a preliminary question: how relevant are legal rules to the activities to the operations of CSIS and the CSE?

THE SIGNIFICANCE OF THE LEGAL REGIME

Some may be of the view that the nature of the operations of security services like CSIS and the CSE and the secrecy in which they are often necessarily cloaked renders legal limits of marginal relevance in understanding the effective constraints on security service operations and how they actually behave. The nature of the regulatory scheme for the security operations of CSIS and the available evidence both suggest that this view is mistaken. With regard to the CSE, there is also evidence to suggest that it operates within the law.

The McDonald Commission, in its exhaustive report on the RCMP security service, repeatedly stressed the importance of a security service having clear legal limits on its activities.[4] Under the Canadian Security Intelligence Service Act[5] (the "CSIS Act"), there is an elaborate system of checks on the behaviour of CSIS that ensures that the legal limits of its authority are constantly borne in mind. It is beyond the scope of this chapter to describe this system in a comprehensive way, and it has been done elsewhere.[6] Nevertheless, identifying the key elements most directly relating to the legal limits of CSIS's powers is sufficient to illustrate the relevance of these legal limits.

The first layer of checks consists of internal review within the executive branch. The Solicitor General is the minister responsible for the operations of CSIS and in that capacity is empowered to give directions to the Director of CSIS.[7] There is also regular interaction between the minister, the department, and CSIS. The Solicitor General's role has been described as the "key" control mechanism.[8]

The Solicitor General is assisted in discharging his or her responsibility for CSIS by the Inspector General. Under the CSIS Act one of the main functions of the Inspector General is to ensure compliance with the legal mandate. The Inspector General is required

to issue a certificate setting out whether he or she is satisfied with the Director's statutorily required annual report to the Minister and whether, in his or her opinion, [CSIS] has engaged in any activities which are either unauthorized by the [CSIS Act] or ministerial directions or have involved an unreasonable or unnecessary exercise by [CSIS] of any of its powers.[9]

The second mechanism designed to ensure that CSIS acts within its legal mandate is the Security Intelligence Review Committee (SIRC). The SIRC is external to the executive branch. It is an independent committee appointed by Cabinet whose function is to "review generally the performance by [CSIS] of its duties and functions"[10] and to arrange for reviews to be conducted for the purpose of "ensuring that the activities of the Service are carried out in accordance with [the CSIS Act], the regulations and directions issued by the Minister ... and that the activities of CSIS not involve any unreasonable or unnecessary exercise of any of its powers."[11]

This mandate expressly extends to reviewing the certificates of the Inspector General and the directions of the Minister.[12] The consensus of those who have studied the role of SIRC is that it has performed its review function effectively.[13]

Two other elements of the statutory scheme governing CSIS deserve mention. Under section 20 of the CSIS Act the Director of CSIS is obliged to advise the Solicitor General when he or she believes that a CSIS employee has acted unlawfully. A copy of each such report must go to SIRC. A review of the annual reports of SIRC shows that the Director takes this responsibility seriously.[14] Also, in order to use certain covert and intrusive investigative methods available under the CSIS Act, such as mail opening and telephone interception, authorization by warrant issued by a federal court judge is required.[15]

The effectiveness of this statutory scheme in ensuring that CSIS personnel operate in accordance with the legal mandate of the Service is confirmed by Lustgarten and Leigh in their exhaustive study of security services in Canada, the U.K., and Australia. The authors concluded that the security services view themselves as subject to a limited statutory mandate, which provides the "ground rules" for their activities.[16] This is also the view that SIRC has expressed in its annual reports.[17]

Even though the CSE has no legal mandate the legality of its actions is not an irrelevant issue. Whenever concerns have been raised regarding CSE's activities, the government has steadfastly maintained that the agency acted within the law, and to the extent that it or any of its personnel did not they would be subject to prosecution.[18] Until recently, the difficulty with such assurances was that one had to take them on faith, since there was no independent oversight of CSE. On June 19, 1996, the federal government appointed a Commissioner whose mandate is to review CSE's activities and to determine their compliance with the law.[19] In 1997, the Commissioner released his first annual report in which he concluded that CSE had acted within the law.[20]

The legality of CSE's operations is safeguarded by other less direct mechanisms as well. CSE, like CSIS, is subject to scrutiny and review by independent bodies such as the Canadian Human Rights Commission, the Privacy Commissioner, the Information Commissioner and the Auditor General. CSE is also accountable to Parliament. The Minister of Defence is responsible to Parliament for CSE and is supported by the reporting structure under which CSE operates. The Chief of CSE reports to the Deputy Minister of National Defence for financial and administrative issues, and the Coordinator of Security and Intelligence in the Privy Council Office for policy and operational matters.[21]

Notwithstanding these mechanisms it is hard to assess how the Canadian legal regime operates in relation to CSE. The agency consistently says that it targets only foreign communications. In his Annual Report for 1995-96, the Privacy Commissioner concluded that CSE operates in compliance with the Privacy Act, that there is no evidence that CSE intentionally targets Canadians or monitors their communications, and that it uses strict procedures to minimize the possibility that information about Canadians is collected inadvertently. To the extent that its activities take place outside Canada, in most circumstances, Canadian law simply will not apply.[22] For communications that originate or end in Canada, there is a process under the Official Secrets Act[23] under which warrants may be issued by the Minister of Justice requiring any such communication to be given to the Minister or any person identified in the warrant. Such warrants may be of broad scope and unlimited duration and might be used to provide CSE with blanket legal authority for a wide range of activities. At the moment there is no way of determining whether activities of CSE have been authorized under this process.

The creation of a statutory scheme to govern CSE was recommended by the Special Committee of the House of Commons that reviewed the CSIS Act in 1990.[24] Such a scheme with a more rigorous warrant-issuing procedure than exists under the Official Secrets Act combined with some form of independent oversight would go a long way toward assuring Canadians that its most secret intelligence agency indeed acts within the law.

THE SCOPE OF THE CSIS MANDATE IN RELATION TO ECONOMIC SECURITY

If the legal mandate of CSIS is important, the next question concerns the scope of the mandate in relation to economic security. The following discussion sets out the relevant features of the CSIS mandate with a view to making such an assessment.

Under the CSIS Act, the mandate of the Service is elaborately defined. The two sections expressing aspects of the mandate that may be relevant to economic security are sections 12 and 16.

The Section 12 Mandate

General
Section 12 establishes the primary mandate of CSIS.[25] Under section 12 CSIS shall

> collect, by investigation or otherwise, to the extent that it is
> strictly necessary, and analyze and retain information and intelli-
> gence respecting activities which may, on reasonable grounds, be

suspected of constituting *threats to the security of Canada* and, in relation thereto, shall report to and advise the government of Canada [emphasis added].[26]

The key to determining when the section 12 mandate is engaged is the phrase "threats to the security of Canada," which is defined in section 2 of the Act to mean

(a) espionage or sabotage that is against Canada or is detrimental to the interests of Canada or activities directed toward or in support of such espionage or sabotage;

(b) foreign influenced activities within or relating to Canada that are detrimental to the interests of Canada and are clandestine or deceptive or involve a threat to any person;

(c) activities within or relating to Canada directed toward or in support of the threat or use of acts of serious violence against persons or property for the purpose of achieving a political objective within Canada or a foreign state; and

(d) activities directed toward undermining by covert or unlawful acts, or directed toward or intended ultimately to lead to the destruction or overthrow by violence of, the constitutionally established system of government in Canada, but does not include lawful advocacy, protest or dissent, unless carried on in conjunction with any of the activities referred to in paragraphs (a) to (d).

Notwithstanding the obvious effort in these sections to be specific, the content of what is a "threat to the security of Canada" is essentially and necessarily elastic.[24] Nevertheless, unlike the British Security Service Act, 1989, which includes "safeguarding the economic well being"[28] of the country as one of the functions of the service, it is significant that there is no express reference to economic interests in section 2. There is, however, ample room within the language of the CSIS Act to permit activities in relation to economic security.[29] A complete analysis of the appropriate scope of the CSIS mandate in this regard would involve consideration of the practical and policy issues that are at the heart of the other chapters in this study and would touch on fundamental political and philosophical questions[30] regarding the purpose of an intelligence service. Nevertheless, for the purposes of this chapter some comments may be made regarding the mandate of the Service.

The Service's mandate under section 12 is defensive; it is limited to situations constituting a threat to the security of Canada. There is no scope for offensive behaviour to enhance Canadian interests. In relation to economic security only the kinds of threats described in subsections 2(a) and 2(b) appear to be directly relevant. Achieving political objectives through violence and subversion of government may have economic dimensions in many circumstances but primarily involve non-economic threats.

Espionage or Sabotage
A threat for the purposes of subsection 2(a) must consist of or be directed toward or be in support of "espionage or sabotage" and must be either "against Canada" or "detrimental to the interests of Canada." "Espionage" and "sabotage" are not specifically defined in the CSIS Act but have traditionally been considered to take their meanings from provisions in the Criminal Code[31] and the Official Secrets Act.[32]

"Sabotage" is defined in the Criminal Code as any act or omission that: "impairs the efficiency or impedes the working of any vessel, vehicle, aircraft, machinery, apparatus or other thing; or causes property, by whomever it may be owned, to be lost, damaged or destroyed, for a purpose prejudicial to the safety, security or defence of Canada."[33] As is obvious from the above, "sabotage," in an economic context, does not involve appropriation of economic information but rather the effective destruction of some property, like a computer on which the information may be stored,[34] as well as, possibly, destroying or interfering with something for a purpose prejudicial to Canadian economic security. As discussed below, information itself is not "property," so its destruction cannot be sabotage.

"Espionage" is not defined in any Canadian statute but has been understood to take its meaning from the treason provisions of the Criminal Code and section 3 of the Official Secrets Act. The word "espionage" is not used in the Criminal Code, but section 46(2)(b) provides as follows:

Every one commits treason who, in Canada, ...

(b) without lawful authority, communicates or makes available to an agent of a state other than Canada, military or scientific information or any sketch, plan, model, article, note or document of a military or scientific character that he knows or ought to know may be used by that state *for a purpose prejudicial to the safety or defence of Canada* [emphasis added].

Section 3 of the Official Secrets Act encompasses a broader, if somewhat overlapping, range of espionage activity:

Every person is guilty of an offence under this Act who for any purpose prejudicial to the safety or interests of the state,

(a) approaches, inspects, passes over, or is in the neighbourhood of, or enters any prohibited place;[35]

(b) makes any sketch, plan, model or note that is calculated to be or might me or is intended to be directly or indirectly *useful to a foreign power*; or

(c) obtains, collects, records, or publishes, or communicates to any other person any secret official code word, or password, or any sketch, plan, model, article, or note, or other document or information that is calculated to be or might be or is intended to be directly or indirectly *useful to a foreign power* [emphasis added].

The McDonald Commission recommended that new legislation be enacted to integrate these provisions of the Criminal Code and the Official Secrets Act.[36] The Commission recommended that this new statutory provision, along with the definition of sabotage from the Criminal Code, should be the operative ones for the purposes of the CSIS mandate.[37] After much debate before the Senate Committee that considered the CSIS Act,[38] no definitions were adopted in the CSIS Act or elsewhere.

While definitions in the Criminal Code and the Official Secrets Act may provide some useful points of reference for thinking about espionage and sabotage, they contain certain limitations that a review of the CSIS Act suggests are inappropriate. The definition of espionage is the more problematic. First, both the Official Secrets Act and Criminal Code provisions only contemplate actions for the benefit of a foreign state, while there is nothing on the face of section 2(a) to require such a limitation. The limitation in the treason provision to "military or scientific" information finds no basis in section 2(a). Both definitions suggest criteria that are not those specifically identified in the CSIS Act. As will be discussed below, in order to be a threat to Canada for the purposes of section 2(a), espionage or sabotage need to be "against Canada" or "detrimental to the interests of Canada." It only creates confusion to superimpose the criteria of "safety, security or defence of Canada," as required in the sabotage section, or "safety and defence," or "safety and interests of Canada," as expressed in the sections dealing with espionage, on the definition of those terms themselves.

If the Criminal Code definition of sabotage is read without the safety and defence criteria, what remains is a workable definition of sabotage for the purposes of section 2(a). Samuel Porteous suggests a definition of espionage for economic purposes that captures the essence of the Criminal Code and Official Secrets Act provisions: "the use of, or facilitation of, illegal, clandestine, coercive or deceptive means by a foreign government or its surrogates to acquire economic intelligence."[39] The only addition one might make to this definition is to include such activities by private actors. There is nothing inherent in the concept of espionage that excludes private actions. In either case it consists of efforts to obtain information that is not generally available by some means other than obtaining the consent of the person who has such information.

Focusing on these definitions alone, however, fails to capture the more relevant component of the CSIS mandate under section 2(a). The Criminal Code and Official Secrets Act provisions are reactive; they impose criminal penalties on actions that have already occurred. To be useful, CSIS must detect activities that are preparatory to actual espionage or sabotage, such as the recruitment of a government employee in a sensitive position, at the earliest possible stage.[40] When actual acts of espionage or sabotage are uncovered, CSIS may bring the matter to the attention of the appropriate law enforcement authorities.[41] This emphasis on the role CSIS plays in early detection is expressly recognized in section 2(a) by the reference to "activities directed toward or in support of" espionage or sabotage. These very broad phrases extend to almost any type of assistance rendered to those engaged or intending to engage in acts of espionage or sabotage,[42] and thus give CSIS a very generous mandate.[43]

In order for espionage or sabotage or acts directed toward or in support of such activities to constitute a "threat to Canada," they must be either "against Canada" or "detrimental to the interests of Canada." "[A]gainst Canada" suggests actions threatening the existence of Canada or its political system. Activities threatening economic security are more likely to be "detrimental to the interests of Canada." It is difficult to give any precise meaning to "detrimental to the interests of Canada"[44] except to say that for interests to be those of the country they must be important to the nation as a whole, in some sense, rather than the interests of any single Canadian or group of Canadians. Clearly some economic interests will rise to this level, such as ensuring adequate supplies of oil and natural gas or protecting the confidentiality of Canadian positions at international negotiation on treaties such as the World Trade Organization Agreements[45] and the North American Free Trade Agreement.[46] Information important to the protection of such interests as well as information relied on by government in economic policy-making should be protected against espionage and sabotage. At the other extreme the commercial interests of a single Canadian enterprise in relation to a single transaction or event are unlikely to rise to this level, even though there may be an identifiable connection to a Canadian national interest, such as employment.[47] Where, for example, a Canadian firm is interested in securing a contract to provide goods or services, the increased employment in Canada resulting from the success of the bid might not justify the involvement of CSIS in protecting the Canadian firm's bid against espionage or even sabotage, though any breach of the law occasioned thereby would be the subject of civil or criminal action. Where the connection to the interests of Canada is sufficiently close, such as where espionage is intended to be carried out against a Canadian corporation involved in classified government projects, CSIS involvement may be justified.[48]

The foregoing suggests that whether, in any particular case, CSIS's mandate gives it a role will depend on the circumstances. Some of the relevant factors may include the following:

(a) whether the information or technology is confidential;

(b) how important the information or technology is to the competitiveness of the firm;

(c) the overall economic significance to Canada of the firm and the transaction or business to which the information or technology relates;

(d) the purpose for which information or technology is being obtained; and

(e) by whom the information or technology is being obtained.

Regarding (d), the significance of the threat will be greater when, for example, the information is going to be used as part of a systematic government-sponsored program to develop a foreign competitor to the Canadian business. Regarding (e), such a use is more likely where the information is being sought by a state-sponsored organization rather than a foreign private sector competitor. Indeed, as a general proposition, where the resources of a foreign state are being employed, the threat will be greater and, at least in relation to private sector targets, the target will be less able to protect itself. This will be so because of the access to and use of sophisticated technological means by government agents.

One final point may be made regarding the interpretation of "detrimental to the interests of Canada." The interests of Canada may be detrimentally affected by activities carried on in or outside Canada and directed at some other state or foreign entity. Indeed it is possible to argue that this is the only meaning to be attributed to this phrase. The phrase was introduced into the CSIS Act by the Senate Committee considering the Canadian Security Intelligence Service in substitution for the words originally proposed, which were "or against any state allied or associated with Canada." The change was made for the limited purpose of ensuring that the Service did not have authority to investigate activities wholly related to another country and unrelated to Canada.[49] Nevertheless, the important point is that the CSIS mandate extends to activities that are detrimental to Canadian interests, even if directed against a foreign state or entity.[50]

Foreign Influenced Activities
The scope for CSIS activities in relation to economic security is somewhat broader under section 2(b). For the purposes of subsection 2(b) a threat must consist of activities that are

- foreign influenced;
- within or related to Canada;
- detrimental to the interests of Canada; and

  - clandestine;
  - deceptive; or
  - involve a threat to any person.

"[F]oreign influenced" covers foreign interest groups, political organizations, individuals, associations, and corporations simply because they are not Canadian, but extends also to any Canadian person or organization influenced by such a foreign person or organization.[51] It is difficult to be specific regarding the meaning of "influenced," but it would appear to contemplate a lesser degree of control than "directed," which was the language employed by the 1975 Cabinet Directive defining the mandate of the Security Service of the RCMP.[52] The Special Committee of the House of Commons that studied the CSIS Act in 1990 was of the view that "directed" was preferable to "influenced." It considered that "influence" was too broad because it may be "distant, indirect and unconscious" and still be sufficient to engage the CSIS mandate.[53] Nevertheless, no amendment was made. In the context of the Criminal Code the Supreme Court of Canada has held that to influence requires some element of actually affecting a decision, course of conduct, attitude, or action.[54]

"[W]ithin or related to Canada" contemplates activities both inside and outside the territory of Canada. There are no criteria in the Act to help determine how much any particular activity must relate to Canada before it falls within the mandate of the Service. It has been suggested by SIRC that all that must be shown is that there be a "reasonable connection" to Canada.[55] To be consistent with the interpretation of section 2(a) suggested above, the connection must be with Canada as a whole, not just a Canadian person or corporation.

"[D]eceptive" suggests some element of dishonesty or at least lack of good faith. Behaviour may be deceptive if the person engaging in it knows that what he or she is doing is false or intends to mislead by some falsehood. The meaning of "clandestine" is less obvious. It encompasses but is not limited to deceptive behaviour. Rather it probably extends to behaviour that is merely secret and, in any event, need not constitute espionage or sabotage.[56] Dictionary definitions suggest that an element of underhandedness[57] is also involved, so "clandestine" would not extend, for example, to the confidentiality surrounding a normal commercial transaction.

"[D]etrimental to the interests of Canada" has the meaning discussed above. It is a principle of statutory interpretation that words used in two places should be interpreted in the same way, so long as nothing in the context requires them to be interpreted differently.[58] This phrase is used in section 2(b) for the same purpose as it is used in section 2(a), to define an essential feature or characteristic of the defined activity, and so should be interpreted in the same way.

Foreign influenced activities that "involve a threat to any person" comprise the last part of the mandate under section 2(b) as an alternative to the requirement that activities be deceptive or clandestine. The reference to threat need not be limited to actions involving violence, either to persons or property, or bodily injury or harm. This view is supported by the decision of the drafters of the CSIS Act to qualify the meaning of threat in section 2(c) with the words "of acts of serious violence." The qualification clearly suggests a legislative intention that threat when used alone in section 2(b) should not be so qualified. Perhaps more significantly, it was specifically suggested to the Senate Committee that the use of threat alone meant that economic threats would be included, and yet the Senate Committee did not recommend any amendment to section 2(b) in this regard.[59]

The only qualification limiting the interpretation of threat is the subsequent reference to "any person." Two questions arise regarding the effect of this qualification: to what extent does "person" embrace corporations and unincorporated institutions, and can a "threat to any person" extend to matters related to property or only to matters of personal safety or well-being? Regarding the first issue the general rule is that "person" includes a corporation.[60] There is nothing in the context of section 2(b) that would suggest that "person" should not extend to un-incorporated entities, political and social organizations, and similar entities. If section 2(b) were interpreted otherwise, activities such as the blackmailing by a foreign state of anyone other than a natural person, even if detrimental to the interests of Canada, would be outside the powers of the Service.

Expressed at its broadest, section 2(b) establishes a mandate for CSIS to collect, analyze, and retain information under section 12 respecting activities that it, on reasonable grounds, suspects are influenced by a foreign person, organization, or state, relate to Canada, are detrimental to economic interests sufficiently important to be considered an interest of Canada as opposed to merely an individual Canadian or group of Canadians, and are carried out in secret, or, even if not carried out in secret, involve any kind of threat to any kind of person.[61]

Other Features of the Section 12 Mandate

Some final observations should be made with regard to the mandate of CSIS under section 12. First, it is generally accepted that the Service has a responsibility under section 12 to keep itself well informed concerning the environment from which threats to economic security may emerge. Such information assists the Service in observing trends and identifying patterns that suggest the development of a threat.[62] It is not clear, how-ever, whether CSIS is permitted to gather information for the purpose of identifying vulnerability in public or private sector actors or activities in the absence of at least some evidence of a threat. Even acknowledging that some evidence of a threat is required when interpreting the CSIS mandate, it is not possible to say with any certainty what constitutes suf-ficient evidence. For example, it is not clear how precisely the threat must be focused on a particular person or activity, or how certain CSIS must be regarding the existence of a threat in order to justify the gathering of information in relation to it.[63] Sometimes CSIS may feel a need to engage in activities that can only be said to be associated with a threat in the most general sense, such as the activities of foreign intelligence agencies in Canada whose purpose is unknown.[64] Indeed, the very concept of a threat is inherently slippery and susceptible to flexible and creative inter-pretation. Second, even where some CSIS action may be justified under the mandate, various authors as well as the government have suggested that activities permitted under the mandate generally must be justified as being in proportion to the threat.[65] Applying this approach to economic security, it has been suggested that even where a threat to economic security is of national significance, the protection of economic interests, particularly individual private interests, cannot be considered to be as important as the more traditional aspects of the security mandate, such as protection against terrorism.[66] While one may debate the relative importance of economic interests, the requirement for the activities of CSIS to be proportionate to the threat to which they relate in terms of their intrusiveness seems beyond dispute. Such an approach is consistent with the Charter of Rights and Fundamental Freedoms and, at least to some extent, is supported by the language of section 12 itself, which permits the Service to conduct its operations only "to the extent strictly necessary."[67]

The Section 12 Mandate in Practice

However "threat" is defined, Porteous shows in his chapter that the threat to Canadian economic security is increasing. Increasing global competitiveness has enhanced the value and importance of economic and commercial information and technology. This has encouraged foreign intelligence services to become more involved in economic intelligence-gathering, including economic espionage.[68] Research by CSIS confirms that foreign intelligence services from several countries, including traditional political allies, are actively gathering economic intelligence in Canada.[69] The primary targets have been a small core of Canadian businesses with leading-edge technologies, but more ordinary commercial information such as plant layouts, client lists, and bid information have also been targeted.

Consistent with the foregoing anaylsis, CSIS itself, with the support of the Solicitor General and SIRC,[70] interprets its mandate as giving it a defensive role in relation to economic security. In its 1993 *Public Report*, CSIS stated: "The protection of Canada's economic security through countering economic espionage is not a new role for CSIS. This responsibility is set out in the Service's legislative mandate, its policy, and reflected in its practice."[71] In the same report CSIS acknowledged some limits on its role in this area. CSIS limits the use of its powers to economic espionage by foreign intelligence services or surrogates of foreign governments as opposed to industrial espionage by private businesses, which is consistent with the view expressed above that a greater risk to national interests is posed by state-sponsored economic intelligence-gathering. Also, CSIS is not concerned with the collection of data from open sources. It is only concerned to protect information or technology of a "proprietary nature" that a Canadian firm chooses not to share with another company believed to be a surrogate of a foreign government or its intelligence service.[72] Again this is consistent with the suggestion made above that the appropriation of open source information is less likely to threaten Canada.[73] More generally, the limits that CSIS has identified seem to reflect the view that its mandate is limited to serious threats to economic interests.

The Section 16 Mandate

As discussed below, CSE is involved in electronically gathering information on foreign states, corporations and persons ("foreign intelligence"), but unlike many of its allies, Canada does not have a foreign intelligence service which generates foreign intelligence by other means, such as through the presence of agents abroad. CSIS does, however, have a limited mandate in relation to foreign intelligence under section 16 of the CSIS Act.[74] Section 16 provides that CSIS "may, in relation to the defence of Canada or the conduct of the international affairs of Canada, assist the Minister of National Defence or the Secretary of State for External Affairs, within Canada, in the collection of information or intelligence relating the capabilities, intentions or activities of foreign states, natural persons or corporations."[75]

The mandate under section 16 is expressed somewhat differently from that under section 12. Though in some ways more open-ended than the section 12 mandate, it is at the same time subject to more stringent limitations. Section 16 gives the Service a broad authority to collect foreign intelligence,[76] subject to the following guidelines:

- CSIS may perform these functions only on the personal written request of the Minister of National Defence or the Secretary of State for External Affairs and with the personal consent of the Solicitor General.[77]

- CSIS may only "assist" the Minister of National Defence or the Secretary of State for External Affairs in performing these functions.

- CSIS may only perform these functions in relation to the "defence of Canada or the conduct of the international affairs of Canada."

- CSIS may only perform these tasks "within Canada."

While matters of economic security will not, in most cases, relate to the defence of Canada, there will be some matters, like international trade negotiations, that relate to the conduct of the international affairs of Canada. In these circumstances the potential role of CSIS may be significant. An important feature of the section 16 mandate is that, unlike section 12, the language of the statute appears not to limit CSIS to a defensive role. For example, CSIS might collect information on the bargaining strategies of a foreign state at a trade negotiation not to protect Canadian interests against threats but to enhance Canada's position.[78] The extent to which information relating to an individual private negotiation would relate to the conduct of the international affairs of Canada is less obvious. All such offensive activities may, however, be fraught with diplomatic, ethical, practical, and, above all, political risks that would have to be considered in relation to any CSIS activities in this regard.

It is clear that any such offensive role is narrowly restricted. CSIS may carry out its collection function only in Canada and only in relation to foreigners.[79] In practice this means that CSIS relies extensively on its network of information-sharing agreements with intelligence services around the world,[80] as well as the signals intelligence-gathering carried out by CSE.[81]

Also, the Service's role is limited to assisting. While all the implications of this limitation are not obvious, one implication has been that, in practice, CSIS does not retain information obtained pursuant to its section 16 function for its own purposes unless the requirements of section 12 are also met.[82] The limitation to assisting also highlights the most important feature of the CSIS mandate under section 16: its content is defined by Foreign Affairs and Defence.

THE SCOPE OF CSE OPERATIONS

CSE has no statutory mandate but operates under a classified 1946 order-in-council amended in 1975. CSE's main task is signals intelligence (SIGINT): the collection and analysis of foreign radio, radar and other signals regarding the capabilities, intentions or activities of foreign states, corporations or persons in relation to the defence of Canada or the conduct of its international affairs. The foreign intelligence gathered may include economic information, as well as political or military information which could have security implications. CSE also provides technical advice and services to help ensure that government telecommunications and electronic data processing operations are secure.[83]

In performing both these functions, CSE may assist CSIS in the fulfilment of its mandate under section 12 of the CSIS Act to defend against the activities of foreign actors gathering economic intelligence. As noted in the preceding section, in connection with the CSIS mandate under section 16 of the CSIS Act, CSE may play an important role as well. It has been claimed, for example, that CSE obtained information that helped the Canadian Wheat Board outbid the United States on a wheat contract with China in 1992,[84] and that it monitored communications from the Mexican embassy in Ottawa during the negotiations that led to the North American Free Trade Agreement.[85] To the extent that CSIS is engaged by the Minister of Defence or, more likely, the Minister of Foreign Affairs to collect intelligence in connection with economic matters, CSE's assistance will be crucial.

Recent disclosures indicate that the Agency had spied on foreign governments, their embassies, consulates and diplomatic staff, both in Canada and abroad, to acquire economic intelligence.[86] As well, CSE has been actively recruiting business school graduates, presumably to enhance its analytical capabilities with respect to economic information and to improve its surveillance of economic targets. Though they may appear somewhat duplicative, the roles of the two agencies are, in practice, complementary. CSIS relies heavily on the SIGINT capabilities of CSE and CSE's ability to act outside Canada.

THE SCOPE OF THE **RCMP** MANDATE
IN RELATION TO ECONOMIC SECURITY

In order to define the role of CSIS and CSE more fully, it is necessary to examine the complementary role of the RCMP. The establishment of CSIS in 1984 marked the separation of the function of security intelligence from security enforcement and protective security in accordance with the recommendations of the McDonald Commission.[87] While CSIS was to assume security intelligence responsibilities, the RCMP was to continue to fulfil its responsibilities for law enforcement in connection with security matters and protective security.[88] These include the following:

(a) preventing, detecting and investigating offenses defined by federal statutes such as the Copyright Act, the Criminal Code, the Official Secrets Act, and the Export and Imports Permits Act;

(b) protective security measures to safeguard important persons, certain federal properties, airports, and vital points from security offenses or threats, including the consideration of threat assessments from CSIS and other sources relevant to such protection; and

(c) providing advice to departments and agencies of the government regarding protective security measures.[89]

In connection with its mandate to enforce the law, the RCMP must be concerned with all foreign intelligence-gathering activities that violate any law, not just those that fall within the purview of "threats to Canada," the requirement to engage the CSIS mandate under section 12 of the CSIS Act. Nevertheless, under the Security Offenses Act,[90] which came into force in 1984, the RCMP has a special role in relation to security offenses. Where an offence under any law arises out of "conduct constituting a threat to Canada within the meaning of [the CSIS Act]," the RCMP have the "primary responsibility to perform the duties assigned to peace officers" in relation to the offence.[91] In effect this displaces the responsibilities of provincial and local police forces.

In discharging its responsibilities in relation to security, the RCMP necessarily engages in intelligence-gathering. It does so through its National Security Investigations Directorate.[92] Unlike CSIS's responsibility to perform intelligence collection, analysis, and advice to government in order to provide advance warning of threats to Canada,[93] however, the law enforcement role of the RCMP is essentially reactive; the RCMP does engage in information-gathering but only, for the most part, after some offence has been committed.[94] This gives the RCMP a different kind of focus from CSIS: the RCMP tends to focus more narrowly on obtaining information for the discrete purposes of apprehension and prosecution; CSIS activities are more open-ended. Significantly, they need not relate to any current or even anticipated illegal activity.[95] Expressed succinctly, the RCMP collects criminal intelligence while CSIS collects security intelligence.

Within CSIS there is a further division of intelligence-gathering activity. CSIS produces operational intelligence addressing discrete concerns for specific consumers or for a narrowly defined purpose usually with a short time horizon. One use of operational intelligence is to produce longer-term, more broadly defined strategic intelligence that is used by a wide range of government consumers.[96]

Though not a law enforcement agency, CSIS can play an important role in assisting the RCMP with its law enforcement responsibilities.[97] CSIS may acquire information in the course of its activities that helps the RCMP. Disclosure by CSIS for such purposes is expressly contemplated by the CSIS Act.[98] In the Memorandum of Understanding between the RCMP and CSIS, the Service is obliged to report incidents in which it is likely that a Criminal Code offence has taken place.[99] Nevertheless, there will be circumstances in which CSIS may be reluctant to disclose information, such as when the use of the information as evidence in criminal proceedings, perhaps introduced through the testimony of CSIS personnel, may jeopardize the identity of a source or in some other way compromise its operations.[100] This risk will arise not only in cases where CSIS provides information that may be used directly in evidence. While any disclosure to the RCMP itself may be of some concern for CSIS, that concern will be increased substantially when the RCMP makes disclosure to the Crown for the purpose of a criminal prosecution, in light of the decision of the Supreme Court of Canada in *R. v. Stinchcombe*.[101] This case has made clear that all relevant information in possession of the Crown, whether or not it will be used in evidence, must be disclosed to the defence.[102]

The RCMP's responsibility to provide advice to departments and agencies of the government regarding protective security measures is of critical importance to the protection of government information against foreign intelligence-gathering. As part of its protective services activity the RCMP does inspections to protect communications from unlawful interception and advises on electronic and physical security systems in a variety of delivery modes. Performing its protective security function effectively requires the development of threat assessments, which in turn require the collection of intelligence. CSIS is an important source of such intelligence. While there would seem to be no impediment to CSE providing information to assist the RCMP, there is no publicly available information showing a practice of doing so.

REGULATION OF FOREIGN INTELLIGENCE-GATHERING

Legal Sanctions on Foreign Intelligence-gathering in Canada

As described above, one of the primary responsibilities of the RCMP is law enforcement, and CSIS has an important supportive role in relation to law enforcement when an aspect of its mandate is engaged. How then may Canadian law be used to discourage and punish foreign agents gathering economic intelligence in Canada? The following discussion addresses not just the relevant provisions of the criminal law in this regard, but also Canadian intellectual property laws, which define the nature and scope of proprietary rights in information and technology and the Canadian export control regime. The purpose of reviewing the application of this legal framework to economic intelligence-gathering is to point out and assess some of the gaps in the current regime of legal protection of commercial and economic information held by Canadian businesses and government. The following discussion is relevant to intelligence-gathering by both state-sponsored and private actors.

Intellectual Property Law Considerations
The Canadian law regarding ownership of and entitlement to information, technology, and other intangible products of mental effort (referred to as "intellectual property" in this chapter) is complex and highly specialized. Patents, copyrights, integrated circuit protection, and trade secrets are the principal forms of intellectual property protection available in Canada that are relevant to economic intelligence. Each provides varying and limited kinds of protection for intellectual property held by

business and government.[103] In relation to economic intelligence, the Canadian regime, like the regimes of most countries, has two critical gaps: neither information nor ideas are protected against appropriation.

Theft of Information: The Supreme Court of Canada held in 1988 that information is not property, and therefore cannot be stolen for the purposes of the Criminal Code.[104] In *R. v. Stewart* the Court refused to consider a list of the names, addresses, and telephone numbers of six hundred employees of a hotel complex to be property, even though the hotel treated it as such by keeping it confidential and protecting it by certain security arrangements. Consequently, while, as discussed below, there may be criminal acts associated with the acquisition of information, such as theft of the media on which the information is stored, breaking and entering, and so on, the information itself and the ideas it contains are not protected unless they are subject to protection under one of the intellectual property laws mentioned above. Such protection is marginal at best.

Copyright is the right that belongs to the creator of an artistic or written work, including a computer program. The creator has an exclusive right to make or to authorize others to make copies of the work.[105] It is a fundamental principle of copyright law that copyright does not protect ideas contained in a work subject to copyright but only the expression of those ideas.[106] The ideas themselves may be freely appropriated. Similarly, facts and information contained in a work are not protected.[107] Where the only way to acquire ideas or information is to copy the expression of those ideas, copyright will provide some protection. For example, it would be an infringement of copyright to copy a document or computer disk in order to obtain ideas or information. If someone obtains possession of an authorized copy of a work subject to copyright, or reads it, and thereby acquires the information and ideas contained in it, there is no infringement.

Patent law does not protect information or bare ideas either. A person holding a patent has the exclusive right to make, use, sell, or otherwise exploit the subject matter of the patent. Patents do not protect mere ideas, mere scientific principles or abstract theorems, phenomena already existing in nature, and inventions that are obvious to those knowledgeable in the relevant field.[108] Patents may only be obtained where the idea is new and has been embodied in a useful device or process (an "invention").[109] The patent system does not limit the acquisition of the information or ideas inherent in a patented invention, only their exploitation. Indeed the patent system requires that information regarding a patented invention be disclosed and made part of the public record as a condition of the grant of the exclusive right to exploit the invention represented by the patent. Such disclosure must be such as to permit a person skilled in the relevant technology to understand it.[110]

Integrated Circuits: The protection of integrated circuits, also called semiconductor chips, under the Integrated Circuit Topography Act[111] gives the right holder the exclusive right to exploit an integrated circuit but, like the Patent Act, does not otherwise extend protection to the ideas underlying the integrated circuit[112] and, moreover, the Act expressly permits private non-commercial acts as well as other uses solely for the purpose of analysis, evaluation, or teaching.[113] Registration of an integrated circuit requires, among other things, filing sufficient information to permit its identification and so promotes dissemination of the ideas and information inherent in it.[114]

The Limits of the Statutory Intellectual Property Regimes and Reliance on Trade Secrets: The statutory regimes for copyrights, patents, and trade secrets do not provide an effective set of rules to deter or punish those intent on appropriating information or ideas. None provides any direct protection of information, and the protection of ideas is limited. While copyright may be used to protect information and ideas by prohibiting the copying of their expression, there will be, in most cases, non-infringing ways of acquiring the information or idea. Ideas are not protected at all under copyright. Under the Patent Act and the Integrated Circuit Topography Act ideas are only protected to the extent that they are embodied in some invention or integrated circuit. Even in such circumstances the protection is only against exploitation by another person in Canada. Regarding commercial exploitation outside of Canada, relief for a patent or integrated circuit rights holder will be available if he or she has taken the necessary steps to obtain patent or integrated circuit rights in the jurisdiction in which the exploitation is taking place. Many uses of the ideas or information, such as taking the next innovative step, are not prohibited. Indeed, the schemes of both Acts require filings that disclose the ideas and information inherent in an invention or integrated circuit with a view to encouraging just such uses.

In addition to these conceptual limitations, however, there are various other problems with reliance on these rights as a way of controlling foreign intelligence-gathering. Enforcement is essentially a matter left to the private parties holding intellectual property rights. While the ability to litigate to prevent infringing commercial exploitation provides a measure of protection against loss of a competitive advantage, private enforcement will be impractical in many cases, because of various impediments inherent in the intellectual property system. Litigation is an uncertain, time-consuming and, most importantly, expensive solution. A survey for the Science Council of Canada found that the costs of obtaining and enforcing these intellectual property rights are so great that only large companies commonly expended money to obtain and enforce them.[115] Also, litigation for the purpose of enforcement would have to be commenced not just in Canada, but also in each foreign jurisdiction in which the infringer sought to do business.

Whether CSIS or the RCMP might have a role in connection with private enforcement is questionable at best. Only a strained interpretation of the RCMP mandate under section 19 of the RCMP Act to "enforce laws" would permit the RCMP to assist private enforcement, not a role it has played historically. With respect to CSIS, the strict disclosure regime under the CSIS Act would not seem to permit the Service to provide information to private parties to assist in the assertion of their intellectual property rights, as discussed below under "Disclosure."

Of the three statutory intellectual property regimes discussed above, only copyright provides for criminal enforcement.[116] While such enforcement is clearly within the mandate of the RCMP, and CSIS may provide information to assist the RCMP in this regard, such enforcement has been extremely rare.

For these and other reasons the legal and practical protection relied on by most businesses is in the category of trade secrets. The law of trade secrets in Canada is "a complex subject,"[117] because there is no statutory framework; trade secrets are protected by a variety of common law rules developed by judges in deciding individual cases. As a result the scope of trade secret rights is uncertain. Information kept secret by businesses may be legally protected through contractual restrictions on disclosure agreed to by persons receiving information, as well as through a variety of practical and technical strategies. Apart from contractual obligations, the common law imposes an obligation not to disclose a trade secret on the person to whom the information has been given and provides a remedy if three requirements have been met:

(i)   the information must have the necessary characteristic of confidence, meaning that the steps must have been taken to keep it secret or to limit its disclosure;

(ii) the communication by the secret owner to the person who disclosed it must have been made in the context of some relationship creating an obligation of confidence, such as the relationship between two parties negotiating a business transaction;[118] and

(iii) there must be some misuse or unauthorized use of the information.[119]

Unlike the other kinds of intellectual property protection described above, the scope of what may be protected is unlimited for trade secrets. Ideas and information may be trade secrets. Nevertheless, the protection afforded by the obligation not to breach a confidence is restricted in several important ways. Critically the requirement for a relationship may mean that information obtained surreptitiously, such as through espionage or reverse engineering, may not be protected.[120] Some writers have suggested that any person who comes into possession of secret information should be prevented from using it if it is reasonable to conclude that the person should have known that it was secret.[121] Undoubtedly such a conclusion would be reasonable in the case of persons engaged in espionage. In the absence of some judicial authority on this point, however, the application of such a duty of confidence to third parties remains an open question. The efficacy of trade secret law for protection against economic and commercial intelligence-gathering is further reduced because it is not subject to criminal enforcement. Trade secret rights may only be enforced by the person who possesses the secret.[122]

Summary: Neither statutory intellectual property law nor common law rules regarding trade secrets and property rights in information will provide a practical basis for defending against foreign intelligence-gathering in most circumstances. In the case of the statutory regimes governing intellectual property the substance of the rights is such that they do not protect against the acquisition or, in most cases, the use of information or ideas by foreign persons or governments engaged in intelligence-gathering. In the case of trade secrets the rights may attach to both information and ideas, but the nature of the right is such that it may not be violated by appropriation without the consent of the holder of the information, such as by espionage. Even where statutory or trade secret rights are infringed, enforcement is left to the private rights holder; neither the RCMP nor the CSIS has any role in this regard. Only in relation to the criminal enforcement of copyright can the RCMP and CSIS be of assistance. These limitations of the legal regime seem to create a hospitable environment for economic espionage.

Criminal Law Considerations

The Criminal Code

As indicated above, in light of the *Stewart* case, taking information is not theft. Nevertheless there are various criminal offences that may be committed in the course of obtaining information. In general, breaking into any premises[123] or taking any tangible object, like paper or computer disks,[124] will constitute an offence.[125]

Where information is acquired through some technological rather than physical means, the acquisition may be an offence, notwithstanding *Stewart*. The use of any electro-magnetic, acoustic, mechanical, or other device (a "listening device") to intercept a private communication and to intercept a radio-based communication "maliciously or for gain" constitutes an offence.[126] Indeed the possession of a listening device and any disclosure of information intercepted with one are both offences.[127] Also, even if a person takes nothing but uses a computer system with intent to destroy or alter data or to render data meaningless or interferes with anyone's use of the system, that person commits an offence.[128]

Certain other offences may be committed in connection with the means used to acquire information. It is an offence to give or offer to give a bribe to any person and to demand or accept a bribe in consideration of the doing or forbearing from doing any act in connection with the business or affairs of any private[129] or public[130] employer. Similarly, any person who commits extortion by using threats or violence to induce any person to do anything, including providing information, is guilty of an offence.[131]

Offences commonly associated with threats to the security of Canada, like treason and sabotage, are likely to have limited application to foreign economic intelligence-gathering activities. As noted above,[132] part of the treason provision has been considered to define "espionage." Treason is committed where, among other things, "any person communicates or makes available to an agent of a state, other than Canada, military or scientific information or any sketch, plan, model, article, note or document of a military or scientific character that he or she knows or ought to know may be used by that state for a purpose prejudicial to the safety or defence of Canada."[133] While certain technological or economic information or documents may be "scientific" within the meaning of this provision, the requirement that the purpose be prejudicial to the safety or defence of Canada suggests that the section would not apply unless the information has some military rather than purely economic significance, although some non-military information or documents might be caught. Information or documents relating to some extreme environmental or health danger might be examples. A further limit is that the treason provision only applies to disclosure to "an agent of a state other than Canada." Disclosure to a foreign private interest is not an offence.

Like treason, sabotage, as defined above,[134] appears to contemplate actions prejudicial to military or political interests rather than economic interests.[135] Unlike the treason section, however, the sabotage provision does refer to prejudice to Canada's "security," not just to "safety or defence," suggesting a slightly broader scope of application, which might include economic security.

The Official Secrets Act

Unlike private information, government information is protected under the Official Secrets Act, in addition to being protected under the provisions of the Criminal Code described above. The Official Secrets Act creates a variety of offenses using very broad language that may have application to threats to economic security relating to the appropriation of government information. As discussed above,[136] section 3 of the Act deals with espionage. Under section 3, obtaining, collecting, and communicating any official secret that might be useful to a "foreign power" for a purpose "prejudicial to the interests"[137] of Canada is guilty of an offence.[138] There are, however, some important limitations on prosecutions under section 3. First, Canadian cases have held that only classified information is protected.[139] Second, the requirement under section 3 that information must have some possible value to a "foreign power" might exclude an acquisition for a merely private purpose. Having noted these limitations, a variety of presumptions and other advantages for the Crown exist that facilitate prosecutions under section 3 as well as the other provisions of the Official Secrets Act.

Under section 4 of the Act, any disclosure of "secret" information to an unauthorized person is an offence by the discloser, as is receiving such information. Information is not made secret simply because someone stamped "secret" on the document in question. The courts have made clear that, to benefit from the protections of the Official Secrets Act, secrecy must lie at the very nature of the document and the surrounding circumstances affecting the document. A document marked "secret" will not be considered secret under the Official Secrets Act if its contents have been widely disclosed within government, or in a public forum such as the House of Commons.[140] Despite these judicial restrictions, the potential scope for the application of the Official Secrets Act remains very broad and has been the target of consistent criticism.[141]

Notwithstanding the potentially wide application of these provisions of the Official Secrets Act to intelligence-gathering activities of all kinds, prosecutions have been rare.[142]

Summary

On the basis of the foregoing it would appear that there is some scope for addressing foreign intelligence-gathering through the criminal law notwithstanding the limits imposed by the Supreme Court's decision in *Stewart*. The Official Secrets Act provides a significant measure of protection for government information. Also, in relation to both government and private information, even though the acquisition of the information itself is not subject to penalties under the Criminal Code, unless the means of acquisition is a listening device, many of the activities associated with the surreptitious acquisition of information, such as

breaking and entering, bribery, and extortion, are. In recognition of its
responsibilities in this area, the RCMP have adopted a client awareness
program to assist government and private sector actors to protect their
computer systems from unlawful intervention.[143]

Limits of the Criminal Law

In practice there are several problems associated with the use of the
criminal law. Two significant ones are the territorial limits of Canadian
criminal law and the diplomatic status of foreign intelligence agents
engaged in criminal activity.

The general principle traditionally applied by the courts to determine the limits of their jurisdiction in enforcing the criminal law is that
a Canadian court only has jurisdiction if the offence is committed in
Canada. Subject to the exclusions discussed below, the nationality of a
person or the basis of his or her being in Canada is not relevant. While
formerly this territorial limitation was strictly enforced, there has been
an long-term trend toward the adoption of interpretative doctrines that
have had the effect of relaxing it. In 1985, the Supreme Court of Canada
catalogued all of these doctrines in *Libman* v. *The Queen*, summing
them up in the following test: a person may be convicted of an offense
under Canadian law so long as there is some "real and substantial connection" between the criminal activity and Canada.[144] Examples of the
situations in which a sufficient connection with Canada would be found
may include the following: formation of criminal intent in Canada,
impact of the crime experienced by a victim in Canada, and enjoyment
of the fruits of a crime in Canada.[145]

It seems likely that in most cases involving actions of economic
intelligence-gathering by foreign agents there will be sufficient connection with Canada to meet the test articulated in *Libman*. The ability to
prosecute in Canada, however, may be of little value if the person alleged
to have committed the offence has left the country. Canada's criminal
laws are not enforceable in foreign jurisdictions. Despite a network of
international agreements in place to assist investigations for the purpose
of enforcing Canadian law[146] and to provide for extradition, criminal
enforcement against persons outside of Canada, especially where state
agents are involved, will be difficult.

An additional impediment to enforcement against foreign agents, in
some circumstances, are the immunities from prosecution which they

may benefit if they are connected to the official presence of their state in Canada under the Foreign Missions and International Organisations Act.[147] Under this act, the staff of foreign diplomatic and consular posts are immune from arrest or detention pending trial except in the case of a "grave crime" and pursuant to a decision of a competent judicial authority.[148] For the purposes of the Act a "grave crime" is any offence created by an act of Parliament for which an offender may be sentenced to imprisonment for five years or more.[149] Consular officers and employees enjoy a more limited immunity than diplomats. In criminal matters immunity is restricted to acts performed in the course of their consular functions.[150] Also, diplomatic and consular premises are inviolable; Canadian police cannot seek to enter such premises or exercise power within them.[151] Canada must permit free communications on the part of the mission or consulate for all official purposes and must maintain the inviolability of the diplomatic bag.[152] The diplomatic bag is any package or container designated by the mission or consulate. Under the Act it is only to contain official correspondence and articles, but Canada may have no right to examine the contents of the bag to determine if this obligation is being honoured.

Some commentators have argued that the provisions of the Act which implement the Vienna Convention on Diplomatic Relations and the Vienna Convention on Consular Relations are not available to protect the staff of foreign missions under circumstances where the provisions of either convention are breached. In support of this position it may be noted that each convention obliges persons enjoying privileges and immunities to respect the laws and regulations of the host state.[153] Though the issue has never been addressed in Canadian law, the British Parliament's Foreign Affairs Committee, in its "Report on the Abuse of Diplomatic Immunities and Privileges," rejected this position. The committee determined that the convention obligations applied even where the Libyan embassy in London was being used for terrorist purposes, an incident which had resulted in the shooting death of an English policewoman.[154] The only remedy that seems to be available when diplomatic privileges and immunities have been abused is the expulsion of any person involved in the abuse and, ultimately, the severing of diplomatic relations.[155] Neither is likely to be very effective in combatting foreign intelligence-gathering.

Export Controls

The third element of the Canadian legal regime relevant to defending against economic intelligence-gathering by foreign agents is the control of exports under the Export and Imports Permits Act.[156] Export controls are an important way of controlling the transfer of technology out of a country and are used by most countries to protect their military, political, and economic interests.[157] The Act authorizes the creation of a list of goods that cannot be exported without authorization (the "Export Control List") and a list of countries to which no exports may be sent without special authorization (the "Area Control List"). The authorization required is a permit issued by the Export Controls Division of the Department of Foreign Affairs and International Trade.

The Area Control List and the Export Control List were based, originally, on the lists developed by the Coordinating Committee for Multilateral Export Controls (COCOM).[158] The COCOM lists were designed primarily to prevent the transfer of weapons and certain technology to states in the former Soviet Bloc and certain outlaw states. Effective March 31, 1994, COCOM was replaced by a new arrangement, which substantially relaxed restrictions on transfers to states in the former group.[159]

While export controls might be used as a means of preventing intelligence from being removed from Canada, they are subject to a serious practical limitation. They only operate in relation to information or technology embodied in goods. They will not be effective to prevent disembodied information from leaving the country.[160] Also, the export control system is not designed to act as a barrier to the export of technology. Especially given the pace of technological change, it would be difficult to recast the export control regime to protect Canadian competitive advantages without creating unnecessary barriers to trade. There would be significant political barriers to doing so as well.

The Effect of Recent Changes to Canada's International Obligations

In recent years, Canada's international obligations have changed substantially with the coming into effect of the NAFTA[161] on January 1, 1994 and the results of the Uruguay Round of negotiations on the GATT[162] (WTO Agreement) on January 1, 1995. Among the wide range of subjects covered by both agreements is the establishment of minimum national standards for the nature and enforcement of intellectual property rights under the laws of the party states.[163]

Although Canada's commitments under both agreements required significant amendments to Canadian intellectual property laws, such amendments are likely to have little impact on the efficacy of using intellectual property laws to deter or punish foreign intelligence-gathering in Canada.[164] The rules regarding the basic categories of intellectual property protection, copyright, patent, integrated circuits, and trade secrets were not affected in ways relevant to the protection of information or ideas, nor were Canadian standards for enforcement significantly changed. No new categories of intellectual property protection were introduced. Aspects of technology and other types of proprietary information and ideas not traditionally protectable under domestic copyright, patent, integrated circuit, and trade secret laws remain unprotectable under NAFTA and the Trade Related Aspects of Intellectual Property Agreement (the "TRIPs Agreement") forming part of the WTO Agreement.[165] What one commentator has called the "know how gap," meaning information and ideas only protectible through trade secrets or by contract, has not been filled.[166]

There will be, however, certain benefits for Canadian intellectual property rights holders. NAFTA and the TRIPs Agreement help ensure that the level of intellectual property rights that Canadians have in Canada will be recognized and enforced under the laws of other countries. This will greatly facilitate actions to protect such rights outside of Canada, particularly in the many countries in which intellectual property rights are weak or their enforcement is deficient. Also, to the extent that rights guaranteed under these international agreements are not protected under the national laws of party states, the new dispute settlement processes in NAFTA and the WTO Agreement permit Canada to obtain a determination to this effect and possible relief. Nevertheless, given the limited scope for using intellectual property rights enforcement as a mechanism for deterring or punishing foreign intelligence-gathering efforts, the impact of these changes in the international regime is unlikely to be significant, and the opportunities for CSIS or the RCMP to provide assistance in this regard will remain limited.[167]

There is one final point that deserves mention in connection with the international legal regime as it relates to the activities of security services in support of private commercial interests. The Subsidies

Agreement,[168] which forms part of the WTO Agreement sets out a comprehensive framework for national laws dealing with subsidies. Both the subsidization practices of national governments and their imposition of sanctions on subsidization by foreign governments are regulated. The Subsidies Agreement establishes, for the first time, a definition of subsidy. The definition is very broad, and possibly could be interpreted to extend to both defensive and offensive activities of national security services directed to helping domestic commercial interests.[169] To the extent that such an interpretation is accepted three consequences could follow. First, each state party to the WTO Agreement would be obliged to report such activities by its security service to the WTO, though, as a practical matter, one may be sceptical regarding the willingness of the state to do so.[170] Second, in some circumstances, goods produced by businesses that benefitted from this form of subsidy could be subject to countervailing duties imposed by states into which such goods were imported. Third, the Subsidies Agreement provides that where goods benefiting from such a subsidy cause "serious prejudice" to the interests of another state that state may seek relief through consultation and ultimately dispute settlement proceedings.[171] If, as a result of such proceedings, serious prejudice is found, the subsidizing state must take steps to remove the adverse effect of the subsidy or withdraw the subsidy. If appropriate steps are not taken within a specified period of time the complaining state may take counter-measures.

Disclosure

A critical issue in connection with the legal regulation of efforts by CSIS to defend against foreign intelligence-gathering is the extent to which information obtained by CSIS in accordance with its mandate may be disclosed. The starting point for considering this issue is section 19 of the CSIS Act which provides the scheme governing disclosure of information obtained by the Service in the course of performing its mandate under the Act. The general rule is that information may only be disclosed by CSIS for the purposes "of performing its duties under [the Act] or the administration or enforcement of [the Act] or as required by any other law." CSIS may also disclose information in the following circumstances:

(a) where the information may be used in the investigation or prosecution of an alleged contravention of any law of Canada or a province, to a peace officer having jurisdiction to investigate the alleged contravention and to the Attorney General of Canada and the Attorney General of the province in which proceedings in respect of the alleged contravention may be taken;

(b) where the information relates to the conduct of the international affairs of Canada, to the Secretary of State for External Affairs or a person designated by the Secretary of State for External Affairs for the purpose;

(c) where the information is relevant to the defence of Canada, to the Minister of National Defence or a person designated by the Minister of National Defence for the purpose; or

(d) where, in the opinion of the [Solicitor General], disclosure of the information to any minister of the Crown or person in the public service of Canada is essential in the public interest and that interest clearly outweighs any invasion of privacy that could result from the disclosure, to that minister or person.

Where any disclosure is made under (d) above the Director of CSIS shall, as soon as practicable thereafter, submit a report to SIRC with respect to the disclosure.[172]

There are several points to note about section 19 in relation to disclosures for the purpose of combatting foreign intelligence-gathering. First, the specifically enumerated grounds for disclosure provide some scope for CSIS to use information for this purpose.[173] Cooperation, including information exchange with law enforcement agencies, including, in particular, the RCMP, for purposes of assisting with the investigation or prosecution of anyone in connection with any of the offenses under the Criminal Code, the Official Secrets Act, the Export and Imports Permits Act, or the Copyright Act described above, is clearly contemplated under (a).[174] Also, disclosure to Foreign Affairs of information relating to foreign intelligence-gathering activities connected with international economic arrangements, like trade agreement negotiations, is permitted because it relates to the international affairs of Canada under (b). Disclosures of information in the public interest pursuant to (d) may be made only to a government minister or a public servant and are intended to be infrequent. The limited nature of section 19(1)(d) is manifest from the requirement that the public interest must "clearly" outweigh any invasion of privacy and the obligation to report any such disclosure to SIRC. This seems to be well understood by CSIS, since such public interest disclosures have been extremely rare.[175]

In order to understand the scope of the general permission granted to CSIS to disclose for the purposes "of performing its duties under the Act or the administration or enforcement of this Act or as required by any other law" one must recall what CSIS's duties are and what the administration and enforcement of the Act involves. As mentioned above, the primary duty of CSIS is to collect, analyze, and retain information regarding threats to the security of Canada and to report to and advise the government regarding such threats under section 12.[176] In order to collect information one must inevitably make certain disclosures. Section 17 of the CSIS Act expressly contemplates cooperative arrangements with other government agencies, police forces, the governments of foreign states, and international organizations. Though information disclosure is not expressly referred to in section 17, disclosure in this context is an integral part of CSIS operations and, obviously, is one type of disclosure contemplated in section 19.[177] Other disclosures would have to be linked similarly to gathering or analyzing information or advising government regarding threats. Applying this standard, all disclosures to government relating to foreign efforts to acquire government information or to facilitate detection or analysis of such efforts would be permitted.

The disclosure regime consisting of sections 12, 17, and 19 of the CSIS Act, gives CSIS limited scope to provide information to private sector actors. It seems impossible to fit disclosure to private parties for the purpose of assisting private litigation to enforce intellectual property rights within the mandate of CSIS under section 12, or any permitted disclosure under sections 17 or 19. Are there some circumstances in which limited disclosure to private parties may be permitted for the purpose of gathering or analyzing information? For example, if CSIS becomes aware of a plan to obtain certain proprietary information from a Canadian high-tech firm, could CSIS disclose the existence of the plan to the firm so that CSIS could find out more about it and analyze it?

Similarly, if CSIS reasonably suspects that a foreign intelligence agency intends to appropriate government information by infiltrating a private business organization that is doing government work under contract, could CSIS disclose information to the organization in order to facilitate its information-gathering and analysis? These questions illustrate that the extent to which CSIS may disclose information to private parties for the purpose of its operations has critical implications for how CSIS carries out its operations.[178] Unfortunately, the statutory scheme gives little guidance in this regard.

One aspect of the disclosure regime that is clear is that CSIS may only disclose the results of its collection and analysis to government.[179] Once information is disclosed, government must make the political decision regarding what further disclosure is appropriate. Thus the government acts as a political buffer for CSIS in relation to disclosure. The discussion above regarding the disclosure regime governing CSIS probably has no application to information gathered under section 16. As discussed above, CSIS's role under section 16 is limited to *assisting* the Minister of Defence or the Secretary of State for Foreign Affairs. If the interpretation given to this limit is correct, CSIS cannot retain information that it has acquired in the course of such assistance for its own purposes, unless such retention can be justified under section 12.[180] If CSIS cannot retain information, it surely cannot disclose it, in accordance with section 19. Consequently, only the disclosure contemplated in section 16, that is, to the Minister of Defence or the Secretary of State for Foreign Affairs, would be permitted. However, some disclosure may be permitted for the purpose of gathering information in the fulfillment of its section 16 mandate.[181]

OFFENSIVE ECONOMIC INTELLIGENCE-GATHERING BY CANADIAN GOVERNMENT AGENCIES

There has been a debate in recent years regarding whether Canada needs a foreign intelligence service, given the enhanced economic security needs described in this study.[182] As discussed above, section 16 of the CSIS Act appears to give CSIS a limited role to gather information not linked to threats to Canada, which I will refer to as offensive economic intelligence-gathering. In particular, section 16 requires that the Service's offensive intelligence-gathering activities for the purpose of enhancing

Canada's economic security, may only be carried out "within Canada." In this section I will raise legal issues associated with offensive foreign intelligence-gathering by CSIS that would become relevant if its responsibilities were expanded in this direction. To some extent these concerns will be relevant to CSIS in connection with its defensive role outside of Canada, and also to the activities of CSE.

The Foreign Legal Environment

It is impossible even to attempt to describe the legal environment in which the gathering of economic intelligence by Canadian government agencies might be carried on outside of Canada, given the diversity of legal systems throughout the world. This diversity itself creates a concern for any Canadian foreign intelligence-gathering operation. The laws in the state in which such an operation is carried out may be very different from Canada's in ways relevant to the operation's legality. In this section I will address two examples of such differences: foreign legal sanctions on intelligence-gathering activities and the implications of foreign intellectual property laws.

Some countries such as China and France[183] have criminal laws with a much broader scope than Canadian laws in terms of what information-gathering activities constitute an offence. Such laws enable foreign states to take action against economic intelligence-gathering by foreign agencies.[184] For example, under French law it is expressly provided that obtaining privately held commercial and industrial information, including some open source information, as well as government information, is a punishable offence. Under Chinese law the state retains an unlimited discretion to determine what is a state secret and therefore protected. By contrast, Canadian law only imposes criminal penalties on the gathering of information in very limited circumstances: copyright infringement,[185] acquiring information using a listening device,[186] and actions contrary to the Official Secrets Act in relation to government information.[187]

Similarly, notwithstanding the movement toward greater uniformity in international standards for protection and enforcement of intellectual property laws evidenced by the TRIPs agreement and the intellectual property chapter of NAFTA, foreign intellectual property laws may be different from Canadian laws in important ways. The standards for substantive protection set out in these international agreements are very general. There is significant scope for national peculiarities both in the implementation of these standards into the law of each party state and in the application of these standards to particular facts in judicial decisions. The result is that there may be substantial differences in the effective level of protection of intellectual property from state to state.[188] This will be particularly true in relation to new technologies, regarding which the scope of protection is uncertain.[189] Another source of differential levels of protection and enforcement is the fact that there are transitional periods during which countries do not have to fulfil all their obligations under TRIPs.[190]

Consequently, should CSIS or CSE engage in economic intelligence-gathering in any state, they must make the difficult assessment of what is legally permitted there. It is unreasonable to expect that laws in any foreign state would approximate the relative openness of Canadian law.[191]

CONCLUSION

The statutory mandates of both CSIS and the RCMP contemplate a role in relation to the protection of Canadian economic security, although neither expressly refers to economic interests. The mandate of the RCMP is clear. In connection with economic security, as with other matters, the primary responsibility of the RCMP is law enforcement and, in that regard, includes but is not restricted to protecting economic security interests that rise to national significance. In support of this role, CSIS is permitted to supply information. Unfortunately, the Canadian legal regime creates an inconsistent patchwork of rules protecting information and technology. Intellectual property rules have a narrow focus and suffer from several other limitations that severely restrict their utility as a means for the RCMP to combat foreign intelligence-gathering in Canada. The Criminal Code creates a variety of offenses that may be committed in the course of economic intelligence-collection, but does not punish collection itself, unless carried out using a listening device. The Official Secrets Act does punish the collection of information, but its application has been limited to classified government information that is collected for "a purpose prejudicial to the safety or interests of the state," and might be at least indirectly "useful to a foreign power." No matter what the substantive basis for taking action against foreign intelligence-collection in Canada, reliance on law enforcement is subject to a number of inherent barriers, including diplomatic immunities and privileges and the limits of Canadian jurisdiction.

The role of CSIS in relation to law enforcement and, indeed, all of its operations, is limited under section 12 to collecting information for the purpose of investigating threats to Canada and advising government regarding them. The CSIS mandate is limited to threats to economic security interests of national significance. In one sense this gives CSIS a more restricted role than the RCMP. But once a threat of this magnitude is identified, the potential role of CSIS is much broader. It is not restricted to operations directed toward the enforcement of the patchwork of laws in Canada, but permits the collection of any information it determines is relevant and consistent with the requirements of section 12. The potential scope for CSIS activities in relation to the protection of private interests, however, appears to be severely limited by the disclosure regime in the CSIS Act as well as the requirement to link such activities to interests of national significance.

This last point is a particular concern since, as Porteous points out so effectively, other states, including our largest trading partner, the United States, are actively engaged in the provision of such information to or for the benefit of their private sectors. A variety of complex issues associated with providing intelligence to the private sector are addressed in the Porteous chapter. These include how to identify what intelligence is needed and to whom intelligence should be disclosed so as to ensure that the benefit of such disclosure remains in Canada. Undoubtedly in times of budgetary constraint, it would be difficult for CSIS or the RCMP to obtain the additional resources needed to develop the capability to assist the private sector in any meaningful way. Nevertheless, in the absence of such a capability Canada seems to be at a serious disadvantage.[192]

If there is any other conclusion that may be drawn from the analysis in this chapter, it must be that Canada's legal regime has not been conceived or adapted to protect government and private interests from foreign economic intelligence-gathering operations in any coherent way. In considering whether the legal regime should be changed to provide specifically for such a role two general constraints must be taken into account. First, there are important policy considerations discouraging the imposition of rigid controls on the flow of information and technology. Protecting information and technology must be balanced with ensuring access in order to promote competitiveness and prosperity. Second, from a practical point of view, at least in relation to intellectual property, it would be difficult for Canada to adopt a scheme of intellectual property-protection significantly different from that of our trading partners because of our international obligations under the WTO Agreement and NAFTA.

Maintaining a balance between protection and access and acting in accordance with our international obligations does not preclude improving our legal regime. On the basis of the foregoing discussion, it is possible to suggest a variety of ways in which Canadian law might be amended to permit a more rational and coherent approach to dealing with the threat of foreign intelligence-gathering. In light of the constraints identified, the focus of such improvements should be on the provision of effective means to punish certain acquisitions of intelligence without the consent of the person in possession of the intelligence. First, the law of trade secrets could be put on a statutory basis that would expressly provide for two changes from the current common law: surreptitious appropriation of trade secrets could be both prohibited and subject to criminal enforcement.[193] Second, the Official Secrets Act could be amended to make clear that the taking of any classified government information is an offence, removing the requirements that the taking be for "a purpose prejudicial to the safety or interests of the state" and "useful to a foreign power."[194] These two changes would help to ensure that all information that the government or a private person wanted to keep secret would be protected by law as enforced by the RCMP and other law enforcement agencies. They would also bring Canadian law more into line with the laws of other states. Such a change to the Official Secrets Act might be thought to render its application both too wide, because it would criminalize the appropriation of even the most trivial classified information, and too narrow, because if would leave out sensitive open source information. To meet this concern it may be preferable to adopt a different approach: the appropriation of any government information that represented a threat to the security of Canada could be prohibited.[195]

Consideration should also be given to whether the mandate of CSIS should be amended to expressly refer to economic interests.[196] Although any expression of an economic mandate would, of necessity, be couched in very general language, it would be helpful to CSIS and to those to whom CSIS is responsible to set out its responsibilities in this area in language specifically and uniquely chosen for this purpose. The current statement of CSIS mandate in the CSIS Act requires divining CSIS's role in relation to threats to economic security from all encompassing language that speaks to military, political, and similar kinds of threats. Although it is undoubtedly true that the present vaguely worded mandate permits the government to shift directions in response to the rapidly changing conditions of today's world, it may be possible to retain sufficient flexibility within a new, clearer, and more specific mandate.

Finally, in light of the increasing evidence of the use of foreign intelligence agencies by many states as an adjunct to their strategic trade policy, the need for a broader foreign intelligence-gathering mandate may need to be reconsidered. An analysis of this issue is far beyond the scope of this chapter. Nevertheless, one may identify some of the ways in which such a mandate may be implemented. The most straightforward, though the least transparent, approach would be for the government to use the section 16 process more frequently. Several alternatives may also be identified: amending the CSIS Act to provide for a more expansive offensive intelligence-gathering mandate, setting up a new agency with its own statutory mandate, and expanding CSE into a foreign intelligence-gathering agency with its own statutory mandate.

APPENDIX

RELEVANT STATUTORY PROVISIONS

I. SELECTED SECTIONS OF THE *CANADIAN SECURITY INTELLIGENCE SERVICE ACT*
R.S.C. 1985, c. C-23, as amended

Section 2

"[T]hreats to the security of Canada" means

(a) espionage or sabotage that is against Canada or is detrimental to the interests of Canada or activities directed toward or in support of such espionage or sabotage,

(b) foreign influenced activities within or relating to Canada that are detrimental to the interests of Canada and are clandestine or deceptive or involve a threat to any person,

(c) activities within or relating to Canada directed toward or in support of the threat or use of acts of serious violence against persons or property for the purpose of achieving a political objective within Canada or a foreign state, and

(d) activities directed toward undermining by covert or unlawful acts, or directed toward or intended ultimately to lead to the destruction or overthrow by violence of, the constitutionally established system of government in Canada,

but does not include lawful advocacy, protest or dissent, unless carried on in conjunction with any of the activities referred to in paragraphs (a) to (d).

Section 12

12. The service shall collect, by investigation or otherwise, to the extent that it is strictly necessary, and analyze and retain information and intelligence respecting activities which may, on reasonable grounds, be suspected of constituting threats to the security of Canada and, in relation thereto, shall report to and advise the government of Canada.

Section 16

16. (1) Subject to this section, the Service may, in relation to the defence of Canada or the conduct of the international affairs of Canada, assist the Minister of National Defence or the Secretary of State for External Affairs, within Canada, in the collection of information or intelligence relating to the capabilities, intentions or activities of
    (a) any foreign state or group of foreign states; or
    (b) any person other than
        (i) a Canadian citizen,
        (ii) a permanent resident within the meaning of the *Immigration Act*, or
        (iii) a corporation incorporated by or under an Act of parliament or of the legislature of a province.

(2) This assistance provided pursuant to subsection (1) shall not be directed at any person referred to in subparagraph(1)(b)(i), (ii) or (iii).

(3) The Service shall not perform its duties and functions under subsection (1) unless it does so
    (a) on the personal request in writing of the Minister of National Defence or the Secretary of State for External Affairs; and
    (b) with the personal consent in writing of the Minister.

Section 17

17. (1) For the purpose of performing its duties and functions under this Act, the Service may,
    (a) with the approval of the Minister, enter into an arrangement or otherwise cooperate with
        (i) any department of the Government of Canada or the government of a province or any department thereof, or
        (ii) any police force in a province, with the approval of the Minister responsible for policing in the province; or

(b) with the approval of the Minister after consultation by the Minister with the Secretary of State for External Affairs, enter into an arrangement or otherwise cooperate with the government of a foreign state or an institution thereof or an international organization of states or an institution thereof.

(2) Where a written arrangement is entered into pursuant to subsection (1) or subsection 13(2) or (3), a copy thereof shall be given forthwith to the Review Committee.

Section 19

19. (1) Information obtained in the performance of the duties and functions of the Service under this Act shall not be disclosed by the Service except in accordance with this section.

(2) The Service may disclose information referred to in subsection (1) for the purposes of the performance of its duties and functions under this Act or the administration or enforcement of this Act or as required by any other law and may also disclose such information,

(a) where the information may be used in the investigation or prosecution of an alleged contravention of any law of Canada or a province, to a peace officer having jurisdiction to investigate the alleged contravention and to the Attorney General of Canada and the Attorney General of the province in which proceedings in respect of the alleged contravention may be taken;
(b) where the information relates to the conduct of the international affairs of Canada, to the Secretary of State for External Affairs or a person designated by the Secretary of State for External Affairs for the purpose;
(c) where the information is relevant to the defence of Canada, to the Minister of National Defence or a person designated by the Minister of National Defence for the purpose; or
(d) where, in the opinion of the Minister, disclosure of the information to any minister of the Crown or person in the public service of Canada is essential in the public interest and that interest clearly outweighs any invasion of privacy that could result from the disclosure, to that minister or person.

(3) The Director shall, as soon as practicable after a disclosure referred to in paragraph (2)(d) is made, submit a report to the Review Committee with respect to the disclosure.

II. SELECTED SECTIONS OF THE *OFFICIAL SECRETS ACT* *R.S.C. 1985, c. O-3*

Section 2

2. (1) In this Act,
"Attorney General" means the Attorney General of Canada;
"document" includes part of a document;
"model" includes design, pattern and specimen;
"munitions of war" means arms, ammunition, implements or munitions of war, military stores or any articles deemed capable of being converted thereinto or made useful in the production thereof;
"offence under this Act" includes any act, omission or other thing that is punishable under this Act;
"office under Her Majesty" includes any office or employment in or under any department or branch of the government of Canada or of any province, and any office or employment in, on or under any board, commission, corporation or other body that is an agent of Her Majesty in right of Canada or any province;
"prohibited place" means

(a) any work of defence belonging to or occupied or used by or on behalf of Her Majesty, including arsenals, armed forces establishments or stations, factories, dockyards, mines, minefields, camps, ships, aircraft, telegraph, telephone, wireless or signal stations or offices, and places used for the purpose of building, repairing, making or storing any munitions of war or any sketches, plans, models or documents relating thereto, or for the purpose of getting any metals, oil or minerals of use in time of war,
(b) any place not belonging to Her Majesty where any munitions of war or any sketches, plans, models or documents relating thereto are being made, repaired, obtained or stored under contract with, or with any person on behalf of, Her Majesty or otherwise on behalf of Her Majesty, and

(c) any place that is for the time being declared by order of the Governor in Council to be a prohibited place on the ground that information with respect thereto or damage thereto would be useful to a foreign power;

"senior police officer" means any officer of the Royal Canadian Mounted Police not below the rank of inspector, any officer of any provincial police force of a like or superior rank, the chief constable of any city or town with a population of not less than ten thousand or any person on whom the powers of a senior police officer are for the purposes of this Act conferred by the Governor in Council; "sketch" includes any mode of representing any place or thing.

(2) In this Act, any reference to Her Majesty means Her Majesty in right of Canada or any province.

(3) In this Act,

(a) expressions referring to communicating or receiving include any communicating or receiving, whether in whole or in part, and whether the sketch, plan, model, article, note, document or information itself or the substance, effect or description thereof only is communicated or received;

(b) expressions referring to obtaining or retaining any sketch, plan, model, article, note or document include the copying of, or causing to be copied, the whole or any part of any sketch, plan, model, article, note or document; and

(c) expressions referring to the communication of any sketch, plan, model, article, note or document include the transfer or transmission of the sketch, plan, model, article, note or document.

Section 3

3. (1) Every person is guilty of an offence under this Act who, for any purpose prejudicial to the safety or interests of the State,

(a) approaches, inspects, passes over, is in the neighbourhood of or enters any prohibited place;

(b) makes any sketch, plan, model or note that is calculated to be or might be or is intended to be directly or indirectly useful to a foreign power; or

(c) obtains, collects, records or publishes, or communicates to any other person, any secret official code word, password, sketch, plan, model, article, note, document or information that is calculated to be or might be or is intended to be directly or indirectly useful to a foreign power.

(2) On a prosecution under this section, it is not necessary to show that the accused person was guilty of any particular act tending to show a purpose prejudicial to the safety or interests of the State, and, notwithstanding that no such act is proved against that person, he may be convicted if, from the circumstances of the case, his conduct or his known character as proved, it appears that his purpose was a purpose prejudicial to the safety or interests of the State.

(3) If any sketch, plan, model, article, note, document or information relating to or used in any prohibited place, or anything in such a place, or any secret official code word or password is made, obtained, collected, recorded, published or communicated by any person other than a person acting under lawful authority, it shall be deemed to have been made, obtained, collected, recorded, published or communicated for a purpose prejudicial to the safety or interests of the State unless the contrary is proved.

(4) In any proceedings against a person for an offence under this section, the fact that that person has been in communication with, or attempted to communicate with, an agent of a foreign power, whether within or outside Canada, is evidence that that person has, for a purpose prejudicial to the safety or interests of the State, obtained or attempted to obtain information that is calculated to be or might be or is intended to be directly or indirectly useful to a foreign power.

(5) For the purpose of this section, but without prejudice to the generality of subsection (4),

(a) a person shall, unless he proves the contrary, be deemed to have been in communication with an agent of a foreign power if
(i) he has, either within or outside Canada, visited the address of an agent of a foreign power or consorted or associated with an agent of a foreign power; or

(ii) either within or outside Canada, the name or address of, or any other information regarding, an agent of a foreign power has been found in his possession, has been supplied by him to any other person or has been obtained by him from any other person;

(b) "an agent of a foreign power" includes any person who is or has been or is suspected on reasonable grounds of being or having been employed by a foreign power, either directly or indirectly, for the purpose of committing an act, either within or outside Canada, prejudicial to the safety or interests of the State, or who has or is suspected on reasonable grounds of having, either within or outside Canada, committed, or attempted to commit, such an act in the interests of a foreign power; and

(c) any address, whether within or outside Canada, reasonably suspected of being an address used for the receipt of communications intended for an agent of a foreign power, or any address at which such an agent resides, to which he resorts for the purpose of giving or receiving communications or at which he carries on any business shall be deemed to be the address of an agent of a foreign power, and communications addressed to that address to be communications with such an agent.

Section 4

4. (1) Every person is guilty of an offence under this Act who, having in his possession or control any secret official code word, password, sketch, plan, model, article, note, document or information that relates to or is used in a prohibited place or anything in a prohibited place, or that has been made or obtained in contravention of this Act, or that has been entrusted in confidence to him by any person holding office under Her Majesty, or that he has obtained or to which he has had access while subject to the Code of Service Discipline within the meaning of the National Defence Act or owing to his position as a person who holds or has held office under Her Majesty, or as a person who holds or has held a contract made on behalf of Her Majesty, or a contract the performance of which in whole or in part is carried out in a prohibited place, or as a person who is or has been employed under a person who holds or has held such an office or contract,

(a) communicates the code word, password, sketch, plan, model, article, note, document or information to any person, other than a person to whom he is authorized to communicate with, or a person to whom it is in the interest of the State his duty to communicate it;
(b) uses the information in his possession for the benefit of any foreign power or in any other manner prejudicial to the safety or interests of the State;
(c) retains the sketch, plan, model, article, note, or document in his possession or control when he has no right to retain it or when it is contrary to his duty to retain it or fails to comply with all directions issued by lawful authority with regard to the return or disposal thereof; or
(d) fails to take reasonable care of, or so conducts himself as to endanger the safety of, the secret official code word, password, sketch, plan, model, article, note, document or information.

(2) Every person is guilty of an offence under this Act who, having in his possession or control any sketch, plan, model, article, note, document or information that relates to munitions of war, communicates it, directly or indirectly, to any foreign power, or in any other manner prejudicial to the safety or interests of the State.
(3) Every person who receives any secret official code word, password, sketch, plan, model, article, note, document or information, knowing, or having reasonable ground to believe, at the time he receives it, that the code word, password, sketch, plan, model, article, note, document or information is communicated to him in contravention of this Act, is guilty of an offence under this Act, unless he proves that the communication to him of the code word, password, sketch, plan, model, article, note, document or information was contrary to his desire.

(4) Every person is guilty of an offence under this Act who

(a) retains for any purpose prejudicial to the safety or interests of the State any official document, whether or not completed or issued for use, when he has no right to retain it, or when it is contrary to his duty to retain it, or fails to comply with any directions issued by any Government department or any person authorized by any Government department with regard to the return or disposal thereof; or

(b) allows any other person to have possession of any official document issued for his use alone, or communicates any secret official code word or password so issued, or, without lawful authority or excuse, has in his possession any official document or secret official code word or password issued for the use of a person other than himself, or on obtaining possession of any official document by finding or otherwise, neglects or fails to restore it to the person or authority by whom or for whose use it was issued, or to a police constable.

NOTES

1. In arguing in favour of support for the GATT, President Clinton stated that "national security as defined in economic terms" was so important that it should be above partisan politics in the same way as "national security defined in military terms." *Globe and Mail*, 17 November 1994, B-2.

2. Samuel Porteous, "Economic Espionage (II)," *Commentary*, No. 46 (1994), 2. He defines "Economic Intelligence" as "policy or commercially relevant economic information, including technological data, financial, proprietary, commercial and government information, the acquisition of which by foreign interests could, either directly or indirectly, assist the relative productivity or competitive positions of the economy of the collecting organization's country." This definition includes information gathered by foreign agents relating to private activities referred to here as "commercial intelligence."

3. A statutory mandate was recommended in *The Canadian Intelligence Community: Control and Accountability, the Report of the Auditor General to the House of Commons, Chapter 27* (Ottawa: Minister of Public Works and Government Services Canada, 1997) at 27-15, 27-18, 27-27. A similar recommendation was made in the *Annual Report of the Privacy Commissioner, 1995-96* (Ottawa: Canada Communications Group, 1996). See endnotes 18-20 and accompanying text.

4. D.C. McDonald, "Freedom and Security Under the Law" (Ottawa: Supply and Services Canada, 2d report, 1981), 423, 428-29, 442.

5. Canadian Security Intelligence Service Act, R.S.C. 1985, c. C-23.

6. *Report of the Auditor General*, 1997; L. Lustgarten and I. Leigh, *In From the Cold: National Security and Parliamentary Democracy* (Oxford: Clarendon Press, 1994), 422-33, 458-67. Lustgarten and Leigh describe the mechanisms for executive review as "comprehensive and complex," 422. See also Solicitor General, *On Course: National Security for the 1990s. The Government's Response to the Report of*

the House of Commons Special Committee on the Review of the Canadian Security Intelligence Security Act and the Security Offenses Act (Ottawa: Supply and Services Canada, 1991), 7-26; *In Flux But Not in Crisis: A Report of the House of Commons Special Committee on the Review of the Canadian Security Intelligence Service Act and the Security Offences Act* (Ottawa: Queen's Printer, 1990), 137-61.

7. All such directions must be in writing and copies forwarded to the Security and Intelligence Review Committee (SIRC) (CSIS Act, ss. 6(2) and 38(2)). Also the Deputy Minister in the Department of the Solicitor General must be consulted by the Director of CSIS on general policy matters (CSIS Act, s. 7(1)).

8. G. Osbaldeston, *People and Process in Transition: Report to the Solicitor General by the Independent Advisory Team on the Canadian Security Intelligence Service* (Ottawa: Supply and Services Canada, 1987), 6, 7, 28. See also *In Flux*, 92-96.

9. CSIS Act s. 22(1) and (2). The Inspector General has a statutory right of access to all CSIS material (other than cabinet documents) for the purpose of fulfilling these functions (CSIS Act s. 31). In the Inspector General's annual assessment released in 1995, the then Inspector General was critical of the level of disclosure by CSIS in its 1992-93 *Annual Report* ("CSIS Report Left Out Information, Watchdog Says," *Globe and Mail*, 27 March 1995, A-3). Regardless of the merits of the Inspector General's concerns, the fact that the 1995 report is addressing the 1992-93 report suggests that his review took place too long after the fact to provide meaningful short-term accountability.

10. CSIS Act s. 38(a).

11. *Ibid.*, s. 40.

12. SIRC has a statutory right to access to information under the control of CSIS and the Inspector General (CSIS Act s. 39(2)).

13. Lustgarten and Leigh, *In From the Cold*, 460; M. Rankin, "The Security Intelligence Review Committee: Reconciling National Security with Procedural Fairness," *Canadian Journal of Administrative Law and Practice* 3 (1990), 173; P. Gill, "Symbolic or Real? The Impact of SIRC, 1984-88," *International and National Security* 4 (1989), 550; Osbaldeston, *People and Process*, 9; *In Flux*, 10.

14. In its 1995-96 Annual Report, SIRC stated that as of March 31, 1996 it had received 13 referrals to the Attorney General, none of which had resulted in prosecutions. In two cases, CSIS dismissed employees who were involved. SIRC *Annual Report for 1995-96* (Ottawa: Minister of Supply and Services, 1995), 39-40.

15. CSIS Act s. 21; Solicitor General, *On Course*, 62. The government concluded that the warrant system was working well.

16. Lustgarten and Leigh, *In From the Cold*, 6, 411. The authors suggest that in addition to the statutory scheme this attitude is due also to the bureaucratic nature of security services. The authors point out that the mandate also serves

THE LEGAL REGIME 181

an important function for security services: it may be used as a "shield" against political pressure to act improperly. See also McDonald, *Freedom and Security*, 513; Report of the Special Committee of the Senate on the Canadian Security Intelligence Service, *A Delicate Balance: A Security Intelligence Service in a Democratic Society* (Ottawa: Supply and Services Canada, 1983 [hereafter the "Senate Report"]), 12.

17. See for example, SIRC *Annual Report for 1988-89* (Ottawa: Supply and Services Canada, 1989), 4; *In Flux*, 199. Since 1991, CSIS and SIRC's operations have been reviewed by the National Security Sub-committee of the Standing Committee on Justice and Legal Affairs.

18. In relation to the disclosures in Michael Frost's book, *Spyworld* (Toronto: Doubleday, 1994), Prime Minister Chrétien and Defence Minister Collenette stated that CSE had not broken any law ("Is Spy Agency's Mission Changing?" *Globe and Mail*, 12 November 1994, A-5). The view of the government expressed in Solicitor General, *On Course*, 54-55, is also that CSE is not above the law. Similarly, in response to allegations by a former CSE employee regarding spying by CSE on embassies of friendly states in Canada and outside, Mr. Chrétien said, "everybody has to respect the law of the land. If the law of the land has been broken, somebody will have to pay the price for it." See "Spies Who Break Law Will Pay, PM Warns," *Globe and Mail*, 15 November 1995, A-4; "Spying on Allies Common Practice, Experts Report," *Globe and Mail*, 14 November 1995, A-2.

19. This appointment was made under Part II of the *Inquiries Act*, R.S.C. 1985, c. I-II, for a term of three years. The Commissioner may also make reports of a classified nature to the Minister of Defence at any time.

20. *Annual Report of the Communications Security Establishment Commissioner, 1996-1997* (Ottawa: Minister of Public Works and Government Services Canada, 1997), 10.

21. Auditor General, *Canadian Intelligence Community*, 27-10.

22. For the purpose of offenses under the Official Secrets Act (R.S.C. 1985, c. 0-3, as amended [hereafter the "Official Secrets Act"]), ss. 13 and 14 of that act deem certain acts to be in Canada.

23. *Ibid*, s. 7.

24. *In Flux*, 152-53.

25. *Ibid*.

26. CSIS Act s. 12. See appendix for the complete text of s. 12.

27. M.S. Friedland began his research report to the McDonald Commission on RCMP activities with the following "confession": "I do not know what national security

means. But then neither does the government." "National Security: The Legal Dimensions," (1979), 1.

28. S. 1(3). The full text of the mandate is "safeguarding the economic well-being of the nation against threats posed by the actions or intentions of those outside the British Isles." This section does not define national security to include national economic well-being, but refers to it separately as part of the statutory mandate. Samuel Porteous states in this volume that the failure to include "economic well-being" as a component of national security suggests a legislative intention not to have "economic well-being" limited to matters of national security. The British have put Government Communications Headquarters (GCHQ), the British equivalent to CSE, on a statutory footing (Intelligence Services Act, 1994 (U.K., 1994, c. 13)). In this Act, the mandate of GCHQ and the Secret Intelligence Service includes "the interests of the economic well-being of the United Kingdom" (s. 1(2) (b)).

29. Lustgarten and Leigh, *In From the Cold*, 390; R. Atkey, "Reconciling Freedom of Expression and National Security," *University of Toronto Law Journal* 41 (1991), 38, 45-46.

30. Solicitor General, *On Course*, 37.

31. R.S.C. 1985, c. C-46, as amended (hereafter "Criminal Code").

32. Official Secrets Act, s. 3.

33. Criminal Code, s. 52. The McDonald Commission suggested that this definition is the appropriate one for determining the mandate of a security service (McDonald, "Freedom and Security," 432).

34. See endnote 94.

35. "Prohibited place" is defined in s. 2 of the Official Secrets Act. See appendix for the full text of s. 2.

36. McDonald, "Freedom and Security," 431.

37. *Ibid.*

38. See, for example, the Submission of the Canadian Bar Association to the Senate Committee, September 12, 1983, 2; Submission of the Hon. B.R.D. Smith, Q.C., Attorney-General of British Columbia, to the Senate Committee, September 21, 1983, 13; Remarks of Senator Firth, Proceedings of the Special Committee of the Senate on the Canadian Security Intelligence Service, September 21, 1983, Issue No. 10, 10:45. New statutory definitions of espionage and sabotage were recommended in *In Flux*, 17-18. The Special Committee suggested that such definitions should specifically clarify whether "industrial and technological espionage also fall within the Service's security intelligence mandate," and whether activities against all governments were caught.

39. Porteous, "Economic Espionage (II)," 2. SIRC has described espionage as including theft of economic and technical secrets, SIRC *Annual Report for 1994-95* (Ottawa: Minister of Supply and Services Canada, 1995), 21.
40. McDonald, "Freedom and Security," 430.
41. This will be discussed in endnotes 160-67 and accompanying text.
42. The following are some examples of such activities:

    (a) participation in planning espionage or sabotage; (b) contributing financial support to acts of espionage or sabotage; (c) knowingly providing facilities, transportation, or equipment for use by those involved in acts of espionage or sabotage; (d) knowingly providing access to premises to persons intending acts of espionage or sabotage; and (e) encouraging others to become involved in acts of espionage or sabotage.
43. There was considerable concern expressed before the Senate Committee regarding the breadth of the mandate in this regard (see, for example, the submissions of the Canadian Bar Association to the Senate Committee, September 12, 1983, 2). The Special Committee of the House of Commons suggested that the words were so broad as to be subject to challenge under the Charter of Rights and Fundamental Freedoms (*In Flux*, 17). The phrase "directed toward" is used throughout the Cabinet Directive of March 27, 1975, on the "Role, Tasks and Methods of the RCMP Security Service," set out in McDonald, "Freedom and Security," 430.
44. The Special Committee of the House of Commons recommended that this phrase be defined in the Act (*In Flux*, 18-19).
45. (1994) 32 I. L. M. 670.
46. (1994) 33 I. L. M. 81.
47. The 1989 Ministerial Direction identified "Economic Security" as a "national interest area" in the following terms: "the conditions necessary to sustain a competitive international position, provide productive employment, and contain inflation." (*In Flux*, 19)
48. The Special Committee of the House of Commons expressed the view that it was not the job of CSIS to protect private sector interests, and doubted whether doing so was within the Service's mandate (*Ibid.*, 95-96).
49. "Senate Report," 12-13.
50. One more point may be made. "Detrimental to the interests of Canada" arguably means prejudicial to the policies and policy objectives of the nation, determined by the Canadian government. This interpretation would be consistent with the decision in *Chandler* v. *D.P.P.* [1964], A.C. 763, in which the House of Lords considered the meaning of "interests of the state" for the purposes of s. 1 of the English Official Secrets Act, 1911.

51. That the section is not limited to actions involving foreign states is apparent from the failure to use this term, which is defined in s. 2 of the CSIS Act.

52. Directive, *supra* note 47. This point was made in *SIRC Annual Report for 1988-89*, 57.

53. *In Flux*, 20. The Special Committee's position was supported by the Canadian Bar Association and SIRC.

54. *R. v. Giguère* (1983), 8 C.C.C. (3d) 1 (S.C.C.).

55. *Ibid.* The Special Committee of the House of Commons recommended that the Act should be amended to limit the mandate to activities which "directly" relate to Canada (*In Flux*, 21).

56. *Ibid.*

57. See the *Concise Oxford English Dictionary*.

58. *Giffels & Vallet* v. *The King*, [1952] 1 D.L.R. 620 at 630 (Ont. H.C.J.); aff'd [1952] 2 D.L.R. 720 (C.A.).

59. Remarks of the Hon. R.R. McMutry, Attorney General of Ontario, to the Senate Committee on the Canadian Security Intelligence Service, August 23, 1983, 13. Such threats might include threats of economic competition, economic retaliation, or other economic sanctions.

60. Interpretation Act, R.S.C. 1985, c. I-21, s. 28.

61. The House of Commons Special Committee recommended that the mandate should be limited to "serious" threats (*In Flux*, 21).

62. Such a role is specifically contemplated in the "Ministerial Direction Defining Threats to the Security of Canada" reproduced in the *SIRC Annual Report for 1991-92* (Ottawa: Supply and Services, 1992), as Annex E at 74.

63. The issue of whether the CSIS mandate extends to vulnerability assessments was raised in the press in 1994. "CSIS Watchdog Finds Possible New Breach: Secrets May Have Been Compromised in Fight Against Corporate Espionage," *Globe and Mail*, 12 December 1994, A-4. In this context the CSIS awareness program may be considered a response to a generally identified threat. Whether it otherwise fits within the Service's mandate under section 12, however, is not obvious, since that section only mandates CSIS to "collect ... and analyze and retain information and, in relation thereto, shall report to and advise the government of Canada."

64. Such activities were contemplated by the McDonald Commission. See "Freedom and Security," 628.

65. Atkey, "Reconciling Freedom"; Lustgarten and Leigh, *In From the Cold*, 15-16; Solicitor General, *On Course*, 6. McDonald, "Freedom and Security," 408-10.

66. Lustgarten and Leigh, *In From the Cold*, 15-16.

67. Both SIRC and the Inspector General must review CSIS operations to ensure that they are not "unnecessary or unreasonable" (CSIS Act ss. 22, 40). In a chapter entitled "Security and Democracy: Interests Requiring Protection and Threats to Those Interests," the McDonald Commission makes no reference to economic security ("Freedom and Security," 39-47). The Commission does, however, refer to economic interests as being appropriate objects of a security service's concern (414-15, 643). The Commission also specifically refers to the need for a security service to balance the intrusiveness of its methods with the seriousness of the threat. See also Osbaldeston, *People and Process*, 23-25.

68. As evidence of this Lustgarten and Leigh, *In From the Cold*, cite a remark that President Clinton's appointee as Director of the CIA made during his confirmation hearings, indicating that the CIA should treat economic espionage as second only to nuclear proliferation as the "hottest topic he faced," 29.

69. "CSIS Assessment of Technology Transfer Between 1980 and 1990" (CSIS Study 91/58), cited in CSIS *Public Report for 1992* (Supply and Services Canada: Ottawa, 1993) and SIRC *Annual Report for 1991-92*, 34.

70. Solicitor General, *Annual Report 1991-92*, 58; SIRC *Annual Report 1988-89*, 37-40. This is also the view of the government (see Solicitor General, *On Course*, 51).

71. CSIS *Public Report for 1993* (Supply and Services Canada: Ottawa, 1994), 8. Economic Security has been included in the Solicitor General's National Requirements Directive since at least 1989 (see SIRC *Annual Report for 1988-89*, 22).

72. *Ibid.* Since at least 1992, CSIS has had a technology transfer unit analyzing technology transfer issues and an awareness program which is designed to promote liaisons between CSIS and private sector high technology and industrial interests in Canada (CSIS *Public Report for 1992*, 6).

73. This is also consistent with Potter's view, as expressed in this study.

74. The House of Commons Special Committee describes the s. 16 mandate as a "secondary" one (*In Flux*, 11).

75. CSIS Act s. 16(1).

76. It is odd that this list of subjects of foreign intelligence-gathering does not extend to non-corporate organizations, though perhaps this gap may be avoided in practice by investigating individuals connected with such organizations.

77. The personal written request of the Minister of National Defence or the Secretary of State for External Affairs and the personal written consent of the Solicitor General is required under s. 16(3) of the CSIS Act. The Senate Committee identified the consent of the Solicitor General as an important safeguard (Senate Report, 19).

78. It is acknowledged that the concept of threat itself is somewhat elastic. One could argue that obtaining information on the positions of other nations at trade talks was necessary because a potential threat to Canada's interests might arise from an agreement unfavourable to Canada.

79. The limited nature of CSIS's foreign intelligence role is emphasized by the government in Solicitor General, *On Course*, 55-56. The various agencies involved in the gathering of foreign intelligence, including CSE, are described at 51-57. See *In Flux*, 39; also Evan Potter's chapter. All foreign intelligence activities of CSIS must be reported separately to SIRC (CSIS Act s. 38(a)(v)). A study conducted by SIRC in 1988-89 determined that the s. 16 mandate is "too restrictive," and that as a result CSIS was not being used effectively in this area. SIRC recommended that the words "within Canada" be deleted (*SIRC Annual Report 1988-89*, 13).

80. For a historical description of the international information-sharing engaged in by the RCMP Security Service see McDonald, "Freedom and Security," 632-38. S. 17 of the CSIS Act authorizes the Service to enter into cooperative arrangements with foreign governments and agencies and, pursuant to s. 38 (a)(iii), SIRC has an obligation to review these arrangements and monitor the provision of information and intelligence pursuant to them.

81. CSE Mission Statement.

82. *SIRC Annual Report for 1993-94* (Ottawa: Supply and Services Canada, 1994), 35.

83. This mandate is sometimes referred to as Information Technology Security or ITS. This discussion of what CSE does is based largely on the *Annual Report of the Communications Security Establishment Commissioner* (Office of the Communications Establishment Commissioner, 1997). For updated information on the CSE (including estimates of its budget), see "The Communications Security Establishment: An Unofficial Look Inside Canada's Signals Intelligence Agency" at HYPERLINK http://watserv1.uwaterloo.ca/~brobinso/cse.html.

84. Frost, *Spyworld*, 224-27.

85. "Spies who break law will pay, PM warns; Japan, Mexico, South Korea ask for clarification on charges," *Globe and Mail*, 15 November 1995, A-4.

86. "Spying on allies, common practice experts report; just too valuable to give up, historian says," *Globe and Mail*, 14 November 1995, A-2.

87. McDonald, "Freedom and Security," 413-26.

88. Royal Canadian Mounted Police Act, R.S.C. 1985, c. R-10. This is part of the general mandate of the RCMP to "enforce laws, prevent crime, maintain peace, order and security" (s. 18). See also Solicitor General, *On Course*, 45.

89. *Ibid.*, 45-46.

90. R.S.C. 1985, c. S-7.

91. Ss. 2 and 6. In performing its law enforcement functions, the RCMP is subject to the fairly rigorous provisions of the Criminal Code governing the issuance of warrants, authorizations for the interception of communications, and other procedural matters in relation to offences under the Criminal Code or any other federal statute. The scheme is intended to balance the needs of law enforcement agencies like the RCMP with the privacy interests of persons under investigation. The RCMP is not subject to oversight by the Inspector General or SIRC or any equivalent body. Such oversight was recommended by SIRC in its *Annual Report for 1985-86* (Ottawa: Supply and Services Canada, 1986), 7, and by the House of Commons Special Committee in Solicitor General, *In Flux*, 153, 185.

92. *Ibid.*, 101-03.

93. CSIS also provides security assessments in support of the government's security clearance program (CSIS Act s. 13) and provides information and advice in support of government citizenship and immigration programs (s. 14).

94. It must be acknowledged that the RCMP has an important role regarding threats in connection with its discrete task of safeguarding certain persons and property.

95. See generally Osbaldeston, *People and Process*, 5. The relationship between the RCMP and CSIS is governed by a Memorandum of Understanding (MOU) that outlines the security responsibilities of CSIS and the RCMP and provides the basis for cooperation between CSIS and the RCMP. The MOU confirms that CSIS is responsible for investigating suspected threats to the security of Canada while the RCMP is charged with preventing security offenses and enforcing the law. It also deals with the arrangements for the exchange of information between CSIS and the RCMP. The MOU was agreed to in 1989 and has been revised several times since then. In 1993 the Inspector General reported on the MOU, concluding that it had improved the exchange of information and intelligence between the two agencies. *SIRC Annual Report for 1993-94*, 54. See Solicitor General, *On Course*, 47-48, and endnotes 172-81 and accompanying text on the regulation of information disclosure by CSIS.

96. Osbaldeston, *People and Process*, 18. In the past CSIS has been criticized for focusing too much on operational intelligence at the expense of strategic intelligence.

97. During its first few years of existence CSIS was criticized for behaving too much like a law enforcement agency (*Ibid.*, 5; *SIRC Annual Report for 1986-87*, 13). The regulation of CSIS investigative activities under the CSIS Act is stringent, though less comprehensive than the regulation under the Criminal Code, and the kinds of investigative techniques available are more intrusive (CSIS Act s. 21). The administrative practices in CSIS flesh out this regulatory scheme. Nevertheless,

how CSIS conducts its operations depends substantially more on judgment, and there is a correspondingly greater need for accountability. See Solicitor General, *On Course*, 59-66. Both the Special Committee on the Review of the Canadian Security Intelligence Service Act and the Security Offenses Act, the government in *Ibid.*, 62 and SIRC have concluded that the warrant process is working well. See Solicitor General, *In Flux*, 109-32. The scheme for issuing warrants survived a challenge under the Charter of Human Rights and Fundamental Freedoms (*Re Canadian Civil Liberties Association and Attorney General of Canada* [1992] 91 D.L.R. (4th) 38 (Gen Div.); *R. v. Atwal* [1989], 79 N.R. 90 (F.C.A.)).

98. S. 19(2)(a). See appendix for a full text of s. 19. See also the discussion under the heading "Disclosure," endnotes 172-81 and accompanying text.

99. *In Flux*, 104.

100. The reluctance of security agency personnel to give evidence in support of prosecutions under the Official Secrets Act was described in V. Goglek, "Secret Trials: A Look Behind Closed Doors" (119) 4 *National* 11 (hereafter "Secret Trials"), 13-18.

101. (1991) 68 C.C.C. (3d) 1.

102. Even where intelligence is supplied it may be difficult to turn it into usable criminal evidence. In some circumstances there may be an issue regarding whether intelligence obtained directly from CSIS sources can be used successfully in court without a challenge under the Canadian Charter of Rights and Fundamental Freedoms.

103. For a brief overview of the Canadian legal regime in relation to intellectual property see J.C. Castel, A.L.C. de Mestral, and W.C. Graham, *The Canadian Law and Practice of International Trade with Particular Emphasis on the Export and Import of Goods and Services* 2/e (Toronto: Edmond Montgomery, 1997), 186-89.

104. *R. v. Stewart,* [1988] 1 S.C.R. 963. For a compelling argument in favour of property rights in information see A.S. Weinrib, "Information and Property," *University of Toronto Law Journal* 38 (1988), 117.

105. Copyright Act, R.S.C. 1985, c. C-46, s. 3 (hereafter "Copyright Act").

106. G. Hammond, "The Legal Protection of Ideas," *Osgoode Hall Law Journal* 29 (1991), 93, 94-106.

107. There is some contrary Canadian authority on this point. In B.C. *Jockey Club* v. *Standen* (1985), 22 D.L.R. (4th) 467, the British Columbia Court of Appeal held that copyright could exist in the "information" and "substantive content" of a work where the author had expended a significant amount of work assembling the information. Commentators have been critical of this aspect of the decision.

108. Patent Act, R.S.C. 1985, c. P-4, as amended by S.C. 1993, c. 44, s. 192, s. 27(3).

109. Patent Act, s. 2. In order to obtain a patent the subject matter also must fit within a recognized category (an art, process, machine, manufacture or composition of matter) (ss. 2, 28.3 and 33).

110. David Vaver has suggested that current patent practice is to minimize what is disclosed in a patent application. See "Intellectual Property Today: Of Myths and Paradoxes," *Canadian Bar Review* 69 (1990), 98, 123.

111. S.C. 1990, c. 37.

112. *Ibid.*, s. 3(3).

113. *Ibid.*, s. 6(2).

114. *Integrated Circuit Topography Regulations*, SOR/93-212, ss. 13-15. I will not deal with trademarks, which have little relevance to the discussion of economic security, though they may have significant economic value, or plant breeders' rights, which have a narrow focus.

115. Price Waterhouse, *Survey of Intellectual Property Rights in Canada: Final Report* (Ottawa: Price Waterhouse, 1989).

116. Under the Copyright Act, R.S.C. 1985, c. C-46, ss. 35-38, 42-43, criminal offenses are punishable by fines up to $1 million or imprisonment for up to five years. These offenses include knowing infringement of a copyright by making or offering infringing copies for sale or lease, distributing such copies for the purpose of trade, or importing them for sale or to exhibit them at a trade exhibit. See generally G. Henderson, *Intellectual Property: Litigation, Legislation and Education: A Study of the Canadian Intellectual Property and Litigation System* (Ottawa: Consumer and Corporate Affairs, 1991).

117. M. Goudreau, "Protecting Ideas and Information in Common Law, Canada and Quebec," 8 I.P.J. (1994), 189, 216.

118. See the decision of the Supreme Court of Canada in *Lac Minerals Ltd.* v. *International Corona Resources Ltd.*, [1989] 2 S.C.R. 574.

119. *Ibid.*, 192-201. Goudreau, "Protecting Ideas," 204-16, discusses the similar law regarding confidential information in Quebec. Trade secrets, as well as statutory intellectual property rights, may have been what CSIS was referring to when it mentioned the need to protect information and data of a "propriety nature" in its *Public Report for 1993*, at 6. See endnote 72 and accompanying text.

120. The Institute of Law Research and Reform, *Trade Secrets* (Edmonton: Institute of Law Research and Reform, 1986), 67. Hereafter *Trade Secrets*.

121. See Goudreau, "Protecting Ideas," 202-04, 215-16.

122. The Institute of Law Research and Reform proposed criminal enforcement of trade secrets in *Trade Secrets*, 218-51.

123. For example, breaking and entering (Criminal Code ss. 348, 350), being unlawfully in a dwelling house (s. 349), possession of house-breaking instruments (s. 352). Also, offenses may be committed in connection with break-ins, firearms offenses (Part III) or offenses related to the use of explosives (s. 81).

124. For example, theft (Criminal Code, s. 322); possession of property obtained by crime (s. 354), theft of mail (s. 356).

125. There may be a small technical problem with relying on the theft of paper or media. It may be difficult to establish that the paper or media, independent of the information recorded on it, is worth more than $1,000, which is the threshold for punishment exceeding two years imprisonment (Criminal Code ss. 322, 334). An interesting example of this problem arose in *R. v. Appleby* (1990), 78 C.R. (3d) 282 (Prov. Ct. J.). Norman Belisle was charged with stealing "Budget in Brief," that disclosed critical details of the soon-to-be-released federal budget. In striking out the charge the court relied, in part, on the fact that the only thing which could have been stolen was the paper on which the document was printed, worth less than $.01.

126. Criminal Code ss. 184 and 184.5. "Electromagnetic, acoustic, mechanical or other device," "private communication," and "radio-based telephone communication" are defined in s. 183.

127. Criminal Code ss. 191, 193 and 193.1.

128. Criminal Code ss. 342.1 and 430.

129. Criminal Code s. 426

130. Criminal Code s. 121.

131. Criminal Code s. 346.

132. See endnotes 31-43 and accompanying text.

133. Criminal Code s. 46. Actions outside of Canada by Canadians can be treason (s. 46(3)).

134. See endnote 32 and accompanying text.

135. Criminal Code s. 52.

136. See endnote 32 and accompanying text.

137. In the view of the McDonald Commission, the language of the Official Secrets Act is too broad and the reference to "interests" should be deleted (D.C. McDonald, Security and Information [1st Report][1979][hereafter "Security and Information"], 17). Compare the treason provision in the Criminal Code set out above, endnote 34 and accompanying text.

138. Ss. 2 and 3.

139. McDonald "Security and Information," 13-14. Some commentators question whether this is the correct view.

140. *R. v. Toronto Sun Publishing* (1979), 24 O.R. (2d) 621 (Prov. Ct. Crim. Div.), 631-2.

141. *Ibid.*, 22-23. See also Rankin, "Reconciling National Security"; Goglek, "Secret Trials," 19.

142. There have been only six prosecutions in the past 30 years. Two examples of prosecutions are *R. v. Ratkai* [1989] N.J. No. 334 (T.D.) and *R. v. Toronto Sun Publishing* (1979), 24 O.R. (2d) 631 (Prov. Ct. J.). See McDonald, "Security and Information," 4-8.

143. See Solicitor General, *Annual Report for 1991-92* (Ottawa: Supply and Services Canada, 1993), 31.

144. *Libman v. The Queen*, [1985] 2 S.C.R. 178, 213. For a description and analysis of this case and the law in this area see E.M. Morgan, "Criminal Process, International Law, and Extraterritorial Crime," *University of Toronto Law Journal* 38 (1988), 245, 268-75.

145. These examples and the English cases from which they derive are found in *Ibid.*, 271.

146. For example, the Mutual Legal Assistance in Legal Matters Act, R.S.C. 1985, c. M-30 (4th Supp.).

147. S.C. 1991, c. 41. The Act implements the Vienna Convention on Diplomatic Relations, the Vienna Convention on Consular Relations and the Convention on the Privileges and Immunities of the United Nations (Schedules I, II, and III respectively).

148. Art. 41(1), Vienna Convention on Consular Relations. This immunity extends to civil liability as well.

149. S. 2. For the purposes of the criminal offense of theft this length of imprisonment may only be imposed if the value of what is stolen exceeds $1000. This may create a problem if the offense is only the theft of media on which information is recorded. See endnote 125 and accompanying text.

150. Art. 43(1), Vienna Convention on Consular Relations. Consuls, although they represent their state, fulfill a different role from diplomats. Instead of being concerned with political relations between two states, foreign consuls in Canada are concerned with administrative matters, such as issuing visas and promoting their state's commercial, economic, scientific, and cultural relations with Canada. Consular activities are defined in Art. 5.

151. Art. 22, Vienna Convention on Diplomatic Relations.

152. Art. 27, Vienna Convention on Diplomatic Relations; Art. 35, Vienna Convention on Consular Relations.

153. Art. 41, Vienna Convention on Diplomatic Relations; Art. 55, Vienna Convention on Consular Relations.

154. See *American Journal of International Law*, 80 (1986), 135.

155. When certain Libyans were expelled from Britain, their diplomatic bag was not searched. R. Higgins, "The Abuse of Diplomatic Privileges and Immunities: Recent United Kingdom Experience," *American Journal of International Law* 79 (1985), 641; J.T. Southwick, "Abuse of Diplomatic Privilege and Immunities: Compensation and Restrictive Reforms," *Syracuse Journal of International Law and Commerce* 15 (1988), 82.

156. R.S.C. 1985 c. E-19.

157. For example, former President Reagan used export controls to ensure that U.S. technology was not exported to the former Soviet Union. See A.L.C. de Mestral and T. Gruchella-Wesierski, *Extraterritorial Application of Export Controls Legislation: Canada and the U.S.* (Netherlands: Kluwer, 1990), 5.

158. For a description of the export control system in Canada, see Castel, *The Canadian Law and Practice of International Trade*, 441-66; Lustgarten and Leigh, *In From the Cold*, 387-89.

159. Dept. of Foreign Affairs and International Trade, *A Guide to Canada's Export Controls* (Ottawa: Supply and Services Canada, 1994), iii.

160. The CSE's SIGINT capability may be of assistance in such circumstances. It has been argued that export controls may have negative effects on domestic competitiveness. See Comment, "National Security Export Controls on Data Encryption: How They Limit U.S. Competitiveness," *Texas Journal of International Law* 29 (1994), 437.

161. (1993) 32 I. L. M. 670 (NAFTA).

162. (1994) 33 I. L. M. 81 (WTO Agreement).

163. Chapter 17 of the NAFTA, and the Agreement on Trade-Related Aspects of Intellectual Property (TRIPs), forming part of the WTO Agreement.

164. Regarding the changes required to implement NAFTA and the WTO Agreement see C. Kent, "The Uruguay Round GATT TRIPs Agreement and Chapter 17 of NAFTA: A New Era in International Patent Protection," *Canadian Intellectual Property Review* 3 (1994), 711; W.N. Sprigings, "The Impact of NAFTA Amendment Act on Canadian IP Statutes," *Canadian Intellectual Property Review* 10 (1994), 745.

165. See J.P. Chandler, "The Loss of New Technology to Foreign Competitors: U.S. Companies Must Search for Protective Solutions," *George Washington Journal of International Law and Economics* 27 (1993-94), 305. Chandler describes the failures of traditional intellectual property laws to protect research and proposes new rules to do so.

166. J.H. Reichman, "Beyond the Historical Lines of Demarcation: Competition Law, Intellectual Property Rights, and International Trade after GATT's Uruguay Round," *Brooklyn Journal of International Law* 20 (1993), 75, 113.

167. See endnotes 188-90 and accompanying text for additional reasons for this conclusion. It is interesting to note that the "national security" exclusion in the NAFTA provides that no party is required to "furnish or allow access to any information the disclosure of which it determines to be contrary to its essential security interests." Also, no party is prevented from taking any action that it considers necessary for the protection of its essential security interests "(i) relating ... to ... traffic and transactions in other goods, materials, services, and technology undertaken directly or indirectly for the purpose of supplying a military or other security establishment" (Art. 2102). Article 73 of the TRIPs Agreement contains a similar exclusion, except that it does not refer to "allowing access" as a basis of failure to comply with the agreement, nor does it refer to "other security establishment."

168. The Agreement on Subsidies and Countervailing Measures forms part of Annex 1A to the WTO Agreement (hereafter the "Subsidies Agreement").

169. The definition expressly refers to "services" provided by government (s. 1.1[a][1][iii]). In this chapter for this study, James Brander describes the economic rationale for characterizing economic intelligence activities by security services as a subsidy.

170. *Ibid.*, Art. 8.2 and Art. 25. Reports must be made to the Committee on Subsidies and Countervailing Measures.

171. *Ibid.*, Arts. 6 and 7. Such prejudice would occur, for example, where the subsidized goods were displacing exports of another state into the subsidizing state or a third state.

172. CSIS Act s. 19(3). See appendix for the full text of s. 19.

173. In order for disclosure to be permitted, the information must have been obtained consistently with the CSIS mandate.

174. See endnotes 116 and accompanying text.

175. A review of SIRC *Annual Reports* from 1988-89 disclosed that only one such disclosure was reported to SIRC (*SIRC Annual Report for 1990-91*, 19).

176. The role of CSIS under s. 16 is limited to assisting the Minister of Defence or the Secretary of State for External Affairs, which suggests that disclosures should only be made to them, although cooperation and information exchange will be a part of information-gathering under s. 16. I will not deal with the duties of CSIS in relation to security assessments (s. 13) or immigration (s. 14).

177. Such arrangements are subject to the scrutiny of SIRC (CSIS Act ss. 17(2) and 38(a)(iii)). S. 38(a)(iii) specifically requires SIRC to "monitor the provision of information and intelligence pursuant to these arrangements."

178. In this regard one may question the basis for the technology awareness program operated by CSIS (see endnote 72). One further concern that may arise is potential liability under s. 4 of the Official Secrets Act in connection with disclosures. See note 140 and accompanying text.

179. Since information gathered under s. 16 may not be retained by CSIS unless it meets the requirements of s. 12, such information presumably cannot be disclosed at all under s. 19. See endnote 82 and accompanying text. Private parties may obtain information subject to certain important exceptions under the federal Access to Information Act (R.S.C. 1985, c. A-1, as amended, s. 2(1)).

180. See endnote 82 and accompanying text.

181. See endnotes 176-77 and accompanying text.

182. Peter Russell, "Should Canada Establish a Foreign Intelligence Service?" (Ottawa: Supply and Services Canada, 1988); T. D'Arcy Finn, "Does Canada Need a Foreign Intelligence Service?" *Canadian Foreign Policy* 1, 3 (Fall 1993), 149-62; Alistair S. Hensler, "Creating a Canadian Foreign Intelligence Service," *Canadian Foreign Policy* 3, 3 (Winter 1995-96), 15-35.

183. *Nouveau Code Penal* (Editions Dalloz, 1993), 1853. In 1996 the United States enacted an economic espionage statute (18 U.S.C., chapter 90).

184. Gathering information by private actors may also be an offense.

185. Endnote 116 and accompanying text.

186. Endnote 126 and accompanying text.

187. Endnotes 136-42 and accompanying text.

188. Like the scope of trade secret protection. See for example the trade secret statutes in many U.S. states and the EEC Directive on Trade Secrets.

189. This is true even of relatively mature technologies. For example, the scope of copyright protection for computer programs is not at all clear. A. Miller, "Copyright Protection for Computer Programs, Databases, and Computer-generated Works: Is There Anything New Since CONTU?" *Harvard Law Review* 106 (1993), 978; C.P. August, D.K.W. Smith, "Software Expression (SSO), Interfaces, and Reverse Assembly," *Canadian Intellectual Property Review* 19 (1994), 679.

190. Under Part VI of the TRIPs Agreement all countries have one year to give effect to their obligations under the agreement. Developing countries have an additional four years, and least developed countries have up to ten additional years in relation to some obligations.

191. There are various other issues that would confront CSIS in relation to any activity outside of Canada. For example, Samuel Porteous has described the foreign activities of national security services such as the CIA in support of domestic commercial interests in his chapter for this study.

192. It should be recognized that, since it has no governing statute, CSE has no legal restrictions on the circumstances in which it may gather economic intelligence for offensive or defensive purposes, or to whom it must disclose any intelligence it does gather.

193. Both were recommended by the Alberta Institute of Law Research and Reform in 1986. See "Trade Secrets," 218-51. The U.S. enacted a law imposing criminal penalties on agents of foreign governments engaged in economic espionage in 1996 (18 U.S.C., chapter 90).

194. This was recommended by the Mackenzie Commission in 1966. See *Report of the Royal Commission on Security* (Ottawa: Supply and Services Canada, 1966), 77.

195. A version of this approach was taken in amending the British Official Secrets Act, the act on which the present Canadian statute is based, in 1989. The amended act criminalizes disclosure of certain types of information where it is likely to cause serious harm to the interests of the nation.

196. As noted above, economic interests are expressly referred to in Britain's Security Service Act, 1989. See endnote 28 and accompanying text.

IV

THE ECONOMICS OF ECONOMIC INTELLIGENCE

James A. Brander

THE TRADITIONAL ROLE of intelligence services is to provide information to governments about threats to national security. Intelligence services as a group have normally focused on military, political, and potential terrorist activity. A typical intelligence service also devotes a good deal of effort to keeping track of other intelligence services. In addition, however, intelligence services have also been involved in the provision of economic intelligence. Sometimes this merely involves the compilation and analysis of publicly available information, but it may also involve economic espionage.

With the decline of East-West tensions, the relative importance of military and political intelligence has diminished. This, in turn, has raised the relative profile of economic intelligence in general and economic espionage in particular. In Canada, the major intelligence services are the Canadian Security Intelligence Service (CSIS), the Royal Canadian Mounted Police (RCMP), and the Communications Security Establishment (CSE). As described in the chapter by Anthony VanDuzer, both CSIS and the RCMP are legally limited to a defensive role with respect to economic espionage; CSE, which is the government's signals intelligence-gathering unit, at present has no statutory mandate, a fact that makes it difficult to ascribe to it a purely defensive posture. CSIS and the RCMP try to prevent foreign intelligence services or their surrogates from obtaining confidential business information, but they do not actively seek such information. As reported elsewhere in this volume, CSE's history of operations has been more ambiguous than that of CSIS and the RCMP. Nonetheless, it can be stated that Canada's primarily defensive posture on clandestine economic intelligence-gathering is in stark contrast to the practices of some other countries. There have been widely publicized cases in which intelligence services from, for example, Russia and Japan, have stolen trade secrets from foreign firms and turned them over to domestic rivals. Several examples are described in the chapter by Samuel Porteous.

The objective of this chapter is to provide an economic analysis of economic intelligence. More specifically, the chapter considers whether there is any reasonable economic rationale for the involvement of state-supported intelligence services in economic espionage or in economic intelligence more broadly. This question is considered primarily from a national point of view, in that I ask whether one country (such as Canada) can gain from state-supported economic intelligence, but I also discuss what form international agreements over economic intelligence might take.

There are three types of economic argument that might provide a rationale for state-supported economic intelligence services. These three arguments are the "strategic trade policy" argument, the "public good argument," and the "police" argument. In order to make these arguments clear the first section provides some background on economic policy analysis. Sections two, three, and four discuss the strategic trade policy, public good, and police arguments respectively. The conclusion comments briefly on the evolution of intelligence service activity in response to a global environment characterized by a proliferation of non-traditional security threats, including greater incentives for economic espionage.

A PRIMER ON ECONOMIC POLICY ANALYSIS

We can think of economic policy analysis as consisting of a series of questions. The most basic question asks what kinds of economic activities the government should undertake. Then, within a general category of activity, we ask what specific projects should be carried out, and how much of each project should be carried out. Going further, we then ask how the projects should be implemented and managed. I cannot provide a very full discussion of these questions here.[1] There is, however, one key point that needs to be made: the economic rationale for government provision of economic goods and services (including intelligence services) is really quite limited.

The starting point for a consideration of the economic role of government is the assertion by Adam Smith that the private pursuit of economic self-interest has impressive efficiency properties that work in the overall collective interest.[2] Thus, as a base-line principle, Smith argued that governments should have a very limited role in the production of economic goods and services. The "default" approach to any particular economic function would be that it should reside in the private sector, although Smith did recognize some exceptions.

FIGURE 7: GOVERNMENT INTERVENTION

```
                   ┌─────────────────────┐
                   │   SECURE SYSTEM OF   │
                   │ VOLUNTARY EXCHANGE   │
                   └─────────────────────┘
            ┌─────────────┼─────────────┐
            ▼             ▼             ▼
    ┌──────────────┐ ┌──────────────────┐ ┌──────────────┐
    │MARKET FAILURE│ │MACROSTABILIZATION│ │EQUITY/FAIRNESS│
    └──────────────┘ └──────────────────┘ └──────────────┘
            │
            ▼
      Public Goods
      Externalities
   Imperfect Competition
  Asymmetric Information
```

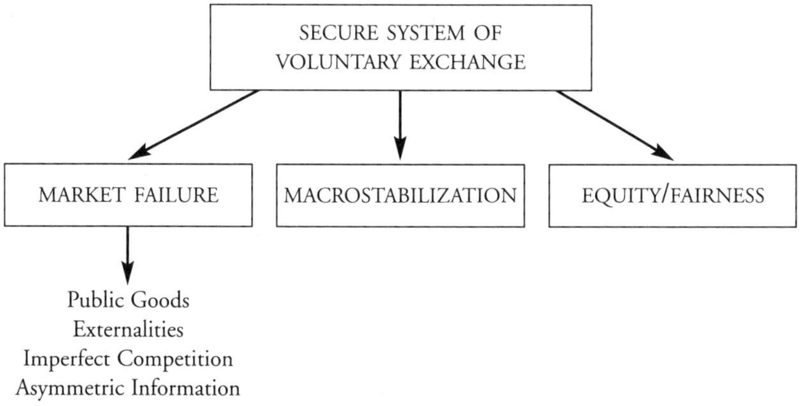

The work of Smith has been formalized by subsequent economists, who have shown that private enterprise has strong efficiency properties under certain conditions. The implication is that market-based economies would be expected to out-perform extensive systems of state control, such as the now dismantled Soviet-style system of central planning. However, modern economic analysis also recognizes (as did Adam Smith himself) that there are situations that call for government intervention. Figure 7 provides a schematic diagram of the justifiable economic role of government.

Following Figure 7, one economic rationale for government action is to provide a secure system of voluntary exchange, because having such a system is what allows the efficiency properties of market-based private enterprise economies to occur. (This is discussed more fully in the fourth section of this chapter.) Even when such a system is in place, governments may still reasonably intervene to deal with macroeconomic stabilization or to undertake economic redistribution for reasons relating to equity or fairness. Also, there are so-called "market failures." These are situations in which private markets fail to achieve efficiency even with a secure system of exchange in place. There are four sources of market failure: public goods, imperfect competition (or "market power"), externalities, and informational asymmetries. Governments may, of course, have legitimate non-economic objectives that lie outside economic analysis, but there is no economic rationale for intervention other than those given in Figure 7.

Very often in political debate one hears that the government should intervene in some industry because it is "important," or that it should carry out some project because the private sector would not do so. These rationales are spurious. Economic importance is no reason, in itself, for government intervention, and the mere observation that the private sector fails to do something (like growing bananas in the Yukon) is, in most cases, a good indication that it should not be done at all, not an argument that governments should do it.

In the case of intelligence services, there are no macroeconomic stabilization issues to consider, and equity-based rationales seem to have modest relevance. This leaves us with the market failure rationales and with overall exchange security. Two of the three arguments, I have suggested, the strategic trade policy argument and the public good argument, derive mainly from market failure considerations. The police argument mainly concerns exchange security, although it also relates to market failure.

ECONOMIC INTELLIGENCE AS STRATEGIC TRADE POLICY

The meaning of the term "strategic trade policy" is not completely self-evident, and different researchers have used the term in slightly different ways. A standard definition is that strategic trade policy is a trade policy that conditions or alters a strategic relationship between firms. This definition implies that the existence of a strategic relationship between firms is a necessary precondition for the application of strategic trade policy.

A strategic relationship between firms is one in which firms have a mutually recognized strategic interdependence. More formally, the payoffs (profits) of one firm must be directly affected by the individual strategy choices of other firms, and this must be understood by the firms themselves. Strategic trade policies would therefore not arise under perfect competition, nor under pure monopoly unless potential entry were an important consideration. Strategic trade policy amounts to the study of trade policy in the presence of oligopoly. In other words, strategic trade policy applies in industries in which a small number of firms are engaged in imperfectly competitive rivalries. Thus it is the "imperfect competition" type of market failure that creates a potential role for government policy of this type.

The analysis of strategic trade policy is part of a broader research agenda that has been very active since the beginning of the 1980s.[3] Since then, international trade economists have sought to incorporate oligopoly and other forms of imperfect competition into the formal analysis of international trade and trade policy so as to make contact with important empirical regularities and policy concerns. The central insight of strategic trade policy is that intervention to alter the strategic interaction between oligopolistic firms can itself be an important basis for trade policy. Economic espionage by state-supported intelligence services is a type of government intervention that can play the role of affecting strategic interactions between oligopolistic rivals.

As is often the case in economics, the academic use of the term strategic trade policy differs from the way the term is used in political debate, where it has at least two other distinct meanings. First, strategic trade policy sometimes refers to trade policy that has direct military implications. Second, the term strategic is sometimes used simply as a synonym for important; thus strategic trade policy is trade policy targeted toward industries that are thought to be important for some reason. An industry that is "strategic" by one of these definitions might also be strategic in the game theoretic sense used here, but neither of these definitions is relevant to the analysis presented here.

The basic idea of strategic trade policy is that government policy can be used to increase the domestic share of the above-normal profits that may be available in imperfectly competitive industries. The simplest case to consider arises when there is just one domestic firm and one foreign firm in an oligopolistic rivalry in world markets. Profits in the world market are the target of the espionage activity. Economic espionage that favours the domestic firm may enhance its competitive position and increase its profits, at the expense of rivals, sufficiently that there is a net gain to the domestic economy over and above the direct cost of the espionage activity. A simple example should make the point clear.

Suppose that two countries are capable of producing a particular good. For concreteness, let us call the good a 150-seat passenger aircraft and let us call the countries America and Europe. Also, assume that there is one firm in each country that can produce the good. We will call the firms Boeing and Airbus respectively. Suppose that the internal market for this product is small in both countries, and that most consumption of the product is in other countries (as it might well be for a particular type of aircraft). We can then take the profit earned as the appropriate measure of national benefit from this product for each of the two countries.

We assume that each firm must choose either to produce the product or not. We also assume that the market is profitable for one firm if it is the only entrant, but that the market will be unprofitable if both firms enter and must share the market. The profits or "payoffs" are shown in the following table. The first number in each cell is the payoff to Boeing (and "America"), while the second number is the payoff to Airbus (and Europe).

		Airbus Enter	Not Enter
	Enter	-5 -5	100 0
Boeing			
	Not Enter	0 100	0 0

In this example, if both and Boeing and Airbus choose to enter, we can see that they both lose 5. If one firm enters and the other does not, the entering firm gets a net benefit of 100, whereas nothing happens to the other firm. Given this payoff matrix, the outcome is indeterminate. If either firm enters, the other would prefer not to. If, for example, Boeing entered while Airbus did not, then Boeing would earn a return of 100 and Airbus would earn nothing. If Airbus did enter, its return would be -5, so it would prefer not to enter. Similarly, if Airbus enters and Boeing does not, then Boeing would prefer not to enter. What can government policy do? Suppose that the European intelligence services are able to obtain the results of early product development by Boeing and turn these results over to Airbus, thereby saving Airbus the cost of doing the early development itself. Suppose this cost is 10. This has the effect of lowering Airbus costs by 10 and therefore increasing its net benefit by 10 if it actually produces the product and enters the market. In other words, this cost saving is just enough to allow Airbus to be profitable even if both firms ultimately enter the market. Assuming that the original payoffs for Boeing were net of its early product development costs, its payoffs are unchanged and the new payoff structure is as follows.

		Airbus	
		Enter	Not Enter
	Enter	-5 5	100 0
Boeing			
	Not Enter	0 110	0 0

In this case, the outcome is clear: Airbus will enter. Furthermore, once Boeing realizes that Airbus is committed to entering, it should cut its losses and decide not to enter at all. The basic reason for this outcome is that the higher benefits derived from stolen information makes entering a "dominant strategy" for Airbus. Entering is the best strategy for Airbus no matter what Boeing does. If Boeing enters as well, Airbus still earns 5, which is better than the zero it gets if it does not enter. If Boeing does not enter then Airbus gains 110 by entering. Thus Airbus should certainly enter. Knowing that Airbus will enter for certain, Boeing should not enter, for it will lose 5 for certain (over and above whatever costs have been sunk in early product development) if it does. Thus Airbus will earn 110 and Boeing will earn nothing.

To make the example very stark, let us suppose that the cost of the espionage activity is very high. Suppose, in fact, that the cost of getting the information through espionage is 10 (the same amount that the information would cost to produce directly). Even in this case, the espionage activity leads to a net benefit of 100 to Europe (which equals 110 minus the subsidy of 10). Profits have been shifted to Airbus by the espionage activity. Even if we assumed that the base case (without the subsidy) gave Airbus a 50 percent chance of getting the market to itself, the espionage still provides net "expected benefits" to Europe.

Note that the espionage activity acts just like a subsidy.[4] Whether the European intelligence service obtained the information by espionage or simply subsidized Airbus to generate the information itself, the effect is the same. The existing work in strategic trade policy considers the subsidy instrument. The new observation in this chapter is that espionage acts much like a subsidy in this setting.

It should be emphasized that the discussion provided here is just an illustration. It does not prove anything formally. However, the corresponding formal analysis of subsidies and other trade policy instruments is contained in the literature cited in endnote 3. The extension to the case of espionage follows directly from this work. The basic point of this example is to demonstrate that one country will typically have a unilateral economic incentive to engage in economic espionage so as to shift profits from foreign to domestic firms. This is true even if the cost of the espionage is as high as the cost of producing the information in the first place. The effect is even stronger if, as one suspects, espionage is a relatively inexpensive way of obtaining information.

Unilateral incentives are not the end of the story, of course. It is fairly clear that the other government, in this case the U.S. government, would also have an incentive to undertake espionage activities. It would have incentives to try to prevent the success of European espionage, but it would also have incentives to undertake direct espionage of its own against the European firm.

It is instructive to consider the effect of successful direct espionage by many governments. Suppose that intelligence services around the world became very good at obtaining confidential economic information. Suppose that they became so successful that it became very difficult for companies to keep R&D results confidential, or to keep product development information from rivals. The net effect would be to reduce the system-wide incentive to undertake R&D and product development. The problem is exactly the same as the problem that would arise if there were no patent protection. Once it becomes difficult for the innovator to obtain a reasonable portion of the benefits arising from innovation, we would expect much less innovation. The formal economic details are a little beyond the scope of this chapter, but it is easy to show that such an environment gives rise to substantial inefficiency.

Thus, in a world where aggressive economic espionage is widespread and successful, each country faces a unilateral incentive to undertake such espionage, but all countries together are made worse off. This is a classic "prisoner's dilemma." (The prisoner's dilemma game has been extensively studied, but one particularly interesting investigation of prisoner's dilemma games is Axelrod [1984].)[5] Thus there would be advantages to entering into international agreements to prevent economic espionage.

Some readers might be aware that the role of intellectual property rights has been a very important subject of negotiation within the World Trade Organization (WTO) in recent years. Economic espionage is a direct affront to the spirit of recent agreements on intellectual property rights, and may be grounds for sanctions under international trade law, although there are no test cases to date.

The case in which espionage is directed at technological information is important, but espionage may also be directed at other types of information, such as bargaining positions, maximum willingness to pay for contracts, and other commercial information that might be useful to a competitor, buyer, or supplier. Provision of all of these types of information by an intelligence service acts like a subsidy to the beneficiary firm, and there are efficiency costs to the international system from this activity over and above the direct cost of undertaking the espionage activity. In addition, covertly acquiring such information violates norms of fairness or ethical conduct. There is, of course, a grey area. If, for example, an intelligence service happens to come across information about market opportunities that it passes along to domestic firms, it is not doing anything very different from what trade missions and consular offices do to help domestic firms. The information still is much like a subsidy, but the detrimental effects of the activity are not so obvious as with the other types of espionage discussed previously.

The discussion so far has been devoted to aggressive or direct economic espionage (using intelligence services to obtain confidential information from rivals) rather than defensive espionage. The analysis here suggests that defensive espionage might be a good thing. Defensive espionage has the effect of protecting intellectual property rights more securely and thereby would be expected to increase the incentives to innovate. Furthermore, it acts as a deterrent to aggressive espionage in the first place. Thus, from a worldwide point of view, there is reason to support the use of defensive counter-espionage.

In addition to the question as to which activities should be undertaken, governments and intelligence services also face the question of how much of each activity to undertake. Thus, even if we decide that defensive espionage is an appropriate activity in principle for intelligence services to carry out, we still need to do a cost-benefit calculation to consider how much, if any, such activity is actually warranted. This is just an example of standard economic policy analysis. Any activity, such as counter-espionage, should be carried out as long as the marginal (or extra) benefits of the activity exceed the marginal costs. In any particular case, an empirical judgment must be made. In this case we must ask whether economic counter-espionage has sufficiently low costs and sufficiently high benefits that it is worth doing.

The main insight of this section is that the theory of strategic trade policy suggests that there is unilateral incentive for governments to provide state-supported aggressive economic espionage so as to shift economic profits or "rents" from foreign to domestic beneficiaries. If followed by many national governments, however, we would expect everyone to be worse off under such a regime, as with a standard prisoner's dilemma. Unilateral incentives do not necessarily maximize collective benefits in "games" of this type.

INFORMATION AS A PUBLIC GOOD

The previous section provides an analysis of economic espionage. This section focuses primarily on acquisition of general economic information. The basic idea is that there is a rationale for governments to provide public goods, and some types of information can be viewed as public goods.

A public good is a good that is "non-rival," which means that many people can consume it without "using it up," and it is "non-exclusive," which means that it is difficult to exclude people from using the good. A classic example of a public good is lighthouse services. When one person sees the light and is warned away from a rocky shore, the services of the lighthouse are not used up. Other people also see the signal. Furthermore, it is very difficult to imagine excluding potential users from the lighthouse services. Anyone in range of the lighthouse will see the signal.

A public good causes market failure because it will not be produced by the private sector, or at best will be underproduced, even when its economic value is very high. This is because of the "free rider" problem associated with public goods. Since they are non-exclusive, users do not need to pay to use them. It would be very difficult for a private sector lighthouse to collect enough revenue from users to survive. For this reason, there is a strong rationale for governments to arrange for the provision of public goods.

It is important to realize that the term "public good" has a strict meaning in economics that, like the term "strategic trade policy," differs from the way the term is sometimes used in ordinary language. Thus a public good is not simply a good that is publicly provided. Goods like health care and education are not public goods, for example, even though they might be publicly provided. A public good is a good that meets the two strict conditions given here: non-rivalry and non-exclusion.

Information is not a strict public good, but it is close to being a public good in some cases. It is non-rival in that information does not get "used up," so it meets one of the two criteria, but it is not completely non-exclusive, as certain types of information can be protected and released only to some users. However, it is often difficult to keep users from passing the information along to others, so information is close to being to a public good. The extent to which people can be excluded from information depends mainly on how difficult the information is to interpret. Information that is easy to understand, such as "the interest rate on government bonds is 7 percent" is hard to keep exclusive, because it is easily transmitted and understood. On the other hand, technical information about the design of a computer processor is easier to keep secret, because most people could not understand the information sufficiently to transmit it accurately.

The basic economic rationale for organizations such as Statistics Canada is the public good nature of information. Statistics Canada gathers information about national income, demography, labour markets, and a host of other things and makes this information widely available. Thus, voters can, in principle, make informed judgments about the economic performance of governments without having to hire private information-providers or undertake extensive research on their own. Note that most of this information is relatively easy to understand and interpret, so it would be close to being non-exclusive. We would therefore expect the private sector to underprovide this type of information.

Governments are one major user of the information provided by Statistics Canada. If information were not a public good (that is, if it were a normal private good), then it might make sense for governments in Canada to buy information from private sector suppliers. After all, Canadian governments use a lot of computers but do not need to be in the computer-manufacturing business. The fact that information is not a normal private good, that it has public good properties, is what allows an economic rationale for government information services. We think of the government providing information much as it provides lighthouse services. These services have a value much higher than the cost of production, but would not be adequately produced by the private sector, because of the free rider problem associated with public goods.

This particular rationale for government-provided information is not very persuasive in providing an economic rationale for intelligence services. Intelligence services do not provide information to the general public, or to a wide range of other users. They provide information to governments for confidential use. Thus, the information they provide is proprietary, and does not have a public good character. Therefore, the public good nature that much information has is not very relevant for the operations of intelligence services.

Intelligence services could acquire general economic information that might be made available to a range of users (as the CIA does), but it is difficult to imagine that intelligence services could provide better general economic information than is provided by national statistical organizations such as Statistics Canada or international (publicly funded) organizations such as the World Bank, the Organization for Economic Cooperation and Development, the International Monetary Fund, and various UN agencies. There are also some private organizations, notably the Economist Intelligence Unit, that provide general economic information for a fee.

Overall, a basic economic analysis of the public good argument as applied to economic information provides a rationale for some kind of government-supported information-gathering activity such as that carried out by Statistics Canada and by publicly funded international organizations. It does not provide much of a rationale for provision of general economic information by intelligence services. If there is an important distinction between intelligence services and other information providers (such as Statistics Canada), it has to do with the confidentiality and even secrecy associated with intelligence service activities. However, this very secrecy implies that the information involved cannot be a public good. Thus the public good nature of some information provides only a very weak potential rationale for the activities of intelligence services.

THE POLICE ARGUMENT

What I refer to as the police argument has two logical steps. The first step is the claim that state supported police services are best provided by the public sector. The second step is the observation that the counter-espionage component of economic intelligence can be viewed as a police-like service. The second step could be put slightly differently by saying that covert acquisition of economic information is an essential and inseparable component of important police-like activities.

Most readers would probably take the first step in the argument for granted. It might come as a surprise that economists regard it as necessary to provide an economic rationale for publicly supplied police services. We can note, however, that it is possible to imagine situations short of anarchy without publicly provided police services. In such a situation we would expect extensive use of private security services. In many countries, including Canada and the United States, a substantial fraction of police-like activity is in fact provided by private security services, and most economic counter-espionage activity is undertaken by firms themselves. Nevertheless, modern states depend heavily on state-supplied police services. The economic rationale for public police is not entirely obvious. It rests on three principle components. One component is a public good argument, one is an equity-based component, and the third (and most important) component relates to overall exchange security.

The public good component can be explained as follows. Many police services are substantially non-rival and non-exclusive. Thus, for example, if police apprehend a violent criminal, many people are protected by this act. It is, moreover, impossible to even identify who the next victims would have been. It would be very difficult for private police to obtain income from potential victims if victims cannot even be identified. We could imagine that private police might sign contracts with potential victims of certain types of crime (such as theft from stores), but most potential areas of police activity would be subject to the free rider problem. What private individual would pay police to carry out traffic control, for example? If we are to have an efficient level of policy activity, it will have to be through collective action of some sort, and government provision is the primary form of collective action in modern economies.

There are also equity-based arguments for making police services part of the public sector. Note that many of the interactions people have with the justice system are involuntary. Suspected criminals may be held against their will, and many other participants (jurors, witnesses, etc.) are brought into the system because of a legal obligation, not because of voluntary action. The equity-based argument is that when people interact in a coercive environment, it is very important that the environment be impartial. Thus, for example, there is no market failure reason why court cases could not be conducted by hired judges who compete as free agents in the marketplace. However, we make the collective judgment that judges should be provided by the state in an effort to provide impartiality. (There are, incidentally, areas of law in several countries where private judges are used.)

The most interesting component of the rationale for police services is what I have referred to as the "exchange security" component. The efficiency properties of private sector economic transactions are based on the principle of voluntary exchange. The main reason why Adam Smith and subsequent economists have been able to demonstrate the benefits of private economic transactions derives from the very simple principle that if two parties to a transaction participate in the transaction voluntarily, it is because they both expect to gain from it. Thus, using Smith's example, when I buy bread from the baker, we both gain from the transaction. In a system where all economic transactions are voluntary, each transaction benefits both parties. This creates a strong force that operates in the direction of overall system efficiency (although the story is a little more complicated that just this). If, on the other hand, the government instructs the baker to supply me with bread, and instructs me to consume the bread, there is little assurance that we will be better off. Perhaps I do not like bread and would prefer rice, and the baker might not receive enough compensation from the government for providing me with bread for it to be worthwhile for him to do so. This is the fundamental problem with command economies such as the former Soviet system.

An even worse alternative is anarchy, where the strong simply take from the weak. The real problem with this is that the weak will not bother to produce much if they cannot protect it, and most people will devote most of their resources to protecting their property rather than producing new things of value.

The principle of voluntary exchange is at the heart of the efficiency of market-based economies. In order for voluntary exchange to work, however, participants in the system must be protected from coercion. If I can go to the baker and demand bread at gunpoint, then the efficiency properties of the system break down. Thus the state needs to provide the environment in which voluntary exchange can take place. This consists of doing things like enforcing contracts, protecting individuals from direct coercion, protecting private property, and the like. In order to achieve this, however, the state must use some coercion. It arrests people, incarcerates them, seizes their property, etc. If the state withdrew from this role and allowed private sector agents to carry out such actions, there is no reason to believe that efficient economic transactions would result. This is where libertarians and classical economists part company. Classical economists implicitly presume a coercive role for the state that serves to protect the principle of voluntary exchange in private transactions.

In any case, these three components of the argument for police imply that there is a role for state police services. I am using the term "police services" broadly to include the entire apparatus that protects the system of voluntary exchange. Part of this apparatus involves the provision of information, and much of the information is inseparable from the police services themselves. For example, police investigate crimes, which is an information-gathering activity. Much of this information is economic in nature, especially in crimes involving economic matters, such as financial fraud. This information is not normally of the public good type, so there is no market failure reason for acquiring it through the public sector. However, we can observe that, simply from a "production" point of view, acquiring information is necessarily linked to police service activities that should be carried out in the public sector and cannot be readily or efficiently contracted out. In other words, a certain amount of information production is an inseparable part of the police activity. As we have agreed that police activity should reside primarily in the public sector for reasons beyond simple market failure, this implies an information-gathering role even when market failure is not present.

So far we have established that police services belong in the public sector and that information acquisition is a necessary part of police services. The final step in the argument is then to observe that some economic intelligence activities that might be carried out by intelligence services are part of a legitimate police activity that is important for overall system security. In the case of counter-espionage this seems a fairly easy case to make. In the discussion of espionage as strategic trade policy we presumed that the information in question was technical information. Protecting this information is just an extension of the basic idea that the state should protect the property rights of private economic agents. In addition, espionage might well be focused on other types of information that might be used to blackmail or intimidate senior executives, and this too should be prevented to the extent that illegal coercion is involved. As a result there is a clear rationale to use counter-espionage to protect participants in international business transactions from such threats.

Counter-espionage of this type might be focused on mitigating or stopping the effects of foreign intelligence agencies. In addition, however, it might be focused on the activities of firms themselves, foreign and domestic.

ECONOMIC INTELLIGENCE
AND THE GLOBAL ECONOMY

During the past two decades the term "globalization" has come into popular usage to describe an important trend in economic affairs. This term refers to the increasing interdependence and interconnectedness of the world economy. Globalization has already had an important impact on several distinct areas of government activity, and is likely to have a major impact on security intelligence services.

Traditionally, intelligence services were supposed to protect "national" security, which, stripped to its essentials, means protecting "us" (domestic nationals) from "them" (everybody else). For example, in the discussion of strategic trade policy we assumed that intelligence services will provide advantages to "domestic" firms at the expense of "foreign" rivals. However, one effect of globalization is that it has become increasingly difficult to distinguish between "us" and "them."

As described by Hart, developments in communications technology and transportation systems, combined with international agreements, have led to fundamental changes in business organization.[6] Large firms are increasingly internationalized. A relatively simple product such as a shoe may have components from several countries, and a car may have components from a few dozen. Sales for large corporations are increasingly diversified around the world, as is ownership. It is therefore very hard to identify corporations with countries. Even quintessentially American companies such as General Motors or Coca-Cola have widely diversified production, sales, and ownership around the world. The same is true of large Canadian corporations, such as Alcan and Cominco, and many of the largest "Canadian" corporations (such as General Motors, Chevron, IBM, and Macdonald's) are foreign-owned subsidiaries in any case. Therefore, when a firm is helped or harmed by espionage activity it is increasingly hard to attribute this cost or benefit to workers or share-holders in a single country. This factor may weaken the national incentive to undertake aggressive espionage, and, more importantly, it causes confusion about exactly whose "side" intelligence services are on.

Divided or unclear loyalties at the individual level are an even greater problem than at the corporate level. Traditionally, intelligence services concentrated on protecting a well-defined national group. Particularly in countries with large immigrant populations like Canada, it is now far from obvious where the loyalties of intelligence services should lie. Take the example of those in Canada who hold dual Canadian and Hong Kong citizenship. Much of this population was born in Hong Kong, and lives and works in Hong Kong. What is the appropriate role of CSIS with respect to this population? Should CSIS be policing it, trying to address tax evasion and other potential problems, or should it perhaps be making plans to protect this population from possible problems that might arise now that control of Hong Kong has reverted to China. With regard to economic assistance, should CSIS help a Hong Kong firm run by a Canadian national in Hong Kong? What if that firm is in competition with a Canadian company that actually oper-ates in Canada? In a world of divided loyalties and divided nationalities it is difficult to choose sides.

In addition to weakening national identification, the rapid evolu-tion of communications and information processing technology has a more direct potential effect on the demand for intelligence services. The volume and flow of commercially-relevant information through elec-tronic media is growing rapidly, especially across international borders, and potential theft or misuse of this information will be an increasing threat to firms, governments, and individuals. Information security has become a major public policy concern. It is possible that existing specialized communications security agencies will grow and gradually displace traditional intelligence services. However, it is also possible that traditional intelligence services will find an expanded role in this area.

We think of globalization as deriving from technological changes, but we should not forget that there is another very basic force underlying globalization, and that is simple crowding. World population continues to grow very rapidly. World fertility is falling, but is still far above the level needed to stabilize population, particularly in Africa. As a result, the world continues to become an increasingly small and crowded place, with some parts, particularly sub-Saharan Africa, facing greater impoverishment than ever before.

The effects of these pressures are made worse by the significant market failures (mostly of the externality type) that affect the natural environment. Responding to these problems are a growing number of governmental and non-governmental international organizations and regimes. In recent years there have been international agreements reached on ozone depletion and, within the North American Free Trade Agreement, on a range of environmental issues. However, international agreements and conflicts over environmental issues remain in their very early phases. The key feature of these conflicts is that they are international in scope. When Spanish or Portuguese fishing vessels overfish ocean-going stocks of Atlantic turbot, this has major implications for Canada. Even something that is apparently an "internal" matter, such as the deforestation of the Amazon jungles in Brazil, has important potential effects on climate and rainfall that would affect neighbouring countries.

I would predict that environmental conflict, with significant ramifications for national and international economic development, will be the major area of conflict in the next century. In the Middle East, for example, it seems likely that religious and ethnically based conflict will decline, but it may be partially replaced by major conflicts over water use and water supplies. Thus, intelligence services could play a major role in conflicts generated by resource use issues. They could, for example, play a role in detecting cheating on international environmental agreements by national governments and by private firms, although it is possible that other specialized agencies will take over this role.

The following quotation from Hart makes an important general point. "We have reached the stage at which economics is increasingly global, but politics continues to be intensely local. Markets today are local, regional and global, that is, anything but national, while governance continues to be national."7 Security intelligence services are currently focused on aiding national governments. However, as argued by Hart, the scope of national governments is declining. The monitoring of international environmental agreements or international information flows may well require that intelligence services serve supranational governmental bodies, rather than national governments. One could even imagine that intelligence services might serve an array of clients, including national governments, but also including sub-national governments and supranational bodies. Presumably, the ultimate authority would have to be a national government, but one could imagine that a national intelligence service might, in effect, contract out its expertise to other jurisdictions.

CONCLUSION

This chapter has provided a conceptual statement of the rationale for economic intelligence service activity. I have argued that there are three general arguments related to economics that might be considered. One argument is the strategic trade policy argument, which shows that individual nations might well have incentives to use espionage to further the interests of domestic firms so as shift benefits from foreign to domestic claimants. Viewed in this way, espionage is much like a subsidy to domestic firms and is formally very similar to a subsidy. At this international level, such activity tends to be harmful to innovative activity as a whole. In essence, when one country gains from economic espionage, the damage done to other countries exceeds the benefit to the country that gains. This suggests that the world as whole would gain if countries could agree not to undertake direct economic espionage.

One difficulty in getting general agreement about espionage is that the role of different countries is highly asymmetric in the international espionage "game." Most countries have relatively little to lose from industrial espionage, because their domestic firms have few secrets. The largest potential loser from industrial espionage is the United States, primarily because it provides a disproportionately high share of the world's innovation and therefore has a lot to protect. Also, the United States has both a relatively open society and business community, making it even more difficult to protect sensitive information. At the level of patent and trademark protection, the Clinton administration is at odds with with countries, especially China, that illegally "pirate" various products. The same problems arise over the role of economic espionage. Canada's role is not dissimilar to that of the United States, although Canadian firms have somewhat less innovation to protect, even after adjusting for the relative sizes of the countries, than do U.S. firms. Therefore, countries such as the United States and Canada will have to undertake more vigorous defensive espionage activities. Intelligence services, for example, could play a role in responding to such issues as the "pirating" of domestic products, patent infringements, trademark infringement, and the like.

The second argument for economic intelligence is the public good argument. The public good argument provides a strong case for the existence of national and international statistical agencies such as Statistics Canada and the Statistical Office of the World Bank. These agencies collect and provide general economic information to governments and to many other users. It is hard to see how covert intelligence services can contribute to this, however. Therefore, while the public good argument provides a rationale for the collection of what might be referred to as economic intelligence, it does not suggest a role for intelligence services.

The third argument, which I referred to as the "police" argument, concerns primarily the role of intelligence services in contributing to the overall security of the system of secure voluntary exchange that underlies the efficiency properties of modern market economies. Most such activities, such as police, courts, and the like, are carried out by the domestic justice system, but there does seem to be an important residual role for intelligence services. In this way, we can see intelligence services as an extension of domestic police services. This is, of course, consistent with the structure of the RCMP, which deals with police and intelligence matters directly.

The chapter also considers three important continuing trends in the world economy and their possible impact on intelligence services. The main point of this section is that the world is becoming a more crowded and more integrated place in which it is increasingly difficult to distinguish between "us" and "them" on a national basis. As a result it will be more difficult for intelligence services to base their activities on an adversarial model of world affairs. Intelligence services will, in my view, have to become more like police. They would start with domestic and international law and would concern themselves mainly with violations of this law. For example, in the economic espionage area they would seek to prevent theft of trade secrets, regardless of the nationalities of the firms involved. Thus the motive would not be to "help" a domestic firm and harm a foreign firm, but rather to enforce a more efficient overall world economic system. The "national" component of national security will not completely disappear, but as we move from an era of geopolitics to one of geoeconomics there will be a greater effort to understand and, in the case of intelligence services, to respond to the economic dimensions of old and emerging national security threats. Canada's intelligence services will likely not be immune from such a trend.

NOTES

1. See James Brander, *Government Policy Toward Business* (Toronto: John Wiley, 1995), for an introductory textbook level treatment.

2. Adam Smith, *An Enquiry into the Nature and Causes of the Wealth of Nations* (Dublin: Whitstone, Chamberlaine, etc., 1776).

3. Some of the early papers associated with this line of analysis are James Brander and Barbara Spencer, "Tariffs and the Extraction of Foreign Monopoly Rents Under Potential Entry," *Canadian Journal of Economics* 14, 3 (August 1981), 371-89; James Brander and Barbara Spencer, "Export Subsidies and International Market Share Rivalry," *Journal of International Economics* 24, 3 (May 1985), 83-100; Paul Krugman, "Important Protection as Export Promotion: International Competition in the Presence of Oligopoly and Economies of Scale," in H. Kierzkowski, ed., *Monopolistic Competition and International Trade* (Oxford: Clarendon Press, 1984); Avinash Dixit, "International Trade Policy for Oligopolistic Industries," *Economic Journal* 94, supplement, 1-16. And see also James Brander, "Strategic Trade Policy," in G. Grossman and K. Rogoff, eds., *Handbook of International Economics* (Amsterdam: North Holland, 1995), for a survey of the area.

4. Samuel Porteous discusses this in his monograph, "Economic Espionage," *Commentary*, No. 32 (Ottawa: Canadian Security Intelligence Service, 1994).

5. Robert Axelrod, *The Evolution of Cooperation* (New York: Basic Books, 1984).

6. Michael Hart, "What's Next: Negotiating Rules for a Global Economy," in American Zampeti and Pierre Sauve, eds., *New Dimensions of Market Access in a Globalising World Economy* (Paris: OECD, 1995), 221-42. See also Michael Hart, "A Multilateral Agreement on Foreign Direct Investment: Why Now?" Occasional Paper No. 37, Centre for Trade Policy and Law (Ottawa: Carleton University, 1996).

7. *Ibid.*, 22.

CONTRIBUTORS

JAMES A. BRANDER is Asia-Pacific Professor of International Trade in the Faculty of Commerce, University of British Columbia. He is the author of the book, *Government Policy Towards Business,* and has published extensively in leading scholarly journals of economics. His research interests are in international trade policy, and renewable resources and economic growth. He is currently the managing editor of the *Canadian Journal of Economics,* and is a Research Associate with the National Bureau of Economic Research. Professor Brander received his M.A. and Ph.D. at Stanford University.

SAMUEL D. PORTEOUS is an advisor to business and government on economic intelligence and transnational crime issues. He served with the Canadian Foreign Service from 1989 to 1992, and with the Canadian Security Intelligence Service from 1993 to 1997. There, as a strategic analyst, he was responsible for examining economic intelligence and transnational crime from an intelligence perspective. He holds an L.L.B. from the University of Toronto, an M.A. from the University of Western Ontario, and an M.B.A. from Dalhousie University.

EVAN H. POTTER holds the Reisman Chair on Research and Analysis at the Treasury Board Secretariat. He has been the Senior Harrowston Fellow in Conflict Management and Negotiation at the University of Toronto, and was the first Norman Robertson Fellow (trade policy) on the policy planning staff at the Department of Foreign Affairs and International Trade. As the founding editor of the quarterly, *Canadian Foreign Policy/La Politique étrangère du Canada,* he has written widely on the administration and directions of Canada's international relations. He holds a doctorate in international relations from the London School of Economics.

J. ANTHONY VANDUZER is an Associate Professor and former Vice Dean of the Common Law Section of the Faculty of Law at the University of Ottawa, and an associate of the Centre for Trade Policy and Law (University of Ottawa/Carleton University). He has written extensively on competition, business and trade law issues, and has conducted trade law courses for Industry Canda and the Department of Foreign Affairs and International Trade, as well as for the governments of China, Russia, the Ukraine and Vietnam. Prior to joining the Common Law Section, he practised corporate and commercial law with the firm now known as Fasken Campbell Godfrey, where he specialized in advising high technology firms. Professor VanDuzer received his L.L.M. from Columbia University.